STEWARDS, PROPHETS, KEEPERS OF THE WORD

STEWARDS, PROPHETS, KEEPERS OF THE WORD

Leadership in the Early Church

RITVA H. WILLIAMS

HENDRICKSON
PUBLISHERS

Stewards, Prophets, Keepers of the Word: Leadership in the Early Church
© 2006 by Hendrickson Publishers, Inc.
P. O. Box 3473
Peabody, Massachusetts 01961-3473

ISBN 978-1-56563-949-2

Except where otherwise noted, Scripture quotations are from the New Revised Standard Version of the Bible, copyright © 1989 by the Division of Christian Education of the National Council of the Churches of Christ in the United States of America, and are used by permission.

Printed in the United States of America

First Printing—November 2006

Cover Art: The painting on the cover was done by iconographer and artist Olga Poloukhine using egg tempura on gesso. The work is entitled "The Prophets" and has been used with permission of the artist.

Library of Congress Cataloging-in-Publication Data

Williams, Ritva H., 1960–
     Stewards, prophets, keepers of the Word : leadership in the early church / Ritva H. Williams.
          p. cm.
     Includes bibliographical references (p.) and indexes.
     ISBN-13: 978-1-56563-949-2 (alk. paper)
     1. Christian leadership—History. 2. Christian sociology—History—Early church, ca. 30–600. I. Title.
     BV652.1.W495 2006
     262'.109015—dc22
                                        2006006364

CONTENTS

ACKNOWLEDGMENTS

THE IDEA FOR THIS book goes back to my graduate student days. As preparation for preparing an outline of my doctoral dissertation, my doctoral supervisor asked me to look over everything I had written up to that point with an eye to common threads or themes. That exercise made it clear that I had spent the two previous years writing about connections between church leadership and the Holy Spirit. The end result was a dissertation called "Charismatic Patronage and Brokerage: Episcopal Leadership in the Letters of Ignatius of Antioch." In that work I argued that for Ignatius the role of bishop was a Spirit-inspired response to particular problems facing early Christian communities. It represented a creative integration of charismatic leadership with patron-broker-client relations that structured so much of ancient Greco-Roman social life.

I am still writing about the relationship between church leadership and the Holy Spirit, building on research undertaken in the dissertation process. In this book I explore the influence and interaction of existing social structures, religious experience, and tradition in the leadership of the Jesus movement and the early churches. My expectation going into this work was that social structures and tradition acted to constrain and eventually suppress religious experience. What I have discovered is that in the Jesus movement and the early churches religious experience seems to have worked frequently to subvert dominant forms of social relations and inspired the creative adaptation and invention of tradition.

This book could not have been written without the support and assistance of many people, many more than I can name in the space allotted for this task. I am particularly grateful to Stephen G. Wilson for introducing me to the letters of Ignatius of Antioch, to Margaret Y. MacDonald for helping me see what was important in my work and supervising my dissertation, to Carl Kazmierski for introducing me to the work of the Context Group, to Jerry Neyrey for inviting me to their meetings. I am indebted to the members of the Context Group and the Social-Scientific Criticism of the New Testament Section of the Society of

Biblical Literature for teaching me so much about the social and cultural worlds of Jesus and the early church, especially to Bruce J. Malina and John J. Pilch who read and constructively critiqued an early draft of chapter three.

A special word of gratitude is due to my institution Augustana College for providing two faculty research grants in support of this project, to my student research assistants: Keith Jagger, Bryn Lawrence, and Laura Johnson, and to Eleanor F. Beach for her meticulous indexing of this text.

I dedicate this book to my spouse, John, and to our children, Anne, Adam, and James. Thank you for your loving patience with this woman whose head is all too often in another century.

ABBREVIATIONS

General Abbreviations

ASC	altered states of consciousness
BDAG	Danker, F. W., W. Bauer, W. F. Arndt, and F. W. Gingrich. *Greek-English Lexicon of the New Testament and Other Early Christian Literature.* 3d ed. Chicago, 2000
BTB	*Biblical Theology Bulletin*
HvTSt	*Hervormde teologiese studies*
JBL	*Journal of Biblical Literature*
JSNTSup	Journal for the Study of the New Testament Supplement Series
List	*Listening: Journal of Religion and Culture*
LSJ	Liddell, H. G., R. Scott, H. S. Jones, *A Greek-English Lexicon.* 9th ed. with revised supplement. Oxford, 1996
NovT	*Novum Testamentum*
NovTSup	Supplements to Novum Testamentum
NTS	*New Testament Studies*
SBLSP	Society of Biblical Literature Seminar Papers
SBLSymS	Society of Biblical Literature Symposium Series
VC	*Vigiliae christianae*

Primary Sources

Old Testament

Exod	Exodus
Deut	Deuteronomy
Josh	Joshua
1–2 Kgs	1–2 Kings
Neh	Nehemiah
Isa	Isaiah
Jer	Jeremiah
Ezek	Ezekiel
Hos	Hosea

New Testament

Matt	Matthew
Rom	Romans
1–2 Cor	1–2 Corinthians
Gal	Galatians
Eph	Ephesians
Phil	Philippians
Col	Colossians
1–2 Thess	1–2 Thessalonians
1–2 Tim	1–2 Timothy
Phlm	Philemon
Jas	James
1–2 Pet	1–2 Peter

Apocrypha

Sir	Sirach/Ecclesiasticus
1 Macc	1 Maccabees

Other Ancient Sources

Ant.	Josephus, *Jewish Antiquities*
Diatr.	Epictetus, *Diatribai (Dissertationes)*
Did.	*Didache*
Ep.	Seneca, *Epistulae morales*
Gos. Thom.	*Gospel of Thomas*
Herm. Vis.	Shepherd of Hermas, *Vision(s)*
Hist.	Tacitus, *Historiae*
Hist. eccl.	Eusebius, *Historia Ecclesiastica* (Ecclesiastical History)
Hom. Num.	Origen, *Homiliae in Numeros*
Ign. Eph.	Ignatius, *To the Ephesians*
Ign. Magn.	Ignatius, *To the Magnesians*
Ign. Phld.	Ignatius, *To the Philadelphians*
Ign. Pol.	Ignatius, *To Polycarp*
Ign. Rom.	Ignatius, *To the Romans*
Ign. Smyrn.	Ignatius, *To the Smyrnaeans*
Ign. Trall.	Ignatius, *To the Trallians*
J.W.	Josephus, *Jewish War*
Joseph	Philo, *On the Life of Joseph*
Mor.	Plutarch, *Moralia*
QE I, 2	Philo, *Questions and Answers on Exodus* 1, 2
QG I, 2, 3, 4	Philo, *Questions and Answers on Genesis* 1, 2, 3, 4
Quis div.	Clement of Alexandria, *Quis dives salvetur* (Salvation of the Rich)
Spec. Laws	Philo, *On the Special Laws*

INTRODUCTION

"Who, then, is the faithful and prudent steward . . ." (Luke 12:42, NAB)

"Think of us in this way, as servants of Christ and stewards of God's mysteries." (I Cor 4:1)

"Prophets are not without honor, except in their hometown . . . and in their own house." (Mark 6:4)

"Those who prophesy speak to other people for their upbuilding and encouragement." (I Cor 14:3)

"Those who love me will keep my word." (John 14:23)

"I handed on to you as of first importance what I in turn had received . . ." (I Cor 15:3)

STEWARD, PROPHET, AND KEEPER of the word are three roles that leaders assumed in the early church. These roles are deeply rooted in the everyday life and cultures of the ancient Mediterranean world. Stewards were slaves or other non-elite persons whom elite masters had appointed to act on their behalf in dealings with others who might be socially inferior or superior to themselves. References to stewards and stewardship appear in the letters of Paul, the Gospel of Luke, the Pastoral Epistles, and the letters of Ignatius of Antioch. Prophets sought to discern the divine will for the human community and its projects through altered states of consciousness and other methods of divination. Prophetic activity marks the ministries of Jesus, his apostles, and the communities they founded, as is evident in a wide spectrum of canonical New Testament documents, the Ignatian correspondence, the *Didache*, and the *Gospel of Thomas.* "Keepers of the word" is a term that I have coined (derived from Jesus' words in John 14:23) to refer to those who engaged in the complex oral and written processes needed to preserve and transmit tradition (collective or social memory) in the predominantly oral cultures in which the early church was born and developed. All of the texts mentioned above may be studied as written artifacts of social memory, providing models of and for the social identity of various Jesus groups.

It is not my intention to argue for the existence of offices associated with the roles of steward, prophet, or keeper of the word, or to write an account of the historical origins and development of these roles in relation to any other set of offices that has emerged in the church over time. Studies focusing on the emergence of the offices of bishop and elder/presbyter in particular dominated the Reformation and its aftermath. Contemporary ecumenical dialogues and agreements have once again brought these issues to the forefront. They are addressed once again in Francis A. Sullivan's recent book, *From Apostles to Bishops: The Development of the Episcopacy in the Early Church,* in which he explains the historical and theological bases for the Catholic belief that bishops are the apostles' successors by divine institution. Sullivan's historical conclusions are unobjectionable. The historical episcopate emerged, he says, in the post-New Testament era in different places and times "from the local leadership of a college of presbyters who were sometimes also called *episkopoi.*"[1] He honestly concedes that the historical documents available to us "do not throw any light on how that transition took place."[2]

Sullivan then turns to theological reflection, affirming that the rise of the episcopacy had been divinely instituted. As evidence, he asserts the consistency of this transition with New Testament developments, the utility of the episcopate in preserving the church from schism and heresy, and faithful members' recognition of bishops as successors to the apostles.[3] It is here that Sullivan fails to persuade. The consistency that he finds in the New Testament documents results partly from his own reading of them and partly as a consequence of the canonization process. Dissenting voices from the early churches were excluded. He treats schism and heresy as if they resulted from external threats rather than intramural conflict. He never asks how much the emerging episcopacy might have contributed to or exacerbated schismatic and/or so-called heretical tendencies. In citing Irenaeus, Tertullian, and Origen as evidence that the faithful acknowledged the teaching of bishops as normative, he appears oblivious to the prescriptive quality of their writings. None of these church fathers dispassionately represents the voices of the faithful. Finally, Sullivan's book ends in a denominational impasse: "Christian ministry, in order to be fully valid, must be related to Christ and his apostles

---

[1] Francis A. Sullivan, *From Apostles to Bishops: The Development of the Episcopacy in the Early Church* (Mahweh, N.J.: Newman, 2001), 217.

[2] Ibid., 223.

[3] Ibid., 225.

through the historic succession maintained in the college of bishops."[4] The historical conclusions do not support the theological conclusions, the non-Catholic reader is left out in the cold, and we do not really learn much that will help church leaders lead in the twenty-first century.

My goal is quite different. Rather than tracing the origins and development of any particular office, I will examine the interaction of three roles or functions that early church leaders assumed or carried out. Each role or function represents a different aspect of social interaction that singly and together shaped and continues to shape church leadership. Stewards in the texts that we will be examining were deeply embedded in ancient Mediterranean hierarchical social arrangements, and thus represent the influence of existing social structures. Prophets were devoted to various religious practices involving some form of altered states of consciousness such as meditation, vision quest, or trance designed to engage spiritual or divine entities. They thus represent the impact of religious experience in church leadership. Keepers of the word are those engaged in the creation and preservation of tradition, namely, the collective memories and wisdom that shape a group's identity and way of life. The end result of my investigations will be a workable, three-dimensional, functional model of leadership in the early church that may provide a starting point for reflection on directions for contemporary church leadership.

Like all scholarly endeavors, I will pick up threads from the work of others and weave them into new configurations. One particularly useful trajectory of study emerging in the twentieth century has sought to understand early church leadership by comparing its forms to those of other ancient institutions, such as the synagogue, the philosophical school, elective associations, and the household.[5] Harry Maier argues persuasively that we ought to look to the household, the social setting in which the churches met, for the origins of its leadership structures.[6] Working within this trajectory, I will begin therefore with a description of ancient Mediterranean houses and households. Followers of Jesus, referred to as Jesus groups, gathered in houses that functioned as centers of production, commerce, religious life, and worship, as well as family residences. Jesus and the movement that grew up around him both critiqued and reordered the patriarchal household,

---

[4] Ibid., 236.

[5] See, for example, Wayne A. Meeks, *The First Urban Christians: The Social World of the Apostle Paul* (New Haven: Yale University Press, 1983); James T. Burtchaell, *From Synagogue to Church: Public Services and Offices in the Early Christian Communities* (New York: Cambridge University Press, 1992).

[6] Harry O. Maier, *The Social Setting of the Ministry as Reflected in the Writings of Hermas, Clement and Ignatius* (Dissertations SR 1; Waterloo, Ont.: Wilfrid Laurier University Press, 1991), 4, 148–53, 155–56, 187.

the very basis of social life in first-century Jewish and Greco-Roman cultures. The earliest Jesus groups functioned as surrogate families or fictive kinship groups in which there was only one father figure, the divine one.

Maier argues that hierarchical social arrangements arising from the household contributed significantly to the emergence of episcopal leadership, but he does not explicate what these social arrangements were.[7] I will further Maier's work by highlighting in the second part of chapter one the ways in which patriarchal authority had been extended beyond the household through a system of patronage relationships. These relationships took the form of fictive kinship associations enabling powerful heads of households to act as "father" figures to persons not connected by blood, marriage, or other familial ties for specific economic, religious, and/or political transactions. An important role within patronage relationships was frequently played by intermediaries or brokers who had access to patrons and their resources and who could on occasion represent and act on behalf of powerful patrons. The organization of the early churches as fictive kinship groups simultaneously restricted patriarchal status to God and the role of patron to the heavenly Father, and cast Jesus, the disciples, and later church leaders most frequently in the role of brokers.

Chapter two begins with an examination of the role of the *oikonomos* or "steward" in ancient Mediterranean societies. The steward was generally a managerial slave or freedman responsible for administering the affairs of elite households, social clubs, and municipalities. Josephus' story of Arion the steward will illustrate the ambiguous and vulnerable status and power of such figures, especially within sometimes quite complex patronage relationships. This analysis will provide the necessary historical context for evaluating references to stewards and stewardship in the early texts of Jesus groups. Among the Gospel writers, only Luke includes parables that explicitly feature stewards and sets them up as examples for leaders of Jesus groups (12:41–48; 16:1–8). These parables explore what it means to be faithful and prudent within the context of the hierarchical social structures and patronage relations that characterized ancient Mediterranean societies. Paul uses steward and stewardship language in relation to his own claims to status and authority within and over the churches that he has established. As we shall see, Paul's strategy offers a subversive critique of the dominant Greco-Roman ideology of benevolent patriarchalism endorsed by his critics. In contrast, the pseudo-Pauline epistles seem to adopt the very stance that the apostle opposes by emphasizing the grace or favor that is bestowed on "Paul" with respect to his role in bringing God's

---

[7] Ibid., 187.

oikonomia or "administration." This trend continues in the Pastoral and Ignatian correspondence, where stewardship language is used to legitimate the status and authority of persons who hold the title, status, and office of bishop without the mitigating effects of Paul's theology of the cross.

Another trend that emerged in the twentieth century has been the adoption and adaptation of insights from the social sciences. Drawing on Weber's ideal types of authority, scholars have explored the evolution of church offices alongside or as replacements for an original charismatic leadership of apostles, prophets, and teachers. Maier, for example, explicitly employs Weber's ideal types of authority as a way to understand the authority of a figure like Ignatius of Antioch.[8] While these ideal types are useful heuristically, they tend to obscure the phenomena under investigation. This obscuration is particularly evident in the way Maier highlights textual references to prophetic speech and spiritual knowledge in order to support his thesis that Ignatius' authority was essentially charismatic.[9] Weber's typology does not help us understand how one acquired (or was thought to acquire) spiritual and/or prophetic insight in the ancient world, and points to a frequently overlooked dimension of early church life—religious experience.[10] Particularly helpful for appreciating this phenomena are David Aune's *Prophecy in Early Christianity and the Ancient Mediterranean World* and several articles by John Pilch alerting biblical scholars to research on altered states of consciousness.[11]

Chapter three, therefore, begins with an introduction to altered states of consciousness (hereafter abbreviated as ASC) and their relation to the phenomenon of prophecy in the ancient world. I will argue that Jesus ought to be seen as a prophetic figure operating outside the structures of Israelite political religion and, to a large degree, outside household religion. ASC experiences were the foundation

---

[8] Ibid., 156–61.

[9] Ibid., 159–61.

[10] Recent calls to correct this oversight may be found in works such as Luke Timothy Johnson's *Religious Experience in Earliest Christianity: A Missing Dimension in New Testament Studies* (Minneapolis: Fortress, 1998) and John Ashton's *The Religion of Paul the Apostle* (New Haven: Yale University Press, 2000).

[11] David E. Aune, *Prophecy in Early Christianity and the Ancient Mediterranean World* (Grand Rapids: Eerdmans, 1983). The following articles by John J. Pilch are most useful: "Visions in Revelation and Alternate Consciousness: A Perspective from Cultural Anthropology," *List* 28 (1993): 231–44; "Altered States of Consciousness: A 'Kitbashed' Model," *BTB* 26 (1996): 133–38; "Appearances of the Risen Jesus in Cultural Context: Experiences of Alternate Reality," *BTB* 28 (1998): 52–60; "Paul's Ecstatic Trance Experience Near Damascus in Acts of the Apostles," *HvTSt* 58 (2002): 690–707; "Altered States of Consciousness Events in the Synoptics," in *The Social Setting of Jesus and the Gospels* (ed. Wolfgang Stegemann, Bruce J. Malina, and Gerd Theissen; Minneapolis: Fortress, 2002), 103–15.

of Paul's claims to apostolic status. Within the communities he established, ASC experiences, such as glossalalia and prophecy, were valued so highly that they inspired rivalry for honor and status, particularly within the assembly at Corinth. In Luke-Acts every innovation in missionary practice—from the first acceptance of Gentiles to the appointment of the Ephesian elders as bishops—is unabashedly legitimated by ASC experience. Ignatius too relies on ASC experiences granted to him on his way to execution, when he attempts locally, although unsuccessfully, to legitimate emerging episcopal leadership structures. Other Jesus-group texts present a more ambivalent attitude toward prophetic activity. The Gospel of Matthew, the *Didache,* and the Johannine corpus all treat the phenomenon with suspicion and advocate various tests to determine the authenticity of prophetic performances. The *Gospel of Thomas* endorses ASC experience while testifying to the hostility aroused by claims to special revelations.

One aspect of ancient Mediterranean cultures that has received little attention in New Testament and Patristic studies until very recently is the complex relationship between orality and writing. This area is particularly helpful for understanding the development and transmission of the Jesus traditions. Our deep immersion in cultures in which communication occurs primarily through print and electronic media that require high levels of literacy, together with the fact that the only extant artifacts of the Jesus movement and its successors are texts, have blinded us to the reality that the latter were produced in predominantly oral cultures. In an effort to provide a corrective lens, chapter four begins with a description of first-century Mediterranean cultures as predominantly oral. Estimates of literacy in the Greco-Roman world range from three percent at the low end to ten or fifteen percent at the high end. Even those who could read and write did so in highly "oral" ways. Not only did authors regularly compose by reciting or dictating to scribes, many, if not most, of their literary productions were intended for oral performance and aural reception.

Recognition that our early Jesus-group texts are in fact more like musical scores or scripts for performance means that we must re-imagine the ways that they make meaning. Particularly helpful in this rethinking are social memory studies, originating in the work of Maurice Halbwachs and continued in the work of contemporary sociologists. Social memory is a significant factor in the establishment, reinforcement, and maintenance of personal and social identities through acts of commemoration, that is, remembering together common *commemoranda,* such as material artifacts, rituals, practices, and productions of the verbal arts. When individuals and groups disagree about the significance and meaning of past persons and events, social memory is contested. Such disagreements remind us that any given commemoration is not so much a window into a shared past as a purposeful performance with specific pragmatic and rhetorical goals. Social memory is thus both malleable and persistent. Through the operations of framing and keying, social memory helps persons and groups make sense of their present experiences by relating them to primary, foundational events in the past. In this way social memory provides models of and for society.

In chapter four I combine these two perspectives—the predominance of orality and the operations of social memory—in order to explore the questions of by whom and for what purposes the words of Jesus were "kept." Given the scope of this work, my assessment is of necessity selective and limited; its results are suggestive rather than conclusive. My process of selection is not overly systematic. For the most part I start with Q sayings and attempt to trace how they are used in various early texts of the Jesus groups (e.g., studying Q/Luke 11:47–51 in its own context, following the work of Alan Kirk, and then in its appearance in I Thess 2:13–16). This chapter includes an assessment of Paul's use of commands or sayings that he attributes to the Lord and the function of Jesus' sayings in the resocialization program of the *Didache* and in the ascetic program of the *Gospel of Thomas*. The chapter closes with a brief assessment of the words of Jesus in the Gospel of John.

The final chapter briefly summarizes my findings and suggests how social structures, religious experience, and tradition might interact creatively to form a model for church leadership today.

1

THE SOCIAL SETTING OF THE EARLY CHURCHES

Houses

"HERE'S THE CHURCH, HERE'S the steeple, open the doors and see all the people!" This chant and its accompanying finger play are familiar to many of us from our Sunday school days. Deeply embedded in this children's game are cultural assumptions, including the idea that people worship in specially designated buildings called "churches." Although this fun little game is often used to make the point that the building alone is not "the church," the connection between people and building is inescapable. So, too, the notion that churches look different from the buildings that surround them cannot be overlooked, since they have steeples and other architectural details that mark them out as places of worship. Large double doors, frequently wooden, are often open only on Sunday mornings. Within the doors one expects to find a vestibule or foyer that church folks refer to as the narthex or gathering place. Through yet another set of double doors one enters into the actual worship space, the nave or sanctuary, that is usually filled with long wooden benches called pews facing a raised area (the chancel) containing an altar, a lectern, a pulpit, and other furniture and equipment. Here the people gather to sing, pray, listen, eat, sit, stand, and kneel, as appropriate. Here people are baptized, receive communion, are confirmed, get married, and are bid farewell at the end of life.

Admittedly, in North America today one can find a fair amount of diversity in church architecture, ranging from the traditional, rural, white-clapboard, steepled buildings to large complexes that look more like college auditoriums. While some congregations worship in buildings designated for other purposes, those settings are most frequently temporary. Congregations in their formative stages may meet in the basement of the pastor's residence, a rented room in a commercial building, a school gymnasium, or even a funeral chapel. Yet one of the goals of most fledgling congregations is to buy or build a "church" of their own. My point here is that we associate "church"—people, worship, and related activities—with specially designated buildings with peculiar features like those mentioned above. This connection of churches with buildings is part of our contemporary North American cultural context. It is often difficult for us to realize that almost all of these features, which we take for granted when talking about "church," do not apply to the people we meet in the pages of the New Testament.

In Galilee. Jesus never went to "church." He grew up in Nazareth, a small Galilean peasant village with a population of two to four hundred persons spread out over about ten acres of land. Archaeological surveys of Nazareth have uncovered olive and wine presses, water cisterns, grain silos, and grinding stones, but "no evidence for public architecture of any kind whatsoever."[1] The village in which Jesus grew up had "no synagogue . . . no fortification, no palace, no basilica, no bathhouse, no paved street."[2] In other words, there was no specially designated "church" or other religious building as far as we can tell from the archaeological remains. This lack does not mean, however, that its residents were not a worshipping community. The presence of two-stepped, plastered pools or ritual baths (*miqwaoth*) and fragments of stone vessels points to a Torah-observant Jewish population.[3] Circumcisions, bar mitzvahs, Sabbath gatherings, recitations of Scriptures, celebrations of festivals, and other aspects of religious life were centered in and around people's homes. Jesus would have worshipped together with his family and neighbors in simple fieldstone dwellings with beaten earth floors and thatched roofs, frequently built around existing hillside caves.[4]

What then should we conclude about of the gospel story of Jesus' teaching "in the synagogue" in his hometown of Nazareth (Mark 6:1–6a//Matt 13:53–58// Luke 4:16–30)? In light of the archaeological evidence, "synagogue" here ought to be read not as a reference to a building but to an assembly of persons. They may have gathered in a room, a courtyard, a storehouse, or perhaps even in the village square.[5] This situation in Nazareth does not appear to have been unique in first-century Galilee. In fact, aside from the synagogue at Gamla in the Golan, there is very little archaeological evidence for specially designated worship buildings in the villages.[6] Thus, when we read about Jesus going "throughout Galilee,

---

[1] John Dominic Crossan and Jonathan L. Reed, *Excavating Jesus: Beneath the Stones, Behind the Texts* (San Francisco: HarperSanFrancisco, 2001), 30.

[2] Ibid., 32.

[3] Ibid., 36.

[4] Ibid., 34–35.

[5] Ibid., 26; Richard A. Horsley and Neil Asher Silberman, *The Message and the Kingdom: How Jesus and Paul Ignited a Revolution and Transformed the Ancient World* (Minneapolis: Fortress, 2002), 44.

[6] Crossan and Reed, *Excavating Jesus*, 25–27; John J. Rousseau and Rami Arav, *Jesus and His World: An Archaeological and Cultural Dictionary* (Minneapolis: Fortress, 1995), 100.

proclaiming the message in their synagogues" (Mark 1:39//Matt 4:23//Luke 4:44), we ought to imagine, not ancient equivalents to "churches," but Jewish Sabbath gatherings that occurred wherever space and weather permitted.

A possible exception to this situation may have been at Capernaum, the seaside village that served as a center, at least for a while, of Jesus' ministry. It was home to about one thousand inhabitants engaged primarily in fishing and agriculture, but with access to both sea and land trade routes.[7] After the division of Herod the Great's kingdom in 4 B.C.E., the area around Capernaum became a place of transition from the political jurisdiction of Herod Antipas to that of Herod Philip, where "traffic was monitored and customs duties paid."[8] It is here that Jesus found Levi working in his "toll booth" (Matt 9:9//Mark 2:14//Luke 5:27; in Matt 9:9 Levi is called Matthew), and where Jesus healed a centurion's slave (Matt 8:5–13//Luke 7:1–10).[9] According to Luke (7:5), this officer of Herod Antipas built a synagogue for the residents of Capernaum. Here archaeologists have uncovered the remains of an impressive limestone synagogue dating to the fourth century C.E. Black basalt walls beneath this synagogue have been identified as the foundation of a first-century synagogue, perhaps the structure referred to by Luke. These discoveries are, however, the subject of intense debate among scholars.[10] Even if those black basalt walls did belong to a first-century "synagogue" building, it was probably a multi-use structure. A first-century synagogue inscription from Jerusalem indicates that the building was used for Torah-reading, teaching the commandments, and lodging for needy strangers.[11]

Yet even at Capernaum it seems that Jesus' ministry was based primarily in the "house of Simon and Andrew" (Mark 1:29).[12] Archaeological evidence indicates that houses in Capernaum consisted of small, one-to two-room, single-story, stone-walled units built around a courtyard. These individual units were built into an enclosure wall that limited visibility and access to the courtyard that served as the main living and working space for multi-generation, extended family groups.[13] Simon and Andrew were sharing a house not only with each other, their wives, and

---

[7] Rousseau and Arav, *Jesus and His World,* 46; Carolyn Osiek and David L. Balch, *Families in the New Testament World: Households and House Churches* (Louisville: Westminster John Knox, 1997), 14.

[8] Horsley and Silberman, *The Message and the Kingdom,* 46.

[9] In John 4:46b–54 the centurion is called a "royal official" and it is his son who is ill.

[10] See, for example, Crossan and Reed, *Excavating Jesus,* 90–91; Rousseau and Arav, *Jesus and His World,* 39–47.

[11] Reproduced in K. C. Hanson and Douglas E. Oakman, *Palestine in the Time of Jesus: Social Structures and Social Conflicts* (Minneapolis: Fortress, 1998), 79.

[12] Matt 8:14//Luke 4:38 identify it as Peter's or Simon's house only.

[13] Crossan and Reed, *Excavating Jesus,* 84; Osiek and Balch, *Families in the New Testament World,* 14.

their children, but also with Simon's mother-in-law, who was healed by and ministered to Jesus.[14] It was to such a house that the villagers brought their sick in hopes
that Jesus might heal them (Mark 1:32–34//Matt 8:16//Luke 4:40–41). On
one occasion, the crowd around the house was so large that some desperate people
actually dug through the thatched, mud-packed roof to help their sick friend gain
access to Jesus (Mark 2:1–12//Matt 9:1–8//Luke 5:17–26, Luke's reference to
tiles is unlikely). Another time the presence of a large crowd in the house pre-
vented Jesus and his disciples from eating (Mark 3:19b–20).

Yes, we find Jesus teaching in the countryside (Mark 1:45), beside the sea
(Mark 2:13), or in a boat by the shore (Mark 4:1). I would like to suggest,
however, that much, if not most, of his ministry—both teaching and healing—
probably occurred in houses and was directed at households. He was criticized for
dining in the homes of tax collectors and sinners, an activity that he justified as
analogous to healing the sick (Mark 2:15–17//Matt 9:9–13//Luke 5:27–32).
Jesus was called to the house of Jairus, a leader of the synagogue, perhaps in
Capernaum, to heal his dying daughter (Mark 5:21–43//Matt 9:18–26//Luke
8:40–56). Even when he was trying to avoid public notice, people sought him out
in houses (Mark 7:24). On several occasions, a house was the venue in which the
disciples sought Jesus for clarifying instructions (Mark 7:17; 10:10; 9:28//Matt
17:19; Matt 13:36). When Jesus sent out his disciples, they were specifically instructed to enter a house and stay there until they left that place (Mark 6:10//
Luke 9:4, 10:7). For them too, houses were to be centers or bases from which they
proclaimed the kingdom of God, cast out demons, and healed the sick. (See also
Matt 10:11–15.)

We need to picture the Jesus movement in rural Galilee and the surrounding
region as operating frequently, if not primarily, within and around houses. Sabbath teaching and healing "in synagogues" probably occurred in homes, courtyards, storehouses, or wherever there was sufficient space for the worshipping
community to gather. This "house" setting would have been the same for the
teaching and healing in rural Judea as well. The primary exception to this modus
operandi would have been in the city of Jerusalem, where Jesus seems to have been
active in and around the temple, the house of God.

In Jerusalem. The Jerusalem temple would have been quite different from any
church building that we may be familiar with, both physically and institutionally.
A vast complex built on a plaza elevated 100 feet above street level, it measured

---

[14] Mark 1:30//Matt 8:14//Luke 4:38. It may have been her house; see Crossan and Reed, *Excavating Jesus*, 94.

1,590 feet on the west, 1,035 feet on the north, 1,536 feet on the east, and 912 feet on the south.[15] Raised walkways connected this plaza to the Upper City and provided easy access for the aristocratic priests who were in charge of the temple, and for other Judean elites living in this upscale neighborhood.[16] Non-elite pilgrims entered the temple complex through gates from the south and climbed windowless, four-story staircases.[17] They would emerge in the Court of Gentiles in front of the Royal Stoa, "a giant basilica made up of four rows of forty columns that extended nearly the entire length of the 900–foot southern wall."[18] Here pilgrims could exchange local currencies for the Tyrian half-shekels needed to pay the temple tax and other tithes as well as arrange for the purchase of sacrificial animals as prescribed in the Torah. At the extreme north end of the plaza stood the Antonia Fortress, a military installation built by Herod the Great and in Jesus' day the headquarters of the Roman prefect. From its walls, political and military authorities could oversee and intervene in events taking place within the courts below. These architectural features of the temple complex point to its role as a social institution deeply embedded in Judean politics and economics.

In between the Antonia Fortress and the Royal Stoa was an extensive plaza of about thirty-five acres consisting of a series of concentric open-air "courts." As noted above, pilgrims entering the temple complex would find themselves in the Court of the Gentiles. Sacrificial animals were penned and prepared for slaughter in the open area between the Antonia Fortress and the temple proper, referred to by Chilton as the "North Court."[19] The space between the Royal Stoa and the temple, which Chilton refers to as the "South Court," was open to all people—Israelites and non-Israelites, believers and non-believers.[20] A stone wall a few feet high, called the *soreg*, marked the beginning of the inner courts and the point beyond which Gentiles (i.e., non-Israelites/pagans) could not pass on pain of death. From the Court of Gentiles, Israelite men and women of all ages passed into the Court of Women. Only men were permitted to enter the Court of Israel to present their sacrificial offerings. Priests and Levites took these offerings into the Court of the Priests, the location of the altar and of the temple building itself. The temple was a white marble and gold structure, 103 feet long, 35 feet wide,

---

[15] M. O. Wise, "Temple Origins and Structures," in *Dictionary of New Testament Background: A Compendium of Contemporary Biblical Scholarship* (ed. Craig A. Evans and Stanley E. Porter; Downers Grove, Ill.: InterVarsity, 2000), 1168.

[16] Hanson and Oakman, *Palestine in the Time of Jesus*, 138.

[17] Bruce Chilton, *Rabbi Jesus: An Intimate Biography* (New York: Doubleday, 2000), 30.

[18] Crossan and Reed, *Excavating Jesus*, 198.

[19] Chilton, *Rabbi Jesus*, 217.

[20] Ibid.

and 69 feet high, divided by curtains into two rooms. The outer room housed a seven-branched lamp stand, a table with twelve loaves of bread, and an altar for burning incense. The inner room, or Holy of Holies, where God's presence or glory was thought to dwell, was empty, save for a small rock on which the High Priest offered incense and the blood of atonement once each year on the Day of Atonement.[21] The temple building faced due east so that on the Day of Atonement, and only on that day, the rays of the rising sun, shining through the open doors of the sanctuary, lit up this inner chamber.[22]

The central activity of Judean worship took place outside the temple at the altar in the Court of the Priests. The altar was a massive stone structure measuring seventy-five feet in length and width and twenty-three feet in height.[23] Bruce Chilton describes this altar as somewhat analogous to "an incredibly complex barbecue pit" where wheat and barley were roasted; where blood, wine, and olive oil were poured over the fire; and where butchered animals, whole or in part, were burnt or roasted as sacrifices.[24] For Israelites (before 70 C.E.), as for all ancient peoples, worship involved the ritual slaughter of animals. Sometimes the worshipper gave the entire animal to the deity for consumption or burning. On other occasions God, priests, and/or worshippers shared the flesh of the animal.[25] The act of sacrifice tangibly demonstrated one's allegiance to the deity. Through this act the worshipper affirmed that "God is the one who controls all"[26] and so has a claim upon all goods in life.[27] The sacrifice served both as a gift celebrating God's favor and as an inducement for continued blessings in terms of maintaining and/ or restoring life for individuals, families, and society.[28] Sacrifices were offered daily in the temple; some were obligatory and others were so-called freewill offerings. Admittedly, sacrifice was accompanied by recitations of Scripture, prayers, songs, dramas, and other features of worship with which we may be well acquainted; yet this central aspect of ancient religious life remains utterly alien to the contemporary believer. The act of Jesus going to the temple in Jerusalem, then,

---

[21] Wise, "Temple Origins and Structures," 1169.

[22] Chilton, *Rabbi Jesus*, 216; Crossan and Reed, *Excavating Jesus*, 198.

[23] Josephus, *J.W.* 5.225 in Chilton, *Rabbi Jesus*, 217.

[24] Ibid., 217–18.

[25] Paula Fredriksen, *Jesus of Nazareth, King of the Jews: A Jewish Life and the Emergence of Christianity* (New York: Alfred A. Knopf, 1999), 51–52; Chilton, *Rabbi Jesus*, 217–18; Hanson and Oakman, *Palestine in the Time of Jesus*, 143–44.

[26] Bruce J. Malina, *The New Testament World: Insights from Cultural Anthropology* (3d ed., rev. and exp.; Louisville, Ky.: Westminster John Knox, 2001), 186.

[27] Hanson and Oakman, *Palestine in the Time of Jesus*, 143.

[28] Malina, *The New Testament World*, 185.

cannot be regarded as comparable to the contemporary act of going to church. A more appropriate analogy might be a visit to a slaughterhouse.[29] Yet, even this comparison fails to take in the whole experience of the temple, since this "house of God" functioned as a centralizing political, economic, and religious institution "organizing and governing the life of Judean peasantry."[30]

Summary. Neither Jesus' participation in the synagogues of Galilee nor his participation in temple worship in Jerusalem is readily comparable to our experience of "going to church." There were very few buildings in first-century Galilee set aside specifically for worship. The worshipping community gathered in houses, storehouses, courtyards, and village squares—wherever space and weather permitted. The same setting characterizes Jesus' own ministry; we find him healing and teaching in houses, in villages, in the countryside, or by the seashore, as the size of the crowd seemed to demand. In Jerusalem, Jesus and his disciples participated in temple worship as pilgrims, celebrating at least one Passover (Mark 14:12–21// Matt 26:17–25//Luke 22:7–14). The writer of John's gospel presents a Jesus who frequently goes up to Jerusalem for the festivals celebrated in the temple complex (John 2:13–25; 5:1–18; 7:10–24; 8:2–11; 10:22–42; 13:1–30). In Jerusalem, the temple courtyards were the venue for Jesus' teaching. Here Jesus sparred with chief priests, scribes, and elders (Mark 11:27//Luke 20:1, and in Matt 21:23 only with chief priests and elders), Pharisees and Herodians (Mark 12:13/ /Matt 22:15), Sadducees (Mark 12:18//Matt 22:23//Luke 20:27), and again with a scribe (Mark 12:28 and in Matt 22:34–35 with a Pharisee who was a lawyer). In its precincts Jesus condemned the elite, ruling priests for turning God's house into a "cave of bandits" (Mark 11:17), that is, into "a redistributive institution benefiting only the few."[31]

Jerusalem Jesus Group. The Jesus group that remained in Jerusalem following Christ's death and resurrection continued to gather in the temple (Acts 2:46). Peter and John healed a lame man before the Beautiful Gate (Acts 3:1–10), that is, the entrance to the Court of Women, and preached in Solomon's Portico (Acts 3:11–26; 5:12), one of the colonnades surrounding the Court of Gentiles. The Apostle Paul, along with four members of the Jerusalem Jesus group, underwent purification rituals and made sacrifice in the temple (Acts 21:26). It was in the temple complex that Paul was seized by an angry crowd of pilgrims and then rescued by Roman soldiers (Acts 21:27–36). The point is that, however strange the

---

[29] Hanson and Oakman, *Palestine in the Time of Jesus,* 145.
[30] Ibid., 156.
[31] Ibid., 155. Their translation.

rituals of the Jerusalem temple may seem to us today, they remained an important part of the experience of Jesus' followers in Jerusalem until the temple was destroyed in 70 C.E.

The temple was not, however, the only venue for the religious life of the Jerusalem Jesus group. The writer of Luke-Acts tells us that they "broke bread from house to house" (Acts 2:46), and gathered for prayer in the house of Mary, the mother of John Mark (Acts 12:12). It was here that Peter fled from Herod Agrippa's prison to leave a message for James before departing for "another place" (Acts 12:12–17). No doubt Mary's was a relatively modest house, perhaps similar to the "Burnt House" with its "small entry courtyard paved with stones, a kitchen, four other rooms of varying sizes and a *mikveh* reached by descending steps."[32] Just as Jesus never went to "church," neither did those who gathered in his name in the city of Jerusalem after his death and resurrection. House and temple remained at the center of their religious experiences.

Pauline Mission. A similar situation pertains to the Pauline mission, in spite the repeated use of the word "church" in our English language Bibles. Paul's letters, each ostensibly addressed to "churches," are in fact addressed to *ekklesiai*—that is, to "assemblies" of Christ-followers (e.g., 1 Cor 1:2; 2 Cor 1:1; Gal 1:2; 1 Thess 1:1; Phlm 2). As we learn from Paul's greeting to Philemon, the assembly is in his house (Phlm 2). Other assemblies met in the houses of Prisca and Aquila at Ephesus (1 Cor 16:19; Rom 16:3–5), Gaius at Corinth (Rom 16:23), and Nympha at Colossae (Col 4:15). Lydia at Philippi (Acts 16:16, 40), Chloe in Corinth (1 Cor 1:11), and Phoebe in Cenchraea (Rom 16:1–13) may also have hosted meetings of Christ-following assemblies in their houses.[33] The house of Onesiphorus in Iconium is also portrayed as the place where the assembly met in the early second-century text known as *The Acts of Thecla.*[34]

These dwellings would not have been the houses of peasants, but the dwelling places of non-elite, urban residents who probably made up no more than seven percent of the population of the Roman Empire.[35] The majority of these city dwellers lived in small apartments. Sometimes these apartments were located above or behind the shops in which they worked. In Ephesus, for example, archaeologists have uncovered a row of shops opening onto a colonnaded

---

[32] Osiek and Balch, *Families in the New Testament World,* 13.

[33] Ibid., 33.

[34] Para. 2–7, reproduced in Bart D. Ehrman, *Lost Scriptures: Books that Did Not Make It into the New Testament* (New York: Oxford University Press, 2003), 114.

[35] Osiek and Balch, *Families in the New Testament World,* 37.

portico running along the street. Above these shops was a corridor providing access to a row of rooms, lighted and ventilated by ceiling windows.[36] Alternatives to this arrangement included multi-unit housing and apartment buildings (*insulae*). Examples of the former include two-story buildings at Ostia near Rome, comprised of four living units per floor, each consisting of four or five rooms and a corridor. Some of these dwellings had their own built-in latrines.[37] *Insulae*, on the other hand, were larger complexes of three or four stories. The ground floor often housed shops, a common well or cistern, and a common latrine. More upscale versions included central courtyards with fountains and mosaics. Apartments ranged in size from one to seven rooms, some with windows open to the street and with access to the central courtyard, if there was one.[38] In such buildings the majority of the members who made up Paul's assemblies lived and worked and, on occasion, met. We can imagine such a location for the gathering in Troas, where Eutyches, sitting "in the window," nodded off to sleep and fell three stories (Acts 20:7–12). In the middle of the second century, Justin Martyr reports that a Christian assembly met in his apartments near a bath house in Rome.[39] Most frequently, however, Christian assemblies seem to have met in houses.[40]

Houses in the ancient world, as today, varied greatly in size. At Pompeii and Herculaneum, for instance, the smallest houses were about twenty-five square meters in size, while the largest measured three thousand square meters.[41] The average houses in these two cities were between 175 and 245 square meters.[42] Ideally, Greco-Roman houses were built around an open central space, called a peristyle or atrium, that would have been impossible to include in the smaller houses. Access from the street to the house was through a narrow doorway that was flanked by a stable and/or shops opening onto the street and, in more affluent houses, by a porter's room. Dining room, guest rooms, and a reception room from which the head of the house conducted business were arranged around the central open space. In Greek houses, a passage at the back of the peristyle led to the *gynaikonitis*, that is, the women's quarters. This section consisted of a second open space surrounded by rooms for women's work and domestic activities, as well as cells for

---

[36] Ibid., 12.

[37] Ibid., 20.

[38] Ibid., 18.

[39] *The Acts of the Martyrdom of St. Justin and His Companions.*

[40] See Osiek and Balch, *Families in the New Testament World,* 16, 24.

[41] Ibid., 15.

[42] Ibid., 201.

storage and slaves' quarters.[43] Access to this private area of the house was by invitation only and limited to intimates of the family.[44] Such segregated spaces would, of course, have been impossible in smaller houses and virtually meaningless in households headed by women. The enclosure or confinement of women in male-headed households was thus a symbol of status and affluence, especially in the eastern Mediterranean among Greeks, Syrians, and Palestinians.[45] This gendered division of household space was virtually nonexistent in Roman society in the western empire.[46]

Thus, when we read Paul's commendation of Gaius for hosting the whole assembly in his house at Corinth (Rom 16:23), we need to imagine a relatively large home such as that described above. The assembly would have gathered in the part of the house that was generally open to the public—the "men's" side of the house. Public accessibility rose in relation to the owner's status and importance in the city.[47] In other words, anyone passing by could have wandered in and observed the activities of the *ekklesia*, as Paul implies in his reference to unbelievers or outsiders who might enter (1 Cor 14:24). The lack of privacy in ancient houses is epitomized in *The Acts of Thecla*, where Thecla overhears Paul preaching in the house next door. She spends three days at her window, watching women and virgins entering Onesiphorus's house and listening to Paul's preaching (*Acts of Thecla* 7–9).

The central activity of the *ekklesia* seems to have been a meal—the Lord's Supper—followed by acts of prophecy, teaching, healing, and speaking in tongues (1 Cor 11–14). Its members would have gathered in the dining room (*triclinium*), which typically would have been equipped for nine diners reclining on three couches arranged as an open-ended square facing the peristyle, where additional diners could be accommodated, either reclining or sitting on chairs or on the ground.[48] The Corinthian Christ-followers are described as sitting (1 Cor 14:30), an adaptation designed perhaps to accommodate larger numbers. Estimates on the size of an *ekklesia* range from thirty or forty people to a few hundred, depending entirely on the size of the house.[49]

Would Gaius' house have had a *gynaikonitis* where women and small children ate and perhaps worshipped apart from the men? Osiek and Balch suggest two

---

[43] Ibid., 6–11, 29.

[44] Ibid., 43.

[45] Ibid., 8–9, 44, 46.

[46] Ibid., 27, 47, although there may have been a temporal division of household use.

[47] Ibid., 24–26.

[48] Ibid., 33–34.

[49] Ibid., 201–3.

possible scenarios for such a gathering. If separate dining facilities for men and women were available and customary, we might imagine the women and children dining apart from the men, but "positioned in such a way as to be able at least to hear the voice of the presider and/or preacher." The other possibility is that a woman presider led the women during the meal after which they joined the men for the teaching, or perhaps only when an important visitor presided."[50]

From Paul's comments in his first letter to the Corinthians it is quite clear that women (and slaves, as will be developed further below) were present in the assembly. In 1 Cor 11:4–5 Paul gives instructions about the proper appearance of men and women who pray and prophesy. The concern that female prophets and worship leaders be veiled suggests that they were active in the "public" assembly and not in the "private" women's quarters. Similarly, 1 Cor 14:34–35, whether taken as original to the letter or as a later interpolation, points to the presence of women in the assembly and a concern that they not speak "in public." The need for such a proscription also indicates that the women felt quite comfortable speaking in that venue! The perceived need to silence the women arises, no doubt, from concerns about the public reputation of these assemblies (1 Cor 14:23; 10:32–33; 5:1).[51] The point, however, is that the Corinthian assembly does not appear to have been segregated on the basis of gender, although the nature of women's participation at these gatherings was an issue for some.

Other Groups. These concerns persisted in the Pauline assemblies, as is evidenced by the authors of the Pastoral Epistles and other Pseudo-Pauline texts. The Pastoral Epistles warn against widows who are "gadding about from house to house . . . saying what they should not say" (1 Tim 5:13) and against false teachers who enter houses and captivate silly women (2 Tim 3:6). In *The Acts of Thecla* Paul himself receives that charge. Paul's preaching to the assembly gathered in Onesiphorus' house is overheard by Thecla who lives next door. Her mother, Theoclia, explains to Thamyris (Thecla's fiancé) that her daughter, "clinging to the window like a spider, lays hold of what is said by him with a strange eagerness and fearful emotion. For the virgin looks eagerly at what is said by him and has been captivated" (*Acts of Thecla* 7–9).

---

[50] Ibid., 33–34.

[51] See discussion S. Scott Bartchy, "Power, Submission, and Sexual Identity among the Early Christians," in *Essays on New Testament Christianity: A Festschrift in Honor of Dean E. Walker* (Cincinnati: Standard, 1978), 68–69; Margaret Y. MacDonald, *Early Christian Women and Pagan Opinion: The Power of the Hysterical Woman* (Cambridge: Cambridge University Press, 1996), 144–45.

The location of Jesus groups in houses was not limited to the Pauline mission. The Johannine elder assumes that the assembly represented by "the elect lady" (*eklekte kyria*) and her children is located in a house. He instructs her not to receive or welcome anyone into the house who does not teach that Jesus Christ has come in the flesh (2 John 7–11). It is not until the late second or early third century that Christ-followers began to convert residential dwellings into specially designated worship spaces.

> The clearest and best-preserved example of this change is the Christian house church at Dura-Europos on the frontier of Roman Syria. Without altering the exterior, a house of eight ground-floor rooms, a staircase to the roof, and a central courtyard was converted before the middle of the third century into a building better suited for group worship and activities. This remodeled *domus ecclesiae* provided a larger rectangular room for worship by the removal of one wall between two rooms. The new room, 5.15 by 12.9 meters, could have accommodated perhaps sixty-five to seventy-five people. A small platform, extending almost a meter from the wall, about 1.5 meters long and .20 meters high, was added to the east, short wall. A built-in baptistery with canopy supported by columns was also added in yet another room. While the wall decoration of the large assembly hall remained traditional, the walls of the baptistery room were adorned with biblical scenes.[52]

Please note that the exterior of the building remained unchanged. To passers-by on the street there was nothing to indicate that this house had become a "church." It was not until the fourth century, when emperor Constantine personally financed the building of Christian worship places and made imperial revenues available to bishops to do the same, that we begin to see a proliferation of specially designated worship spaces.

Implications. Contemporary readers need to bear in mind that the persons they meet in the pages of the New Testament and other early Christian texts did not experience "church" in the way that we do. Jesus groups gathered in houses that are quite different physically from the homes in which middle- and upper-class North Americans live. The majority of people in the Greco-Roman world lived in "small, dark, poorly ventilated, crowded buildings where privacy was unavailable, adequate sanitation impossible, and the spread of disease inevitable."[53] These dwellings served functions that most of our homes do not. For most of us, our homes are places of privacy and relaxation where we escape from the demands of work.

---

[52] Osiek and Balch, *Families in the New Testament World*, 35.

[53] Ibid., 32.

This was absolutely not the case in the ancient world where the family residence was a center of production and business activities. The vestibule, peristyle, and/or atrium were parts of the house to which everyone—invited or uninvited—had access, and which functioned more like commercial than domestic spaces.[54]

Ancient houses were also centers of religious life and worship, not just for the followers of Jesus, but as a matter of course for all ancient peoples. The reason for these inseparable functions is that "religion" did not exist as a social institution on its own, but was embedded in the two institutions—the house/kinship and the city/politics—that dominated ancient life. Religious life that was embedded in the realm of politics was carried out in public buildings—temples—that were generally controlled by the elites.[55] As we have seen, this part of religious life meant that for first-century Judeans, while certain religious activities such as sacrifice were limited to the temple in Jerusalem, most other religious experiences fell under the rubric of "domestic" religion. Prayer and fasting, celebrations of life changes (birth, coming of age, marriage, death), and observance of the Sabbath and other special festivals all occurred within the household. Israelite purity practices related to food, menstruation, sexual behavior, childbirth, and the burial of the dead would have been the particular responsibility of women in the home. The Sabbath rituals of preparing special bread and lighting candles or lamps were also the province of women, as were preparations associated with annual festivals.[56] Children had their own special roles to play in the Passover liturgy.

Domestic religion among Greeks and Romans functioned similarly. In Greek and Roman houses, the hearth was associated with the goddesses Hestia and Vesta respectively. It represented the center of family life and was the site for domestic offerings and rites designed to integrate family members. Greek families looked to Zeus Ktesios or Zeus Herkios to guard the boundaries of their domicile and to ensure its food supply; Romans honored the *Penates* for their protection in this area. In addition, Roman families venerated the *Lares*, the deified spirits of dead ancestors, and the *Genius*, who represented the generative power of the *paterfamilias*. Prayers, libations, and simple offerings of food and incense were the regular features of domestic rituals honoring the powers that influenced the household's welfare.[57] Women, children, and slaves regularly participated in family worship,

---

[54] Ibid., 54, 25; see Vitruvius *De Architectura* 6.5.1.

[55] Malina, *The New Testament World*, 83.

[56] Ross S. Kraemer, *Her Share of the Blessings: Women's Religions among Pagans, Jews, and Christians in the Greco-Roman World* (New York: Oxford University Press, 1992), 93–105.

[57] John M. G. Barclay, "The Family as the Bearer of Religion in Judaism and Early Christianity," in *Constructing Early Christian Families: Family as Social Reality and Metaphor* (ed. Halvor Moxnes; New York: Routledge, 1997), 67.

and even had special roles in certain rites. The housewife, serving as the priestess of the home, performed prescribed rituals at weddings and funerals, while children most frequently assisted with ceremonial meals.[58]

In the ancient world "every kinship group was a worshiping group."[59] Houses had altars and sacred sites at which fathers and mothers officiated daily in leading family members to honor the household gods and ancestors who saw to their well-being, prosperity, and fertility.[60] It was quite natural and normal, therefore, for Jesus, his disciples, and the assemblies that formed in Jesus' name to worship at home instead of going to "church."

Households

Characteristics. Houses were the physical spaces in which many, if not most, Jesus groups met. These constructions were not just empty shells of residential buildings taken over for meetings, but households of functioning families.[61] Early Christian worship occurred not only in houses but within the context of family life. Just as our houses do not bear much resemblance to the houses in which our ancestors in the faith lived, our families look and function differently than ancient households in significant ways. The most significant difference is the very concept of what comprises a "family." We tend to associate the word *family* with the notion of a nuclear family, consisting of a husband and wife with one or more children. This definition not only represents blindness to the increasing diversity of family and household configurations that occur today in our own culture, but also renders our reading of biblical texts anachronistic and ethnocentric. None of the pertinent ancient languages—Hebrew, Greek, or Latin—has a term that refers to our notion of the nuclear family.[62] The Hebrew *bayit*, Greek *oikos*, and Latin *domus*

---

[58] Lillian Portefaix, *Sisters Rejoice: Paul's Letters to the Philippians and Luke-Acts as Received by First-Century Philippian Women* (Stockholm: Almquist and Wiksell, 1988), 42–48.

[59] Osiek and Balch, *Families in the New Testament World*, 82.

[60] See discussion in Bruce J. Malina, *The Social Gospel of Jesus: The Kingdom of God in Mediterranean Perspective* (Minneapolis: Fortress, 2001), 15–23; Bruce J. Malina, "Daily Life in the New Testament Period," in *Life and Culture in the Ancient Near East* (ed. Richard E. Averbeck, Mark W. Chavalas, and David B. Weisberg; Bethesda, Md.: CDL, 2003), 355–70; Philip A. Harland, *Associations, Synagogues, and Congregations: Claiming a Place in Ancient Mediterranean Society* (Minneapolis: Fortress, 2003), 61.

[61] Philip F. Esler, "Family Imagery and Christian Identity in Gal. 5:13 to 6:10" in *Constructing Early Christian Families: Family as Social Reality and Metaphor* (ed. Halvor Moxnes; New York: Routledge, 1997), 135.

[62] Halvor Moxnes, "What Is Family? Problems in Constructing Early Christian Families," in *Constructing Early Christian Families: Family as Social Reality and Metaphor* (ed. Halvor Moxnes; New York: Routledge, 1997), 20; Osiek and Balch, *Families in the New Testament World*, 6.

all refer to a residential building and the household associated with it, including material goods, slaves, and immediate blood relatives. Even the Latin term *familia*, from which the English word "family" derives, referred to all persons and possessions—material as well as human—under the legal authority of the *paterfamilias* or "head of the household."[63]

In North America today the ideal family is frequently portrayed (e.g., the Simpsons and other television families) as a jointly headed, two-generation, conjugal family that functions as an independent and autonomous, social, residential, and consumption unit.[64] Ancient Mediterranean households, by way of contrast, were much more likely to be co-resident, multigenerational groups, related by kinship, marriage, or other social arrangements, that functioned as units of both production and consumption.[65] These families were patriarchal, that is, headed by the father or oldest male in direct line of patrilineal descent. The father represented and was responsible for maintaining and, if possible, enhancing the family's public honor and social status in the village, town, city, or region in which the *oikos* was located. Within the household, he was responsible for maintaining order, adjudicating disputes, arranging marriages, providing for widowed or divorced female relatives, and settling matters of inheritance within the family. The authority of the Israelite patriarch has been described as "significant but not absolute,"[66] in contrast to that of the Roman *paterfamilias*, who held the power of life and death over both freeborn and enslaved members of the *familia* for the duration of his lifetime.[67]

In our cultural context, newlyweds ideally set up their own autonomous households. Elite Romans did frequently set up nuclear households at marriage, based on a practice facilitated by the custom of giving an adult son a *peculium*, a share of the family fortune either in the form of real estate, movables, money, or slaves to administer on his own. While this custom provided for a degree of economic and social independence, the property was still legally owned by the *paterfamilias*, who also retained the right to contract and dissolve his children's marriages. It was not until well into the second century C.E. that Roman fathers were forbidden by law to end happy marriages. Relatively short life expectancies in the ancient world

---

[63] Moxnes, "What Is Family?" 20–21; Osiek and Balch, *Families in the New Testament World*, 6.

[64] Malina, *The New Testament World*, 139.

[65] Leo G. Perdue, "The Israelite and Early Jewish Family: Summary and Conclusions," in *Families in Ancient Israel* (ed. Leo G. Perdue, et al.; Louisville: Westminster John Knox, 1997), 168; Malina, *The New Testament World*, 139–40.

[66] Perdue, "The Israelite and Early Jewish Family," 174.

[67] Eva Marie Lassen, "The Roman Family: Ideal and Metaphor," in *Constructing Early Christian Families: Family as Social Reality and Metaphor* (ed. Halvor Moxnes; New York: Routledge, 1997), 105–9.

served to mitigate patriarchal control to a certain extent. It is likely that only one in five adults over the age of thirty had a living father.[68]

It was more common in the ancient world for newlyweds to live with or near the groom's family. This preference for patrilocal residence meant that sons generally remained in the parental household even after marrying in their twenties or thirties. Their sisters, however, left their natal homes while still children or adolescents by our contemporary standards. A Judean or Greek girl passed out of her father's legal authority into that of her husband at marriage, which usually occurred between the ages of twelve and eighteen. Elite families tended to marry their daughters off at younger ages; among Romans, as early as nine and ten years of age. A Roman daughter in this period was likely to be married *sine manu*, meaning that she remained under her father's guardianship even after marriage. The adolescent bride joined her husband's family as an "outsider" of questionable quality, only beginning to shed her marginal status when she bore a son.[69]

Because ancient households were units of production as well as consumption, family members not only lived together but worked together. To facilitate production, relationships were further organized around gender and age. From the age of seven or eight, a son related directly to his father to whom he owed obedience and whose role he expected one day to inherit.[70] Under his father's direction, the son would work in the fields, labor in the workshop, and conduct business and other matters related to maintaining and enhancing the family's "public" reputation and status. Female family members, young children (male and female), domestic servants, and slaves (male and female) worked under the direction of the "mother" or senior woman, usually the wife of the patriarch. She normally acted as the household's "financial administrator with the key to the family chest,"[71] overseeing the rearing of children, the processing of food, and the production of textiles and clothing. Ideally, women worked "inside" the residential complex; normal exceptions were made for visits to communal wells and ovens, and in the case of rural households, to assist with harvesting. Women ideally contributed to a family's public reputation by scrupulously guarding their sexual integrity and the family's secrets.[72] As noted above, strict seclusion of women was really only possible in

---

[68] Lassen, "The Roman Family," 106.

[69] Malina, *The New Testament World*, 144.

[70] See Moxnes, "What Is Family?" 34–35; Bruce J. Malina, "Mother and Son," *BTB* 20 (1990): 57–61.

[71] Malina, *The New Testament World*, 48.

[72] Juliet du Boulay, "Women: Images of Their Nature and Destiny in Rural Greece," in *Gender and Power in Rural Greece* (ed. Jill Dubisch; Princeton: Princeton University Press, 1986), 130, 133; MacDonald, *Early Christian Women*, 72.

more affluent households. Many women worked in and sometimes ran family enterprises of various sorts (e.g., Lydia the seller of purple, Acts 16:14–15).

The most important cross-gender relationship in these ancient households was
that between a mother and her son(s). The Mediterranean mother-son bond has
been described as the "closest equivalent in intensity" to the love relationships of
North American marriage partners. This maternal-filial symbiosis was made possible by the gender division of work and space in ancient households whereby the
care and raising of young children was the exclusive domain of women. A mother
pampered her son(s), going to great lengths to safeguard and preserve his life during his vulnerable years of infancy and early childhood. She would remain the one
nurturing figure he could rely on once he entered the rough and tumble world of
men. The special treatment that sons received from their mothers arose out of the
simple fact that sons were the primary source of security and status for women in
their husbands' households. As a son grew and matured, he became his mother's
supporter and defender, first against his father and later against his own wife.
Mothers needed their sons and ensured that their sons would always need them.[73]

The household served as each individual member's primary group of identification and was the immediate source of his or her ascribed honor and status in society.[74] The maintenance and extension of a family's collective honor was of
paramount concern for all family members, arising out of and reinforcing their social and material interdependence. The needs of the household as a whole
superceded the needs of its individual members.[75] Family solidarity, presenting a
united front to the world outside the *oikos*, was regarded as crucial, and demanded
uncompromising loyalty, respect, and obedience, first to one's parents and then to
each other.[76] The Greek writer Plutarch (50–120 C.E.) clearly expresses these sen-
timents in his treatise on brotherly love, *Peri Philadelphian*. With respect to parents,
he asserts that "both Nature and the Law, which upholds Nature, have assigned to
parents, after gods, first and greatest honor" (*Mor.* 479F). The best demonstration

---

[73] Ritva H. Williams, "The Mother of Jesus at Cana: A Social-Science Interpretation of John
2:1–12," *Catholic Biblical Quarterly* 59, no. 4 (1997): 681–82 following du Boulay, "Women," 147,
158–59; Malina, *The New Testament World*, 144; Moxnes, "What Is Family?" 35; Bartchy, "Power,
Submission, and Sexual Identity," 68–69; Andries G. van Aarde, "Fatherlessness in First-Century
Mediterranean Culture: The Historical Jesus Seen from the Perspective of Cross-Cultural Anthropology and Cultural Psychology," *HvTSt* 55, no. 1 (1999): 97–119.

[74] See Moxnes, "What Is Family?" 23; Barclay, "The Family as Bearer of Religion," 66; Perdue,
"The Israelite and Early Jewish Family," 166, 178. See also Malina, *The New Testament World*, 32–48;
Esler, "Family Imagery," 124.

[75] See Esler, "Family Imagery," 123–24; Perdue, "The Israelite and Early Jewish Family," 167.

[76] Malina, *The New Testament World*, 44; Esler, "Family Imagery," 124.

of one's love toward one's parents, Plutarch declares, is to show "steadfast good-will and friendship toward a brother" (*Mor.* 480A). It is, after all, with one's brother that one shares "sacrifices and the family's sacred rites . . . the same sepul-cher, and in life, perhaps the same or a neighboring habitation" (*Mor.* 481D).

In addition to various members related by blood or marriage, households in the ancient Mediterranean world might also include slaves. About two million slaves lived in the Roman Empire, distributed unevenly between rural and urban areas. For example, in the rural villages of Egypt less than seven percent of the popula-tion was enslaved, while in larger cities one might find a slave for every two adult citizens.[77] It is particularly important for us not to read into ancient Greek, Roman, and Christian texts assumptions based on the experience of slavery in pre-Civil War America. Slavery in the Mediterranean world was "neither race-specific nor racist."[78] Unlike slaves in eighteenth- and nineteenth-century North America, slaves in the Roman Empire "were not allowed to marry, they were employed in virtually all the professions, they were individually manumitted, and no one race was enslaved."[79]

Prisoners of war were a major source of slaves. Julius Caesar is reported to have shipped nearly one million enslaved Gauls to Italy during his campaigns between 58 and 51 B.C.E.[80] The city of Sepphoris in Galilee was burned and its inhabitants were sold into slavery in 4 B.C.E. for taking part in uprisings following the death of Herod the Great. Another hundred thousand Judeans were enslaved following the Judean Revolt that ended in 70 C.E. with the destruction of the Jerusalem temple. Enslavement could also result from kidnapping by pirates or brigands, the expo-sure of unwanted infants, selling oneself or family members to pay debts, or being born to slave parents.[81] Slaves were not segregated in work or by the types of jobs performed,[82] nor were they required to wear clothing that set them apart from the free persons among whom they worked and lived.[83] Many, if not most, slaves worked as domestics and personal servants, living within the walls of their mas-ters' houses and sleeping in small, dark, poorly furnished rooms called "cells"

---

[77] Osiek and Balch, *Families in the New Testament World,* 76.

[78] Carolyn Osiek, "Slavery in the Second Testament World," *BTB* 22 (1992): 174.

[79] Osiek and Balch, *Families in the New Testament World,* 74.

[80] J. A. Harill, "Slavery," in *Dictionary of New Testament Background: A Compendium of Contemporary Bibli-cal Scholarship* (ed. Craig A. Evans and Stanley E. Porter; Downers Grove, Ill.: InterVarsity, 2000), 1125.

[81] Alison Burford, *Craftsmen in Greek and Roman Society* (London: Thames and Hudson Ltd, 1972), 44–45, 49; Harill, "Slavery," 1125.

[82] Harill, "Slavery," 1124.

[83] Osiek and Balch, *Families in the New Testament World,* 77.

(*cellae, cellulae*) that might also be used for storage.[84] Other slaves worked as laborers and artisans in family enterprises, sometimes inhabiting a room behind, above, or close to the shop in which they worked. Educated slaves served as private tutors, physicians, entertainers, and secretaries to household members. As the appointed agents and administrators of family businesses, managerial slaves played important roles in the patron-client social system to be discussed below.[85]

Legally slaves were regarded as *res*, that is, "property." The quality of life for slaves varied greatly. Although slaves were not legally allowed to marry, evidence points to the existence of long-term, stable relationships within slave families, especially within large, elite Roman households.[86] Similarly, Roman law prohibited slaves from owning anything. The custom, however, of setting aside a *peculium* for sons and/or slaves enabled some slaves to enjoy a degree of economic and social independence by operating shops and businesses of various sorts.[87] As we shall see in the next chapter, some slaves became quite wealthy, even owning slaves of their own. Slaves were not segregated in household religion for they were expected to participate in the worship of the household gods, the *Lares Familiares*. Indeed, from the beginning of the first century C.E., slaves were ministers in this household cult, even wearing a *toga praetexta*. The primary locus of slave worship was in fact "inside the house within the collective family."[88] Although some slaves led what appear to have been relatively "normal" lives, it would be a mistake to assume that slavery in the Greco-Roman world was a benevolent institution.[89] Even the wealthiest and most powerful slaves were vulnerable to the whims of their masters who did not flinch from degrading, sexually exploiting, physically abusing, and torturing these "talking tools."[90]

Organization of the Jesus Movement as "Household." Not only did the houses in which Jesus and his earliest followers met look quite different from our homes, the households that resided in them were organized and functioned quite differently than our families. Selecting our own marriage partners in adulthood, we establish households that are legally, economically, socially, and residentially independent

---

[84] Ibid., 29.

[85] Dale B. Martin, *Slavery as Salvation: The Metaphor of Slavery in Pauline Christianity* (New Haven: Yale University Press, 1990), 10–12, 166–67; Harill, "Slavery," 1124; M. J. Carey and T. J. Haarhoff, *Life and Thought in the Greek and Roman World* (London: Methuen & Co., 1971), 144.

[86] Martin, *Slavery as Salvation*, 2.

[87] Ibid., 7.

[88] Osiek and Balch, *Families in the New Testament World*, 82.

[89] Martin, *Slavery as Salvation*, 1.

[90] Osiek and Balch, *Families in the New Testament World*, 80; Peter Garnsey and Richard Saller, *The Roman Empire: Economy, Society, and Culture* (Berkeley: University of California Press, 1987), 116.

of our parents. As families we are consumers of products and look to the privacy of our homes to escape the pressures of work. Ancient households were patriarchal, patrilineal, and patrilocal units of production. Marriages were arranged by the heads of households with an eye to securing and improving the family's economic, social, and/or political fortunes. While sons married relatively late and brought their brides into their parental households, daughters married out of their childhood homes once they reached puberty. Ancient households were multigenerational groups, consisting of freeborn, freed, and enslaved persons who not only lived together, but also worked and worshipped together.

Given the centrality of the household in the ancient world, it should be no surprise that the movement that grew up around Jesus in Galilee was comprised of members of several families. We have already met the brothers Simon and Andrew, whose home in Capernaum functioned as Jesus' temporary base of operations. Here he healed and was ministered to by Simon's mother-in-law (Mark 1:29//Matt 8:14//Luke 4:38). The brothers James and John, sons of Zebedee and possibly business partners with Simon and Andrew, were among Jesus' first disciples (Mark 1:19–20//Matt 4:21–22//Luke 5:10). When they left their father to run the family's fishing venture with hired hands, their mother traveled with them and Jesus to Jerusalem (Mark 10:32–40//Matt 20:17–23). The household of Martha, Mary, and Lazarus in Bethany was particularly dear to Jesus (Luke 10:38–42; John 11:1–3; 12:1–3). Jesus' own family members—his mother, brothers and sisters—were never far from him, even though they were occasionally at odds with him (Mark 3:19b–21; 3:31–35//Matt 12:46–50//Luke 8:19–21; John 2:1–11; 7:1–9; 19:25–27). Jesus' family members were part of the group that gathered in Jerusalem following his death and resurrection (Acts 1:14; 15:13–21; Gal 1:19; 2:9). All of these examples involve siblings and/or their mothers, those members of ancient Mediterranean cultures with the closest affective bonds. One reason that we may not hear of fathers joining the Jesus movement is that in this culture "a son always remained a son vis-à-vis his father: consequently it would be impossible for a father to join a movement led by a son."[91]

Challenge of the Jesus Movement to "Traditional" Households. The nature of the ancient household as a multi-generational unit organized around the categories of gender and age is reflected in a number of Jesus' sayings. One of the consequences of discipleship, Jesus warns, will be enmity within households because he came to "set a man against his father, and a daughter against her mother, and a daughter-in-law against her mother-in-law" (Matt 10:34–56//Luke 12:51–53//*Gos. Thom.* 16;

---

[91] Moxnes, "What Is Family?" 34.

see Mark 13:12). This comment presupposes a household consisting of a father and his wife, their son and his wife, and an unmarried daughter. The son is under the father's authority, while the daughter-in-law and daughter function under the mother's direction. Jesus does not affirm this pattern of relationships but rather promises to set it awry. A similar scenario is presupposed in Jesus' insistence that "whoever comes to me and does not hate father and mother, wife and children, brothers and sisters, yes, and even life itself, cannot be my disciple" (Luke 14:26// Matt 10:37//Gos. Thom. 55). Again, the family is depicted as a multi-generational, extended unit that must be set aside in the interests of discipleship. Jesus himself turned a deaf ear to the demands of his own mother and brothers in order to iden-tify himself with "whoever does the will of God" (Mark 3:31–35//Matt 12:46–50//Luke 8:19–21). He expected his followers to do the same. When he called the brothers James and John, we are told that "they left their father Zebedee in the boat with the hired men" (Mark 1:20//Matt 4:22).

We often miss the radicalism of such behavior in the first century because we grow up expecting to leave our parents' households in order to pursue educational and career opportunities that may require moving to another city, state, or even country where we will establish our own households. The vast majority of people in ancient Mediterranean societies had no such expectations. The preference for patrilocal residence meant that men spent their entire lives in or near their places of birth and brought home brides from neighboring communities.[92] While girls were brought up knowing that they would spend their early adult years as marginal members of their husbands' households, their brothers grew up expecting to live in and take over their parents' houses. A man's voluntary departure from his fa-ther's household to follow his dreams would have been interpreted as a sign not of growing up but of filial impiety that would bring shame and dishonor to the fam-ily.[93] Jesus' parable of the "prodigal and his brother" explores the pain and distress caused by such behavior.[94]

Other parables feature father-son relations too. The expectation of filial obedi-ence is reflected in the example of the two sons whose father asks them to go and work in the vineyard (Matt 21:28–32). The recognition of a son's delegated au-

---

[92] van Aarde, "Fatherlessness," 99.

[93] Karl Olav Sandnes, "Equality within Patriarchal Structures: Some New Testament Perspectives on the Christian Fellowship as a Brother- or Sisterhood and a Family," in Constructing Early Christian Families: Family as Social Reality and Metaphor (ed. Halvor Moxnes; New York: Routledge, 1997), 154, reporting from Seppo Syrjanen, In Search of Meaning and Identity: Conversion to Christianity in Pakistani Muslim Culture (Vammala: The Finnish Society for Missiology and Ecumenics, 1984).

[94] Luke 15:11–32; see Richard Q. Ford, The Parables of Jesus: Recovering the Art of Listening (Minneapo-lis: Fortress, 1997), 90–121, 134–39.

thority as his father's representative and agent undergirds the parable of the "wicked tenants" (Matt 21:33–41//Mark 12:1–12//Luke 20:9–19//*Gos. Thom.* 65). These aspects of the father-son relations shaped the way that early Christian writers described Jesus in relation to God (e.g., John 5:17, 19–23). Although Jesus came to be acclaimed as the Son of God among his followers, an analysis of his behavior and teaching suggests that he did not "act according to the expected role of the eldest son in a patriarchal family, but rather like that of a wife of the absent husband."[95]

The primacy of the multi-generational, patrilocal household for individuals in the ancient world is reflected in Jesus' response to Peter's alleged complaint that "we have left everything and followed you" (Mark 10:28). Jesus defines Peter's "everything" as "house or brothers or sisters or mother or father or children or fields" (Mark 10:29). His parents, siblings, and children, together with the house where they resided and the fields that they worked, constituted a man's "family." The absence of a reference to a wife may reflect the fact that the wife was frequently regarded as an outsider and a stranger to this group, or alternatively that wives traveled with the apostles and hence were not put aside.[96] The group bound together by kinship bonds, common residence, and shared livelihood was "everything" in the world of the first-century followers of Jesus. Without a place in a household acquired either at birth or adoption or some other social arrangement, a person quite literally had no social identity.[97] To leave this family—willingly or unwillingly—was to become radically marginalized in a culture where the household was the primary source of social identity.

In response to this ancient social reality, the Jesus movement presented itself as a surrogate household. Jesus promises Peter that he and others who leave everything for the sake of the gospel will receive a hundredfold of what they have abandoned (Matt 19:29//Luke 18:30). Specifically, they will receive "houses, brothers and sisters, mothers and children, and fields" (Mark 10:30). Those who leave their homes and families to follow Jesus will be compensated with a new family, based not on biological kinship relations, but on "personally chosen, intentionally

---

[95] Van Aarde, "Fatherlessness," 104, following D. Jacobs-Malina, *Beyond Patriarchy: The Images of Family in Jesus* (New York: Paulist, 1993), 2.

[96] See 1 Cor 9:5; for alternative explanations see Ross S. Kraemer, "Mark 10:29–30: Sisters and Mothers Left for Jesus' Sake," in *Women in Scripture: A Dictionary of Named and Unnamed Women in the Hebrew Bible, the Apocryphal/Deuteroncanonical Books, and the New Testament* (ed. Carol Meyers; Grand Rapids: Eerdmans, 2000), 430–31.

[97] John Dominic Crossan, *The Historical Jesus: The Life of a Jewish Mediterranean Peasant* (San Francisco: Harper, 1991): 269; van Aarde, "Fatherlessness," 102, quoting V. C. Matthews and D. C. Benjamin, *Social World of Ancient Israel 1250–587 B.C.E.* (Peabody, Mass.: Hendrickson, 1993), 10; Moxnes, "What Is Family?" 23.

embraced and shared commitment to the will of God."[98] Like the households that the disciples left, this new family will consist of brothers, sisters, mothers, and children. It will even include houses and fields. It will not, however, have any human fathers. This exclusion of human fathers is affirmed in Jesus' statement that those who do the will of God are his brother and sister and mother (Mark 3:31–35//Matt 12:45–50//Luke 8:19–21), and even more forcefully in his instruction to call no man "father" (Matt 23:9). In this new family, no one is to assume the role, the privileges, or the power of a father because it recognizes only one father—the one in heaven (Matt 23:9). The members of this household are to relate to each other as brothers and sisters and mothers. This orientation would have been a significant challenge to all members of Jesus groups, but perhaps especially for male disciples who had been socialized with the expectation that they would eventually inherit the powers and privileges of patriarchy. Jesus' teaching, then, was not so much "anti-family" as it was "anti-patriarchy."[99]

The Jesus movement was born in a group-oriented world where the household/family was regarded as the very basis of social life. Patriarchal, patrilineal, and patrilocal in character, its collective needs superceded those of its individual members. It was an institution criticized by Jesus and yet recreated according to his vision of God's reign. The group that gathered around Jesus in his lifetime consisted of family members, most frequently siblings and/or their mothers, who left the households of their fathers and husbands. In the Jesus movement they found a surrogate family or fictive kinship group in which no human person held the power and privileges of a father. As disciples they were all *adelphoi*, brothers and sisters, recognizing only the Father in heaven (Matt 23:8–9). The use of familial language to describe relationships within the Jesus movement was deliberate and inevitable; Jesus' audiences would have understood nothing else.

Challenge of Post-Resurrection Groups to "Traditional" Households. The same trends that emerged before Jesus' death and resurrection continued in the Jesus groups. We learn from Paul that the apostles, the brothers of Jesus, and Cephas were accompanied by "sister-wives" (*adelphe gynaika,* I Cor 9:5), whose presence points to the familial nature of missionary teams. Paul identifies the pre-eminent apostolic couple, Andronicus and Junia, as his "kin" who were "in Christ" before he was (Rom 16:7). Paul also had a sister in Jerusalem, whose son alerted him to a plot against his life (Acts 23:16). Were they members of the Jesus movement too? We can only speculate.

---

[98] Bartchy, "Power, Submission, and Sexual Identity," 69.
[99] Ibid., 73.

Early missionary activity seems to have been directed toward households. Cornelius and his entire household were saved (Acts 10:2; 11:14); Lydia and her household were baptized together (Acts 16:15); and the prison guard in Philippi and his entire family were baptized together (Acts 16:31–34). Crispus, the synagogue official in Corinth, became a believer "together with all his household" (Acts 18:8). Paul himself admitted to baptizing the household of Stephanas (1 Cor 1:16). Many Christ-confessing assemblies, thus, began with the "conversion" of a *pater-*or *materfamilias* and his or her household. Given the emphasis on family solidarity within ancient Mediterranean cultures, we can expect that some, if not most, family members accepted baptism out of loyalty or obedience to the head of the household rather than out of personal conviction. This baptism of households inevitably meant that differing levels of commitment to the Jesus movement lay within these ostensibly "Christian" households.[100]

Individuals could and did join the *ekklesia* on their own, apart from other family members, producing a situation that frequently led to problems. Paul advises church members in "mixed marriages" not to divorce their unbelieving spouses as long as the unbeliever consents to live with them (1 Cor 7:12–13). Paul assures his readers that remaining in such a relationship will not defile the believer, but will make his or her spouse and their children "holy" (1 Cor 7:14). It is even possible that the unbeliever might be saved (1 Cor 7:16). The inherent potential for evangelism within mixed marriages, thus, justifies their preservation. MacDonald astutely points out that Paul's teaching has the effect of legitimizing the existence of "the house divided against itself" contrary to the highly prized Mediterranean value of family solidarity.[101] She draws our attention to the implications for married women in particular:

> By welcoming the wives of unbelieving husbands as members of the community, Paul is sanctioning what might be understood as a type of marital infidelity . . . a Greco-Roman wife's faithfulness to her husband included faithfulness to his gods: a dutiful wife would ensure that children also shared in the religion of the household.[102]

The discipleship of women in unbelieving households could be, and was, regarded as socially subversive, as MacDonald demonstrates in her analysis of Greco-Roman writers' treatment of the subject. She notes that their texts depict Christianity as promoting seditious behavior, immorality, and infidelity among women and children.[103]

---

[100] Sandnes, "Equality within Patriarchal Structures," 152.

[101] MacDonald, *Early Christian Women*, 192.

[102] Ibid., 189; see Plutarch, *Mor.* 140D.

[103] MacDonald, *Early Christian Women*, 122–23.

Paul's instructions to his congregation in Corinth suggest that some members who were married to unbelievers were experiencing hostility, suffering, and abandonment.[104] In such cases, Paul assures the believing spouse that he or she is not bound to try to preserve the union, since "it is to peace that God has called you" (I Cor 7:15). In such circumstances the need to live in peace and security justifies separation or divorce. Writing at least twenty years later to church members in the five Roman provinces of Asia Minor, the author of I Peter takes a different approach. He exhorts wives to accept the authority of their unbelieving husbands, so that they "may be won over without a word by their wives' conduct, when they see the purity and reverence of your lives" (I Pet 3:1–2). For this author the possibility of converting the husband outweighs the personal risks. Undoubtedly, these teachings acknowledge and reinforce patriarchal authority structures within the household in a way that neither Jesus nor Paul did. Yet even as the author does so, he indirectly affirms the wife's power to act effectively as a "quiet evangelist" in her home.[105] As she went about her daily activities, the Christ-confessing wife had the opportunity to influence not only her husband, but her children, slaves, and perhaps even clients and business associates.[106] Submission to patriarchal authority is encouraged not as an end in itself, but as a defensive strategy designed to enable covert evangelism within households.

Contemporary anthropological studies of conversion in Mediterranean cultures highlight the difficulties faced by individuals joining the churches apart from their households. In societies that place a high value on collective honor and family solidarity, the defection of an individual from household religion demonstrates a lack of filial piety. The individual is shamed together with his or her family who are perceived to have failed in their duty to instill the proper values and attitudes.[107] Family honor can be restored only partially by either winning back the "sinner" or committing acts of revenge that may include severe beatings, death threats, or ostracism.[108]

The *Acts of Thecla* illustrates rather well the consequences for women who join the church against their families' wishes. Thecla overhears Paul's preaching about the blessings of chastity in the house next door and is entranced. Theoclia, alarmed by her daughter's obsession with Paul (*Acts of Thecla* 5–6), tries to recall Thecla to her filial duties by inviting Thamyris, her fiancé, to speak with her. He

---

[104] I Cor 7:15; see MacDonald, *Early Christian Women*, 192.
[105] MacDonald, *Early Christian Women*, 195–202.
[106] Ibid., 202–3.
[107] Syrjanen, *In Search of Meaning and Identity*, 167.
[108] Ibid., 177, 170.

interprets her fixation as a lack of shame, incompatible with the modesty expected of a virgin (*Acts of Thecla* 3).[109] Thecla's refusal even to acknowledge him results in "a great outpouring of lamentation in the house," as Thamyris weeps for the loss of his wife, Theoclia for the loss of her child, and the maidservants for the loss of their mistress (*Acts of Thecla* 10). Her family interprets Thecla's fascination with Paul's message as a rejection of her household roles and responsibilities.[110]

Although Thamyris immediately seeks to avenge the loss of Thecla's devotion by arranging for Paul's arrest, even this action fails to restore Thecla to her senses (*Acts of Thecla* 11–16). If anything, her behavior becomes even more reprehensible. During the night she bribes first the gatekeeper of her mother's house to let her out, and then the jailer at the prison to let her join Paul in his prison cell, where she is discovered the next morning "bound together with Paul in affection" (*Acts of Thecla* 19). When she is arraigned with Paul before the governor, Thecla steadfastly refuses to answer the governor's questions. Her frustrated mother publicly denounces her, crying out, "Burn the lawless one! Burn the one who will not be a bride, burn her in the midst of the theatre! Then all the women who have been taught by this one will fear!" (*Acts of Thecla* 20). We may shudder in horror that a mother would call for her only daughter's execution. In Theoclia's eyes, however, her daughter's night time adventure has besmirched not only Thecla's reputation but that of the entire family. Honor can only be restored by creating as much social distance as possible between herself and her daughter.

Bereft of her family's protection, Thecla becomes vulnerable to public suspicion, hostility, and violence. While the governor has Paul scourged and cast out of the city, he condemns Thecla to burn. She is stripped naked in public, "the ultimate symbol of the shameless woman."[111] When she is miraculously saved from the fire, she is banned from the city (*Acts of Thecla* 26). Arriving in Antioch with Paul, she is accosted on the street and has to fight off a would-be rapist. Her successful defense of her virginity and honor results in her assailant's charging her with "sacrilege"—failing to show proper respect for her superiors. Thecla, aided by female animals and humans, eventually prevails in her desire to go and teach the gospel. To ensure her physical safety, she cuts off her hair and dresses as a man. This text promotes the baptizing and teaching ministries of celibate Christian women and does so by valorizing what would be considered quite shameless behavior in ancient Mediterranean societies.

---

[109] See MacDonald, *Early Christian Women*, 175.

[110] Ibid., 172.

[111] Ibid., 176.

At least partially in response to the Greco-Roman perception of the churches as encouraging such seditious and immoral behavior, early Christian texts, such as the Pastoral Epistles, seek to curtail the preaching and teaching activities of Christian women (1 Tim 2:8–15), and to limit the number of widows on a congregation's payroll (1 Tim 5:3–16). Bishops and deacons (male and female) are to have demonstrated their ability to manage their children and their households well (1 Tim 3:1–13). Within these late first- and early second-century, Christ-confessing households, patriarchal relations are reintroduced—wives, children, and slaves are called to submission and obedience to the male head of the household (Col 3:18–25; Eph 5:22–6:9). The adoption of such rules ought to be seen as a defensive strategy in a society where Christ-followers were increasingly scrutinized for signs of immorality and subversion.[112] However pragmatic such rules may have been, they were prompted more by fear than faithfulness to the teaching of Jesus or Paul.[113]

As we have seen, Jesus proclaimed an alternative community in which there were no fathers and no patriarchs to whom one owed obedience and submission. Bartchy argues, correctly I believe, that in this respect Paul and Jesus were on the same page.[114] A quick review of Paul's vocabulary shows that he addresses his readers and hearers as "brothers," "sisters," or "brothers and sisters" some 118 times in the undisputed letters. Bartchy describes this sibling language as "an essential image" in Paul's rhetorical strategy of community building.[115] In spite of their origins in different social classes and ethnic groups, members of the *ekklesia* are to regard each other as brothers and sisters. Paul draws upon Mediterranean values of sibling solidarity when he castigates the better-off in the Corinthian congregation for taking their brothers and sisters to court, for wronging and defrauding their brothers and sisters, and for relying on unbelievers—outsiders—to do so.[116] Five chapters later, Paul criticizes elite members of the Corinthian congregation for "humiliating" their brothers and sisters at the Lord's Supper, a behavior that displays their contempt for God's church (1 Cor 11:22). Paul urges these members to view the assembly as analogous to a human body with many parts that support and cooperate with each other (1 Cor 12:12–26).

---

[112] Ibid., 233.

[113] E. Elizabeth Johnson, "Ephesians," in *The Women's Bible Commentary* (ed. Carol A. Newsom and Sharon H. Ringe; Louisville: Westminster John Knox, 1992), 341.

[114] S. Scott Bartchy, "Undermining Ancient Patriarchy: The Apostle Paul's Vision of a Society of Siblings," *BTB* 29 (1999): 71.

[115] Ibid., 70.

[116] 1 Cor 6:1–8; see Bartchy, "Undermining Ancient Patriarchy," 71–72.

While this discussion of the Corinthian community may seem to be drawing upon a metaphor unrelated to family solidarity, the human body metaphor is in fact one of the models that Plutarch uses in his essay on brotherly love, *Peri Philadelphian.*[117] Bartchy concludes his analysis of Paul's rhetoric in I Corinthians 11–12 by asserting:

> For Paul a house-church functions as the "Body of Christ" when and only when patriarchal values are reversed by giving its weakest and least honorable members the greatest honor (I Cor 12:22–24). Paul conceives of the Church as a family of brothers and sisters in which the strong do not use their strength to dominate the weak in a hierarchy that the strong control. Rather the strong are to pay special attention to the weak, gently empowering them to become strong.[118]

Paul's goal, like that of Jesus, was to create a surrogate family dominated by the values of general reciprocity and mutual support that ideally defined sibling relations in the ancient Mediterranean world.[119]

Esler makes a similar case with respect to Paul's use of family imagery in Gal 5:13–6:10, where Paul seeks "to create an identity for his congregations very different from that of the dominant groups outside their boundaries, especially in his rejection of the usual struggle for honor."[120] Paul urges these new brothers and sisters in Christ to be enslaved to one another through love (Gal 5:13–14), a statement evoking a domestic context in which siblings and slaves lived and worked under the same roof.[121] Paul admonishes them not to "bite and devour one another" (Gal 5:15) like animals searching for food, a behavior that the Greek writer Plutarch explicitly condemns as inappropriate for brothers in *Peri Philadelphian.*[122] Esler argues that Paul's list of "works of the flesh" (Gal 5:19–21) characterizes how people in ancient Mediterranean cultures behaved toward outsiders, while the list of "fruits of the spirit" (Gal 5:22–23) depicts the type of existence one expects within a harmonious family.[123] Paul obviously wants church members to behave toward one another as members of a harmonious family, a point that Paul

---

[117] Plutarch, *Mor.* 478D–E, 481C, E; see also Reidar Aasgaard, "Brotherhood in Plutarch and Paul: Its Role and Character," in *Constructing Early Christian Families: Family as Social Reality and Metaphor* (ed. Halvor Moxnes; New York: Routledge, 1997), 171.

[118] Bartchy, "Undermining Ancient Patriarchy," 76.

[119] Ibid., 77.

[120] Esler, "Family Imagery," 122.

[121] Ibid., 138.

[122] Plutarch, *Mor.* 486B; see Esler, "Family Imagery," 139.

[123] Esler, "Family Imagery," 140.

emphasizes in his exhortation not to "become conceited, competing against one another, envying one another" (Gal 5:26). As Esler points out,

> What we have here is virtually a summary of Mediterranean man, always envious of the success of others outside the family circle and seeking to provoke them to social contests of challenge and response in order to win honor and to be able to boast as a result.[124]

What Paul wants believers to do is to jettison this central aspect of local culture in their dealings with one another and replace it with behavior that is appropriate towards siblings.[125]

A brief examination of Paul's letter to Philemon supports my contention that Paul, like Jesus, was attempting to construct an anti-patriarchal community. The subject of this brief letter is the ongoing relationship of Philemon and his slave Onesimus who has come to Paul for help after having wronged his master in some unspecified manner (v. 18). While staying with him, Onesimus has served Paul and has become a follower of the Way of Jesus. Paul would like to retain Onesimus' services but wishes to obtain Philemon's approval. By addressing the letter, not to Philemon alone but also to the assembly that meets in his house (vv. 1–2), Paul makes Philemon answerable before the congregation for his treatment of Onesimus.[126] Paul reminds Philemon that they are brothers (vv. 1, 7, 20), coworkers (v. 1), and partners (v. 17), and urges him to receive Onesimus—who has now become Paul's child (v. 10) and brother (v. 16)—as he would Paul himself (v. 17). Paul challenges Philemon to welcome his formerly "useless" slave (v. 11) as "a beloved brother" (v. 16). Although it is unclear whether Paul is asking Philemon to manumit Onesimus, there can be no doubt that he is pressuring him to change the nature of their social relations in a way that will be visible to his household and the church that gathers there.[127]

Paul's letter to Philemon is cautious and open-ended, probably because Paul knew he was intruding into Philemon's business but was hoping to use all possible avenues to influence Philemon to change his relationship with Onesimus. In later Christian texts, however, the trend to accept and endorse traditional Greco-Roman household values continues with respect to slaves. In the pseudo-Pauline epistles, slaves receive exhortation to obey their masters in "fear and trembling,"

---

[124] Ibid.

[125] Ibid., 142.

[126] Sandnes, "Equality within Patriarchal Structures," 157.

[127] Bartchy, "Undermining Ancient Patriarchy," 73; Sandnes, "Equality within Patriarchal Structures," 156–61.

rendering service with enthusiasm as if to the Lord rather than to their human owners (Eph 6:5–8; Col 3:22–23). The Didachist goes even further in affirming the submission of the enslaved by urging Christian slaves to regard their owners as "types of God" (*Did.* 4.11). The author of 1 Peter holds up Christ's innocent suffering as a model for slaves to imitate when dealing with unjust beatings at the hands of harsh, possibly heathen, masters (2:18–22). Ignatius forbids the use of common assembly funds for manumitting Christian slaves (Ign. *Pol.* 4.3).

Jesus, Paul, and Their Successors. The point that I am making here is that, just as Jesus encouraged his disciples to leave their fathers' houses, Paul welcomed women, children, and slaves into the fellowship of the church apart from, and sometimes over the objections of, their families. In this respect I share the conclusions of Scott Bartchy:

> Jesus of Nazareth and Paul of Tarsus were on the same page in their intentions to undermine the authority and social cohesiveness of the blood kin group and patriarchal family, to offer an alternative form of social bonding in place of the patrilineal biological family, and to make viable a first-century Mediterranean person's choosing to live in such an alternative, trust-based form of social relations by restructuring the traditional Mediterranean social codes of honor and shame.[128]

Both Jesus and Paul rejected patriarchal household arrangements as an adequate model for organizing first the Jesus movement in Galilee and later the *ekklesia* in the cities of the eastern Mediterranean. Members of these Jesus groups were challenged to see themselves and behave toward one another as siblings, that is, children of a common Father in heaven, regardless of their ethnic, status, or gender differences. Christ-followers who embraced this alternative vision of social relations faced unrelenting opposition, hostility, and even physical violence from their blood kin, their neighbors, and government officials. It is no surprise that many church members were unable to stand against the unrelenting pressure of a world where patriarchal dominance was systemically embedded in every level of society from the household to the empire itself (since the emperor was the *pater patriae*). Hence we find the authors of later Christian texts such as 1 Peter, the pseudo-Pauline Epistles, and the Pastoral Epistles reintroducing the very values rejected by the founders of the Jesus movement, albeit as a survival strategy and in a modified form, as some have argued.[129] Yet conforming for the sake of survival was not the

---

[128] Bartchy, "Undermining Ancient Patriarchy," 71.

[129] See Gerd Theissen, *The Social Setting of Pauline Christianity: Essays on Corinth* (Minneapolis: Fortress, 1982) on "love patriarchalism."

only possible response, as is evident from texts like *The Acts of Thecla* that continued to valorize the overturning of Greco-Roman household norms and expectations.

Patronage

Social Networks. In cultures such as this one, where kinship is the primary organizational model, the most important ingredient for survival is "belongingness." Without a family, without kin, one is nobody. Success in the Greco-Roman world consisted "in having and making the right interpersonal connections, in being related to the right people."[130] These were societies in which all available resources were controlled by numerically minuscule but disproportionately powerful elites made up of "properly pedigreed persons from only the 'best' families."[131] Access to goods and services really depended on "who you knew" rather than on what you knew or how much money you had available. Greco-Roman individuals and families deliberately cultivated and maintained networks of interpersonal connections—patronage relations—designed to facilitate access to scarce goods and services. For those who controlled these resources and access to them, the development of such relationships enabled them to extend patriarchal authority over manumitted slaves, poor relatives, neighbors in want, needy tenants, immigrants in need of protection, and others.[132]

Patronage refers to both a social relationship and a social system. A patronage relationship is a personal, reciprocal, and asymmetrical arrangement for the exchange of goods and services between two parties of unequal status in which different types of resources are exchanged usually in a "package deal." While such relations are informal, and in principle voluntary rather than legal or contractual agreements, they carry a strong sense of moral obligation that contributes to their often binding and long-range nature.[133] The superior party in this relationship is,

---

[130] Malina, *The New Testament World,* 29.

[131] Ibid., 83; David A. deSilva, "Patronage and Reciprocity: The Context of Grace in the New Testament," *Ashland Theological Journal* 31 (1999): 33; see also Garnsey and Saller, *The Roman Empire,* 112–25; Crossan, *The Historical Jesus,* 45.

[132] Burford, *Craftsmen,* 37–50, 136–41; John E. Stambaugh and David L. Balch, *The New Testament and its Social Environment* (Philadelphia: Westminster, 1986), 63–64.

[133] Richard P. Saller, *Personal Patronage Under the Early Empire* (Cambridge: Cambridge University Press, 1982), 1; Andrew Wallace-Hadrill, "Introduction," in *Patronage in Ancient Society* (ed. Andrew Wallace-Hadrill; London: Routledge, 1990), 3; idem, "Patronage in Roman Society: From Republic to Empire," in *Patronage in Ancient Society* (ed. Andrew Wallace-Hadrill; London: Routledge, 1990), 49; John K. Chow, *Patronage and Power: A Study of Social Networks in Corinth* (Sheffield: Sheffield Academic Press, 1992), 31–32; S. N. Eisenstadt and L. Roniger, *Patrons, Clients, and Friends: Interpersonal Relations and the Structure of Trust in Society* (Cambridge: Cambridge University Press, 1984), 48.

of course, the patron who acts as a "father" figure in economic, political, religious, and other social relationships.[134] The patronage relationship is, thus, a form of fictive kinship, connecting persons not related by blood, law, or other traditional ties, for specific social interactions.[135] A patronage system is simply a chain or network of patronage relationships that functions as a primary mechanism for the allocation of scarce resources, including power and its legitimization.[136]

Patrons are persons who have direct control over "first order resources"—such as arable land, financial assistance, jobs, promotions, protection, and other necessities—that are occasionally or nearly always in short supply. Patrons can make these available to others, if they choose, as "favors" or "benefactions."[137] Ideally, the Greco-Roman patron was motivated to do so by the grace, goodwill, and generosity (*charis*) inherent in his or her noble disposition. In other words, the patron grants favors out of a gracious and beneficent desire to help "someone in need, not in return for anything, nor for the advantage of the helper himself, but for that of the person helped."[138] Yet this capacity to give what others need or want is a source of prestige and honor in Mediterranean societies.[139] Failing to help when help is needed mars a potential patron's reputation for faithfulness, dependability, and trustworthiness.[140] Granting favors also serves to build up social networks that provide insurance against hard times. While urging disinterested giving, Roman writers clearly saw patronage as essential to household security: "It is only through the interchange of benefits that life becomes in some measure equipped and fortified against sudden disasters."[141]

The favors of patrons are sought by clients who do not have guaranteed access to resources that are in short supply, either permanently or due to some natural or economic emergency. The goods and services received from a gracious patron are

---

[134] Andrew Drummond, "Early Roman *Clientes*," in *Patronage in Ancient Society* (ed. Andrew Wallace-Hadrill; London: Routledge, 1990), 102; John J. Pilch and Bruce J. Malina, *Handbook of Biblical Social Values* (Peabody, Mass.: Hendrickson, 1998), 151–55; Osiek and Balch, *Families in the New Testament World*, 38.

[135] Osiek and Balch, *Families in the New Testament World*, 53–54.

[136] Terry Johnson and Christopher Dandeker, "Patronage: Relation and System," in *Patronage in Ancient Society* (ed. Andrew Wallace-Hadrill; London: Routledge, 1990), 220–26; Wallace-Hadrill, "Patronage in Roman Society," 71–72.

[137] Jeremy Boissevain, *Friends of Friends: Networks, Manipulators and Coalitions* (Oxford: Basil Blackwell, 1974), 147; Pilch and Malina, *Biblical Social Values*, 151–55; Chow, *Patronage and Power*, 31.

[138] Aristotle, *Rhetorica* 2.7.1 [1385a16–20].

[139] T. F. Carney, *The Economics of Antiquity: Controls, Gifts, and Trade* (Lawrence, Kans.: Coronado, 1987), 153; Saller, *Personal Patronage*, 126; Garnsey and Saller, *The Roman Empire*, 149.

[140] deSilva, "Patronage and Reciprocity," 46.

[141] Seneca, *De Beneficiis* 4.18.1.

charitas, that is, gifts, favors, or benefactions, for which the client is indebted or ob-ligated to respond with *charis.* The grace that the client is expected to return is the gift of gratitude. Failure to do so is the worst of crimes, comparable to sac-rilege.[142] A grateful response ought to include public testimony that aims toward increasing the fame and honor of the giver; faith understood as devoted commit-ment, loyalty, and trust in the patron; and timely gifts and services as needed.[143] These services might include political support, information, or other goods and services, as determined by the patron.[144]

While a large number of clients was considered desirable and visibly displayed a person's power to grant favors,[145] Greco-Roman patrons "did not enter into re-lationships with their social inferiors indiscriminately."[146] Kin, especially by mar-riage, and friends and neighbors from the same village, city, or geographical region were the most frequent recipients of favors, followed by friends and acquaintances acquired at school or during military service.[147] A favor might be extended to a person with whom the patron had no previous relations, provided that the pro-spective client was "a friend of a friend."[148] The language of friendship often dis-guised patronage relations, especially when the client was of the same, or close to the same, social status as the patron.[149]

An important role in many patronage relationships, therefore, is played by the broker who acts as an intermediary between client and prospective patron. Brokers have access to and control over "second order resources," that is, strategic contacts with those who control scarce goods and services. The broker knows how to con-tact and/or influence persons able to grant favors. In relation to the patron, the broker functions as a client asking for favors on behalf of another. In relation to the client, the broker acts as a patron granting the gift of influence and access to his or her own higher level patron. Patron, broker, and client are social roles that

---

[142] See deSilva, "Patronage and Reciprocity," 38–39, 42; Bruce J. Malina, "Patron and Client: The Analogy behind Synoptic Theology," *Foundations & Facets Forum* 4, no. 1 (1988): 5 note 7.

[143] deSilva, "Patronage and Reciprocity," 44–46.

[144] Pilch and Malina, *Biblical Social Values,* 151–55; Robert Paine, "A Theory of Patronage and Bro-kerage," in *Patrons and Brokers in the East Arctic* (ed. Robert Paine; Institute of Social and Economic Re-search, Memorial University of Newfoundland, 1971), 15–17; Eisenstadt and Roniger, *Patrons, Clients, and Friends,* 213–14.

[145] Wallace-Hadrill, "Patronage in Roman Society," 82.

[146] Garnsey and Saller, *The Roman Empire,* 156.

[147] Saller, *Personal Patronage,* 135–37, 182–84.

[148] Ibid., 153–54.

[149] Ibid., 10–11; Richard P. Saller, "Patronage and Friendship in Early Imperial Rome: Drawing the Distinctions," in *Patronage in Ancient Society* (ed. Andrew Wallace-Hadrill; London: Routledge, 1990), 52, 57; Osiek and Balch, *Families in the New Testament World,* 50.

can be embraced alternately or in combination by the same person.[150] The ability to act as a broker derives from physical and/or emotional proximity to sources of patronage. Clients frequently seek out as brokers members of a patron's immediate family (spouse and children), personal friends, and employees who work in close proximity to him. By acting as brokers, persons who otherwise lack status and authority in society, such as women, slaves and ex-slaves, can and do acquire and exercise power, a situation that is deplored by their social superiors.[151]

Patronage relationships and systems pervaded Greco-Roman cultures, structuring social interactions at all levels of society.[152] Senatorial and equestrian appointments in the Roman empire were normally secured through the direct "friendship" or patronage of the emperor, or through the "commendation" or brokerage of the emperor's friends and family.[153] Roman governors and officials provided channels of patronage and brokerage for urban and provincial aristocrats seeking citizenship, various status honors and offices, and other administrative decisions under imperial jurisdiction.[154] Wealthy urban residents granted favors to their home towns by financing public building projects, community festivals, and famine relief in exchange for municipal offices and titles.[155] Well-to-do urbanites sponsored and supported trade guilds, religious societies, and social clubs as acts of patronage.[156] In rural areas wealthy landowners, civilian and military officials, and local "strong men" provided channels of access to goods and services needed by peasants.[157] Freed slaves were legally obliged to continue as clients in relation to their former masters.[158] Within the extended household the *paterfamilias* acted as a patron to various family members.[159]

---

[150] Boissevain, *Friends of Friends*, 147; Paine, "Theory of Patronage," 8, 9, 21; Crossan, *The Historical Jesus*, 59–60.

[151] Saller, *Personal Patronage*, 64–66.

[152] deSilva, "Patronage and Reciprocity," 37; Johnson and Dandeker, "Patronage," 227, 235; Crossan, *The Historical Jesus*, 59–60; Eisenstadt and Roniger, *Patrons, Clients, and Friends*, 181–82; Carney, *The Economics of Antiquity*, 66.

[153] Saller, *Personal Patronage*, 42–45, 64.

[154] Ibid., 75, 150–69.

[155] Osiek and Balch, *Families in the New Testament World*, 50; Chow, *Patronage and Power*, 63.

[156] Osiek and Balch, *Families in the New Testament World*, 50; Garnsey and Saller, *The Roman Empire*, 156–57; Chow, *Patronage and Power*, 66.

[157] Peter Garnsey and Greg Woolf, "Patronage of the Rural Poor in the Roman World," in *Patronage in Ancient Society* (ed. Andrew Wallace-Hadrill; London: Routledge, 1990), 162–64; Keith Hopwood, "Bandits, Elites and Rural Order," in *Patronage in Ancient Society* (ed. Andrew Wallace-Hadrill; London: Routledge, 1990), 181–84.

[158] Crossan, *The Historical Jesus*, 43; Chow, *Patronage and Power*, 70; Saller, *Personal Patronage*, 9.

[159] Osiek and Balch, *Families in the New Testament World*, 54.

Jesus as Broker. Given the pervasiveness of patronage systems in the Greco-Roman world, it should come as no surprise that human-divine relations were conceived of in the same terms. The system of vertical stratification placed the ordinary person far below the level of human rulers, let alone the nonhuman beings—divine and demonic—that controlled the universe. With respect to both earthly and heavenly resources, individuals and households faced the same difficulty: how to gain access to resources controlled by a tiny but excessively powerful elite. Religious activity focused on the "mediation, the transportation, as it were, of goods and services" between the human and divine realms.[160] Priests, prophets, diviners, holy men, magicians, and others acted as brokers between humans and gods, striving to attract to earth much needed resources, such as rain for crops, fertility for humans and animals, victory in war, prosperity in peace, healing for the sick, good fortune in daily life, and so forth. All of these provisions of resources were conceptualized as favors that the deities granted in exchange for human gratitude and praise.[161]

It was not only polytheistic Greeks and Romans who imagined the human-divine relationship as analogous to human patron-client interactions. The Judean historian Josephus describes the relationship between God and Israel "in terms of the dominant form of social relations in the Roman world in which he was living at the time of writing: the patron-client relationship. God is Israel's patron. Israel is God's favored client."[162] God's generosity is the basis of this relationship, epitomized in the giving of the Torah, which for Israelites is a gift (*Ant.* 3.223), indeed the "greatest of all God's benefactions" (*Ant.* 4.213). Israel's response is one of wholehearted gratitude, expressed as obedience and loyalty, which in turn ensures its ultimate prosperity.[163]

Jesus' habit of addressing God as "father" falls under the same cultural pattern. The application of kinship terminology to the God of Israel is an example of the "kin-ification" typical of patron-client behavior.[164] In the Judean political religion of Jesus' day, the Temple in Jerusalem was the place to encounter God. Its hereditary priests were the official brokers or mediators of access to this deity whom

---

[160] See Jack Lightstone, "Christian Anti-Judaism in Its Judaic Mirror: The Judaic Context of Early Christianity Revisited," in *Anti-Judaism in Early Christianity,* Volume 2: Separation and Polemic; Studies in Christianity and Judaism 2 (ed. Stephen G. Wilson; Waterloo, Ont.: Wilfrid Laurier University Press, 1986), 111–12.

[161] Saller, *Personal Patronage,* 23.

[162] Paul Spilsbury, "God and Israel in Josephus: A Patron-Client Relationship," in *Understanding Josephus: Seven Perspectives* (Journal for the Study of the Pseudepigrapha Supplement Series 32; Sheffield: Sheffield Academic Press, 1998), 179.

[163] Spilsbury, "God and Israel," 190–91.

[164] Malina, "Patron and Client," 9.

they usually addressed in political terms as "lord" and "king."[165] As we shall see in chapter three, Jesus was a prophet and holy man operating outside these official structures. As such, he was a broker providing access to God's favor in the form of healing, liberation from demonic possession, and an alternative wisdom. When persons in the gospel texts glorify or praise God in response to being healed by Jesus, they are acknowledging Jesus' role as a broker for God (Mark 2:12//Matt 9:8//Luke 5:25–26; Luke 7:16; 13:13; 17:15; 18:43). Similarly, Jesus' alleged instructions to the healed Gerasene demoniac point to his role as a broker: "Return to your home, and declare how much God has done for you" (Luke 8:39// Mark 5:18–19). Ironically the man goes off proclaiming to all what Jesus had done for him (Luke 8:39//Mark 5:20).

A number of texts describe persons kneeling or prostrating themselves at Jesus' feet, a typical gesture made by a client—an inferior—seeking the favors of a superior they hope will act as a broker or patron.[166] A leper kneels at the feet of Jesus (Matt 8:1–4; Mark 1:40–45) or bows his face to the ground (Luke 5:12) and begs. A Syrophoenician woman approaches Jesus in the same way, asking for help with her demon-possessed daughter (Mark 7:25//Matt 15:25). When Jesus arrives in Bethany following the death of Lazarus, his sister Mary kneels at Jesus' feet (John 11:32). Afterward she anoints those same feet, out of gratitude for the raising of her brother (John 12:3). Even the demon-possessed seem to recognize Jesus' superiority by falling at his feet (Mark 5:1–20//Luke 8:26–39). These texts indicate that people in need entreated Jesus as they would any other potential patron or broker. Neither Jesus nor the gospel writers make any comment, positive or negative. Jesus, in all but one instance, grants the request.

When the mother of James and John kneels and asks that Jesus grant her sons the favor of sitting at his right and left hands in the coming kingdom she is told that God alone has the power to grant such places of honor (Matt 20:20–23). The brothers themselves receive the same response in Mark 10:35–45. In this way Jesus makes it clear that he is not the patron of the coming kingdom.[167] His task is not to distribute first-order resources, such as positions of honor and status.

Requests for mercy indicate that the petitioner believes that the other person is not only in a position to show mercy and grant favors but is also morally obligated to do so.[168] On learning that Jesus is passing by, blind Bartimaeus cries out, "Jesus,

---

[165] See Geza Vermes, *Jesus in His Jewish Context* (Minneapolis: Fortress, 2003), 35.

[166] Bruce J. Malina and Richard L. Rohrbaugh, *Social-Science Commentary on the Synoptic Gospels* (Minneapolis: Fortress, 2003), 151, 165, 177.

[167] Ibid., 103, 193.

[168] Ibid., 194.

Son of David, have mercy on me!" (Mark 10:46–52//Luke 18:35–43//Matt 20:29–34). As the Son of David, that is, God's anointed one or Messiah, Jesus is morally obligated to grant favors to members of the house of Israel who recognize and honor him.[169] Jesus responds by indicating that it is Bartimaeus' "faith" that has made him well (Mark 10:52; Luke 18:42).[170] "Faith" here should be understood as referring to Bartimaeus' trust that, as the Son of David, Jesus has the good will and ability to heal.[171] Bartimaeus appropriately demonstrates his gratitude by following Jesus (Mark 10:52; Matt: 20:34). In Luke 18:43 the blind man not only follows Jesus but glorifies God, so that all who see him do the same. Public testimony honors not Jesus, but God, the divine patron, who gives the power to heal.

When a Canaanite woman in the district of Tyre and Sidon accosts Jesus with shouts of "Have mercy on me, Lord, Son of David" (Matt 15:21–22), she is making the same appeal. She is asserting that, as the Son of David, God's anointed one or Messiah, Jesus is morally obligated to show mercy by granting favors. Jesus initially objects, since he "was sent only to the lost sheep of Israel" and is under no obligation to help this Gentile woman (Matt 15:24). Jesus does grant her request, but only after exchanging polite insults that reveal that the woman's "faith," which displays trust in the good will of Israel's God who empowers Jesus, is great (Matt 15:25–28).[172]

None of these texts uses the explicit terminology of patron-broker-client relations, but these relations are indicated by cultural cues such as kneeling or bowing before a potential broker or patron. Such gestures point to the suppliant's awareness that, as the one in need, he or she is in the inferior position. Cries for mercy operate similarly but convey a more explicit challenge to the potential patron's or broker's honor. We might think of the plea as somewhat closer to a demand than supplication. In our gospel texts Jesus recognizes such gestures and cries as requests for favors and as indicators of "faith" or trust in his willingness and ability to supply what is needed. It is often in response to the latter that the person is healed. Jesus' response to the sons of Zebedee and/or their mother makes it clear that he is not the patron of the coming kingdom. That role is reserved for God, the only Father and Patron whom Jesus recognizes (Matt 23:9). As prophet and holy man, Jesus brokers God's patronage in the world.

---

[169] Ibid.

[170] Matt 20:29–34 tells about two blind men whom Jesus heals because he is moved by compassion.

[171] See deSilva, "Patronage and Reciprocity," 46.

[172] See Malina and Rohrbaugh, Social-Science Commentary on the Synoptic Gospels, 84.

Luke 7:1–10 is a classic illustration of patronage relations in Roman Palestine. The patronage roles that each character plays in the text may be summarized as follows:

Character	Situation "A" (prior to the slave's illness)	Situation "B" (arising from the slave's illness)
Centurion	Acts as patron to village elders, brokers Herodian resources	Client
Village Elders	Clients	Brokers
Friends	Clients	Brokers
Jesus		Acts a patron to centurion, brokers access to God's healing power

Prior to the slave's illness, the centurion built a synagogue, a place for Sabbath gatherings and other community meetings, in the village of Capernaum. In doing so, he acted as a patron and benefactor to the village and its inhabitants. As a non-Israelite military officer representing Herod Antipas and his administration, he had control over or access to various government funds, building materials, and labor that he made available to the villagers.[173] By accepting this favor, the village elders, that is, the heads of the leading households, became the centurion's clients. As such, they were obligated, if they were honorable men, to respond with gratitude by giving the centurion public honor, testimony, loyalty, trust, and timely gifts or services. The centurion effectively, and without overt violence, extended his authority over the villagers, who may have been initially suspicious or even hostile to his presence in their community.

When the centurion's highly valued slave becomes mortally ill, unidentified informants tell him about Jesus. The centurion sends his Judean clients to solicit the services of Jesus (7:3), presuming that their shared heritage will enhance their success with this Judean healer. The elders aptly display their gratitude to their patron by "earnestly" appealing to Jesus and testifying to the centurion's love and generosity toward "our people" (7:4–5). In fulfilling their obligations as clients,

---

[173] It is commonly assumed that the centurion is a non-Israelite and a Roman officer (e.g., deSilva, "Patronage and Reciprocity," 49–50) or alternatively an Israelite serving in the Roman army (Malina and Rohrbaugh, *Social-Science Commentary on the Synoptic Gospels,* 252). Historical evidence indicates that during Antipas' rule there were no permanently stationed Roman officials in Galilee. If this incident is historical, the officer must be serving under Antipas and is presumably a non-Israelite. Why otherwise would Luke refer to the elders as "Judeans" (see Crossan and Reed, *Excavating Jesus,* 87–89)?

the elders are here acting as brokers, facilitating "access to someone who has what the centurion needs."[174] Jesus apparently agrees to the request as he heads toward the centurion's house in the company of the village elders, but is intercepted by "friends" of the centurion (7:6). These "friends" may be persons of equal status to the centurion or clients who enjoy a higher social status than the village elders. They too act as brokers on behalf of the centurion by relaying the message that this military officer considers himself unworthy to receive Jesus in his house, but entreats Jesus to "only speak the word, and let my servant be healed" (7:7). Their communication concludes with the centurion's description of himself as one who is "set under authority, with soldiers under me" (7:8) which is given as an analogy to Jesus' situation as healer. Just as his soldiers and slaves obey him because he represents a higher authority and acts as a broker for the Herodian administration, illnesses and demons obey Jesus because he represents God, a higher authority whose favors he brokers. The high status "friends" (clients) of the centurion stress their patron's humility before, respect for, and trust in Jesus. Astonished by this non-Israelite officer's "faith," Jesus grants the request (7:9–10). "Faith" here should be understood as referring to the centurion's unprecedented and unexpected trust in Jesus' good will and ability to broker God's healing power to a person to whom he is not morally obligated.[175]

The difficulty of avoiding patron-client interactions in the social world of Jesus and his followers is highlighted in the story of the wedding in Cana (John 2:1–12). When the wine runs out, the mother of Jesus sees an opportunity to enhance her family's honor and extend its web of reciprocal relationships. Implicit in her statement to Jesus that "they have no wine" (2:3) are a request that he rectify the situation and a reminder of his obligations as head of the family. Using her privileged access to her son, the mother of Jesus seeks to broker a favor that would establish him as a patron of a local family. Jesus responds with a double query: "What concern is that to me and to you, woman? Has not my hour come?" (2:4, author's translation). Jesus means something like "Why should I (or we) get involved in these local competitions for honor? Is it not time for me to get on with what God has called me to do?" Jesus and his mother appear to be at cross-purposes. She is ready to function as a broker, using her privileged relationship with him (she is a Mediterranean mother!) as a conduit for establishing him as a local patron. Jesus, as an obedient son, grants his

---

[174] deSilva, "Patronage and Reciprocity," 50.

[175] In Matt 8:5–13 the centurion approaches Jesus directly without the use of intermediaries, but does make the analogy between his own role as broker for the administration and that of Jesus. John 4:46–54 has neither of these nuances.

mother's request; but only his disciples witness this revelation of his "glory" and have faith in him (2:11).[176]

Although Jesus could not avoid engaging in patron-broker-client relations, he could and did redefine how they functioned in the movement that he initiated. The conception of the Jesus movement as a fictive kinship circle or network is an element and adaptation of the patronage system.[177] If Jesus conceived of this surrogate household in anti-patriarchal terms, the result would have been anti-patronage as well. Jesus insisted that in this fictive family there is only one father figure, the divine one (Matt 23:8–9), thereby effectively limiting patron-client relations to interactions between God and humans. Humans are to relate to one another as siblings and as children of a common parent. They are not to lord it over one another like kings and benefactors, that is, patrons, but are to serve one another (Matt 20:24–28//Mark 10:41–45//Luke 22:24–27). In a reversal of traditional roles, "masters" serve diligent and watchful slaves (Luke 12:35–38). In the Jesus movement patron-broker-client relations that grow out of the vertical stratification of patriarchy are to be replaced with a sibling solidarity that emphasizes general reciprocity and mutual support.

Jesus' followers must continue practicing the traditional pious acts of almsgiving, prayer, and fasting, but in private only, never in public, never with the intention of winning public acclaim (Matt 6:1–18). They must look to their divine patron for the basic necessities of life, including food, drink, and clothing (Matt 6:25–34//Luke 12:22–32; 10:41), as well as the special favors of participating in God's coming reign, ownership of the earth, comfort, justice, access to the divine presence, and a great reward in heaven (Matt 5:3–11//Luke 6:17, 20–23; Mark 3:13; John 6:3). Most importantly, they are commissioned to act as brokers of God's power by proclaiming the kingdom, healing the sick, raising the dead, cleansing lepers, and casting out demons in exchange for food (Matt 10:5–15// Mark 6:8–11//Luke 9:2–5).

Epistle of James. These values reappear dramatically in the literature of early Christ-confessing groups in Palestine and Syria. The epistle of James begins by pointing "to God as the authentic Patron of Christians."[178] Christ-followers can be assured that they will lack nothing (1:4) because they have a divine patron "who gives to

---

[176] For a detailed treatment of this incident and a discussion of why this text should be rendered in this way, see Williams, "The Mother of Jesus at Cana," 679–92.

[177] Osiek and Balch, *Families in the New Testament World*, 54.

[178] Nancy Jean Vyhmeister, "The Rich Man in James 2: Does Ancient Patronage Illumine the Text?" in *Andrews University Seminary Studies* 33:2 (1995): 273.

all generously and ungrudgingly" (1:5). They are instructed to ask God "in faith, never doubting," without double-mindedness and instability (1:6–8), and with commitment, loyalty, and trust in God alone. Those whose faith endures temptation will be rewarded with a crown of life (1:12), "not merely a golden leaf from a praetor's crown as might a Roman client be given."[179] James reminds his audience that "every generous act of giving, with every perfect gift, is from above, coming down from the Father of lights, with whom there is no variation or shadow due to change" (1:17). The mind of the divine Patron, unlike that of earthly counterparts, does not change "according to the day's mood."[180] The "worship" or "devotion" (*threskeia*) that is appropriate to this Father/Patron consists in acting as patrons/brokers for the less fortunate, such as orphans and widows in distress (1:27). It is through a person's faith and the works they produce that one's identity as a "friend" or client of God is revealed (2:23).

This exhortation to faithful and exclusive devotion to the divine Patron is immediately followed by a condemnation of *prosopolempsis,* an attitude of partiality, favoritism, or deference toward persons of high rank.[181] Members of the assembly are all too willing to toady to a man wearing gold rings and fine clothes while humiliating a poor man in dirty clothes (2:2–3). The gold rings and fine clothes identify the first man as a person of status and means, and a potential patron to be courted. Yet this human patron will oppress them and drag them into court (2:6), presumably to recover loans.[182] He will blaspheme their heavenly patron (2:7), defraud them of their wages in order to finance his own luxurious lifestyle (5:4–5), and even murder the righteous (5:6). As noted by Kloppenborg Verbin,

> This catalogue conforms quite precisely to the principal economic exchanges between patron and client that guaranteed the peasant farmer or smallholder basic subsistence: the granting of loans for seed requirements and emergency situations, the timely payment of wages, the sharing of surpluses, and the providing of protection. On each point, the rich fail to live up to the moral norms of patronage. . . .[183]

For James, to show partiality to such persons is sin, a violation of the "royal law" that commands each person to love his neighbor as himself (2:8–9). In this way James seeks to undo or prevent the development of patronage relations within the

---

[179] Ibid.
[180] Ibid.
[181] John S. Kloppenborg Verbin, "Patronage Avoidance in James," *HvTSt* 55:4 (1999): 764.
[182] Ibid., 772.
[183] Ibid.

Christ-confessing assembly.[184] His persistence in addressing hearers as brothers and sisters, which occurs twenty times in a document of less than two thousand words, coupled with his emphasis on caring for the unfortunate (1:27, 2:14–17), respecting the poor (2:5), and upholding the commandment to love one's neighbor (2:8–9) serve to emphasize the mutual obligation and reciprocity of sibling relations instead.[185]

Paul's Undisputed Letters. Paul's situation is more complex. With respect to his status and authority as an apostle of Christ, Paul adamantly denies having any human patrons. He claims to be an envoy sent "neither by human commission nor from human authorities, but through Jesus Christ and God the Father" (Gal 1:1).[186] Paul claims to have been personally called through God's grace or generous beneficence to proclaim Christ to the Gentiles (Gal 1:15–16). The acknowledged pillars of the Jerusalem church—James, Cephas and John—recognized and acknowledged that this "grace" (gift or favor) had indeed been given to him (Gal 2:9). In other words, the leaders of the Jesus movement affirmed his status as a favored client and broker of their Lord and his Patron.

In relating to his congregations, Paul alternates as need demands in emphasizing his status as a broker and as a patron. In Corinth where divisions have arisen over rival status claims and loyalty to the patrons who baptized various households and members of the community (1:10–17), Paul emphasizes his role as a broker.[187] He and his rival Apollos are both *diakonoi*, agents or intermediaries through whom the Corinthians came to believe (3:5), and coworkers (*synergoi*) who work together in God's field and God's building (3:9).[188] They are servants and stewards of Christ and of God's mysteries (4:1). The Corinthians erred in trying to accord the status of patrons to these brokers. Yet Paul is their "father"— their patron—in Christ; hence his hearers ought to imitate him (4:15–16) and listen to his "beloved and faithful child" Timothy, whom he has sent as a broker to remind them of his teaching (4:17).

The success of Paul's missionary efforts depended on establishing local networks in which those whom he personally baptized (Crispus, Gaius, and the household of Stephanas in Corinth, for example) regarded him as a patron (1 Cor 1:14–15). These new clients responded by providing Paul with material resources, such as

---

[184] Ibid., 779.

[185] Ibid., 784.

[186] This is a claim that he makes consistently; see 1 Cor 1:1; 2 Cor 1:1; Rom 1:1.

[187] Osiek and Balch (*Families in the New Testament World*, 99) suggest that Paul became a patron to those whom he personally baptized.

[188] BDAG, 230.

meeting places and access to their social networks. In relation to the assemblies that
met in their homes, people like Stephanas were to be seen as patrons who deserved
recognition for the services they provided to the saints (1 Cor 16:15–18).[189]
Similar roles would have been played by Prisca and Aquila in Corinth, Ephesus,
and perhaps Rome; by Lydia in Philippi; and by Philemon in Colossae. These relationships were complicated, as has been demonstrated by Whelan's analysis of
Paul's commendation of Phoebe. Letters of recommendation were usually written
by social superiors on behalf of their clients, sometimes on behalf of social peers
for whom the letter writer temporarily assumed the role of broker, but almost
never on behalf of a superior.[190] What is striking about Paul's commendation of
Phoebe is that "no language that might imply inferiority or even equality even in
the simplest sense is employed. On the contrary, Paul underlines her social prominence."[191] Paul identifies Phoebe as a *diakonos*, a title that in Whelan's estimation
means she is "a local leader in the church at Cenchraea,"[192] but perhaps more accurately emphasizes that she is an agent of that congregation.[193] More significantly, however, Paul describes Phoebe as a *prostatis*—a benefactor or patron—of
many persons, including Paul himself. In this way he raises his hearers' expectations
that Phoebe will also be their patron.[194] Whelan argues that Phoebe would have
been "a wealthy and independent woman, likely educated, and patron to one or
more clubs. . . . As a member of the upper classes, she was able to secure connections for Paul and his church which . . . could only be beneficial."[195] Paul's commendation of his "sister" Phoebe serves to introduce her to his circle of clients,
an entire network of people of lower status "who would be more than grateful to
extend their hospitality to a wealthy patron."[196] Paul's motive for doing so is to establish in Ephesus (not Rome according to Whelan) a "socially influential *amica
Pauli* capable of securing his interests in that city while he was in the west."[197]

A similar complexity of reciprocal patron-broker-client interactions is evident
in Paul's letter to Philemon, where Paul requests the services of Philemon's slave
Onesimus. Philemon is a patron both to an assembly that meets in his house (v. 2)

---

[189] See Osiek and Balch, *Families in the New Testament World*, 97.

[190] Caroline F. Whelan, "*Amica Pauli*: The Role of Phoebe in the Early Church," *Journal for the Study of the New Testament* 49 (1993): 80–82.

[191] Ibid., 82.

[192] Ibid.

[193] See BDAG, 230.

[194] Whelan, "*Amica Pauli*," 79.

[195] Ibid., 84–85.

[196] Ibid., 85.

[197] Ibid., 85. See also Osiek and Balch, *Families in the New Testament World*, 99.

and to his slave Onesimus. Paul identifies Philemon as his dear friend, coworker, partner, and brother (vv. 1, 17, 20). He claims the role of patron by reminding Philemon that he could command him to do his duty (v. 8) but prefers to ask for a voluntary good deed (v. 14). Reminding Philemon that he is indebted to Paul with the words "owing me even your own self" (v. 19), he urges Philemon to let him have the benefit for which he asks (v. 20). Paul's careful rhetoric here serves to remind Philemon that he is morally obligated to release Onesimus so that he can serve Paul in Philemon's place (v. 13). But in order to do so, Paul must first act as a broker and reconcile the slave and his owner. Hence, because he informs Philemon that his formerly useless slave (v. 11) is now Paul's "child" or client, he is, therefore, someone who ought to be received as a "beloved brother" (v. 16) with all the honors that Paul himself would be received (v. 17). By addressing his request to the entire assembly that meets in Philemon's house rather than to Philemon alone, Paul makes Philemon "publicly" accountable for his response.[198]

Paul's reliance on well-connected persons who were his social superiors was a necessity but one that was potentially problematic, as John Chow has argued in his analysis of patronage networks in the Corinthian congregation. For example, Paul's refusal to accept financial support was probably regarded as a violation of patronage relations. Chow demonstrates how other conflicts in that congregation, such as divisions at the Lord's Supper, the controversy over eating idol meat, lawsuits and even the case of the man marrying his stepmother, could have arisen from existing patronage relationships.[199]

Johannine Texts. The actual day-to-day ministries of Jesus and his earliest followers were deeply rooted in patronage relationships. Patron-broker-client relations also shaped the theology and ecclesiology of the Jesus and post-Jesus movements. Jesus spoke of God as a "father" or patron. The gospel writers identified him as God's son and favored client. Nowhere is this designation as God's son more pronounced than in the Gospel of John, where the word *father* refers to God one hundred and twenty-three times.[200] In this gospel Jesus declares emphatically that he is the exclusive agent of access to God (14:4–11). In the first farewell discourse the disciples are presented as successors to the powers and place of Jesus on earth (14:12–26). Their authority is a mediated authority derived from the indwelling Paraclete, or Spirit of truth, whose primary function is to "recall" the

---

[198] See deSilva, "Patronage and Reciprocity," 50–51; Osiek and Balch, *Families in the New Testament World,* 99.

[199] Chow, *Patronage and Power,* 83–140.

[200] Compare with Matthew's 45 times, Mark's 5 times, and Luke's 17 times.

words of Jesus.[201] The disciples function as brokers in a hierarchy of intermediary figures. Jesus is the only legitimate broker for the Father (14:6), while the Paraclete mediates access to Jesus in heaven (14:16–17), thereby enabling the disciples to function as Jesus' brokers on earth.

The character of the beloved disciple epitomizes this role. At the Last Supper (John 13:1–38), this figure is portrayed as enjoying a direct, intimate relationship with Jesus that parallels Jesus' own relationship with the Father. Peter is depicted as the eager but ignorant spokesman for the twelve, who must appeal to the beloved disciple to relay his question to Jesus. It is the beloved disciple who facilitates Peter's entry into the high priest's courtyard following Jesus' arrest (John 18:15–18). He provides historical testimony to the final words and deeds of Jesus, who confers on him the status of a "brother" by placing in his hands the welfare of his mother (John 19:25–27). At the scene of the empty tomb (John 20:1–10), the beloved disciple arrives first and concludes that Jesus is risen. In the post-resurrection context, the beloved disciple continues to display his unparalleled insight and discernment by recognizing the risen Lord (John 21:4–7). He is described as a truthful witness, recalling and reinterpreting the words of Jesus for the Johannine community (John 21:24). [202]

Each of the Johannine writers presents himself as the leader and spokesman for a group that mediates access to God and Jesus (1 John 1:3; 2 John 2; 3 John 8, 12) and appears to be a prophet or teacher. The Elder's letters reflect a situation in which powerful householders acting as church patrons can and do refuse hospitality to itinerant ministers and to emissaries from sister congregations. The Elder himself claims a personal authority arising from his age or seniority, his ability to recall what was from the beginning, and his possession and mediation of divine gifts. On the basis of these claims, he relates to his readers as a father or patron, referring to his audiences as his "children" (3 John 4). Even more importantly, he depicts the churches as "women and children" (2 John 1, 13), whom he represents in their dealing with each other and in their interactions with the divine realm.

Pastoral Epistles and Ignatius of Antioch. Patron-broker-client relations dominate Paul's understanding of the human-divine relationship, as is evidenced by the dominant use of grace and faith terminology. Pauline assemblies are led by "gifted" persons (1 Cor 12). In the Pastoral Epistles Jesus is explicitly named as the "the one medi-

---

[201] Bruce D. Woll, *Johannine Christianity in Conflict: Authority, Rank and Succession in the First Farewell Discourse*, (SBLDS; Chico, Calif.: Scholars Press, 1981), 89–91, 96–105.

[202] See Kevin Quast, *Peter and the Beloved Disciple: Figures for a Community in Crisis* (JSNTSup 32; Sheffield: Sheffield Academic Press, 1989), 55–70, 80–89, 125–56.

ator between God and humankind." In these texts, effective household management (including the maintenance of social networks) becomes a prerequisite for leadership in the church. The same theological and ecclesiological pattern continues in the letters of Ignatius of Antioch.

Ignatius, a bishop from the city of Antioch, was arrested and condemned to die by fighting with beasts in the arena at Rome in the latter years of Emperor Trajan's reign (98–117 C.E.). The circumstances that led to his conviction and execution remain a mystery; whether he was a victim of pagan persecution or internal church conflict is a matter of speculation.[203] What is known, however, is that as a small military detachment transported Ignatius in chains through the province of Asia Minor, members of five local churches visited with him. To each of these congregations he sent a letter thanking them for their kindness to him, warning them against deviant teachings and practices, urging them to stand in solidarity with church leaders, and asking them to pray for, or to send messengers to, the church in Antioch.[204] Ignatius wrote two other letters during his journey. One contained personal advice for his fellow bishop Polycarp of Smyrna. The other asked the church in Rome to do nothing to prevent his martyrdom. Since these seven letters are among the very few post-Jesus-group writings to have survived from the early second century, they are important sources of information about the early church.

According to the letters of Ignatius, God's mind is made known through Jesus Christ, the divine mediator, whose purpose includes and is articulated by human bishops established by the Holy Spirit (Ign. *Eph.* 3.2–4.1; Ign. *Phld.* 1.2). These bishops act as brokers, enabling church members to be recognized and heard by the divine patron (Ign. *Eph.* 4.2). Solidarity with the bishop ensures access to the "bread of God," answers to prayer, and protection from the destructive forces of Satan (Ign. *Eph.* 5.2, 13.1–2). Ignatius envisions the bishop as the Lord's steward (Ign. *Eph.* 6.1) and the heavenly Father's representative (Ign. *Trall.* 3.1), who exercises the grace, power, and supervisory capacities of God on behalf and in place of the divine patron (Ign. *Magn.* 2.1–3.1, 6.1). Therefore, on the level of practically

---

[203] Glanville Downey, *Ancient Antioch* (Princeton: Princeton University Press, 1961), 292–94; P. N. Harrison, *Polycarp's Two Epistles to the Philippians* (Cambridge: Cambridge University Press, 1936), 229; William R. Schoedel, *Ignatius of Antioch: A Commentary on the Letters of Ignatius of Antioch* (Hermeneia; Philadelphia: Fortress, 1985), 11; Simon Tugwell, *The Apostolic Fathers* (London: Geoffrey Chapman, 1989), 109; J. Ruis-Camps, *The Four Authentic Letters of Ignatius the Martyr* (Rome: Pontificium Institutum Orientalis Studiorum, 1980), 142; Christine Trevett, "Ignatius 'to the Romans' and I Clement LIV–LVI," *VC* 43 (1989): 35–52.

[204] Virginia Corwin, *St. Ignatius and Christianity in Antioch* (New Haven: Yale University Press, 1960), 21.

every matter of congregational life, the bishop acts as a patriarchal or patronal figure. He is the guardian of widows (Ign. *Pol.* 4.1), a paternalistic overseer of slaves (Ign. *Pol.* 4.3), and the approver of marriages and other personal arrangements (Ign. *Pol.* 5.1). Like any patriarch or patron, the bishop is expected to protect the community's integrity from both internal and external threats (Ign. *Phld.* 2.1). Ignatius' position represents quite a dramatic departure from the sibling relations advocated by Jesus.

Conclusion

In this chapter on the social setting of the early churches, I have highlighted three interrelated concepts, the house, the household, and patronage, which together functioned as a primary organizational structure in the ancient world. The Jesus movement and its successors were formed by and in reaction to these existing domestic arrangements. Houses that functioned not only as private residences but as sites of religious life and worship and as places of production and commerce provided the physical spaces in which the followers of Christ met. Family members who not only lived together, but worshipped and worked together often formed the nuclei of *ekklesiai,* which also attracted individuals apart from their families of origin or marriage. Congregations were in turn encouraged to think of themselves as fictive kinship groups in which all members were siblings, children of a common Father in heaven, regardless of their ethnic or status or gender differences. Just as there was only one heavenly Father, so there was to be only one divine patron. Church members were challenged to replace patron-broker-client relations that grow out of the vertical stratification of patriarchy with a sibling solidarity that emphasized general reciprocity and mutual support.

That later followers of Jesus were unable to maintain such a counter-cultural stance in a world where patriarchal dominance was systemically embedded in every level of society from the household to the empire itself is evident in the literature that emerges from late first and early second century groups. In time church leaders came to be chosen because of demonstrated competence in household management and the maintenance of social networks, As we will see in the following chapter, the figure of the *oikonomos* or steward was intimately connected with household administration in the ancient world. It seems quite natural, therefore, that this social role would have been taken up in the early church as one way of describing congregational leadership.

2

STEWARDS

Stewards in the Greco-Roman World

IN THIS CHAPTER WE will examine the role of the *oikonomos* in ancient Mediterranean societies, namely, the "household steward" or "manager." This contextualized description will enable us to assess how early Christ-followers used this term and its cognates and the concepts to which they refer, particularly in relation to leadership over and within Jesus groups. The word *oikonomos* itself derives from the language and functions of the ancient household. This title extended beyond persons who managed households so that it was also used to designate administrative roles and positions within governments and elective associations. The prevalence of *oikonomoi* in both public and private organizations in the ancient Mediterranean world is rooted in the centrality of the household as a model for the organization of society in general.

Household Management as the Basis of Civic Offices. Philo's remarks comparing households and cities highlights the primacy of the social institution of kinship as a model for society at large:

> Organized communities are of two sorts, the greater which we call cities and the smaller which we call households. Both of these have their governors; the government of the greater is assigned to men under the name of statesmanship, that of the lesser, known as household management, to women. (*Spec. Laws* 3.169–175)

> . . . a house is a city compressed into small dimensions, and household management may be called a kind of state management, just as a city too is a great house and statesmanship the household management of the general public. . . . the household manager is identical with the statesman, however much what is under the purview of the two may differ in number and size. (*Joseph* 38–39)

I would like to draw two points from Philo's comments. First, in the vast majority of households, household management was the domain of women. The wife normally acted as the household financial administrator "with the key to the family chest."[1] It is not surprising, therefore, that Xenophon wrote *Oikonomikos* to instruct his wife on how to run a household. Larger, high-status households, however, were managed by a skilled slave or freedman who bore the title of *oikonomos*, that is, "steward" or "manager" of the household.[2] To the best of my knowledge, this title was not given to women, even when they did the actual managing.

Second, the organization and governance of households and cities were considered to be direct analogues. The city was a "household writ large with the same relations and functions as a family but on a larger scale."[3] In fact, politics was understood to be rooted in and modeled on an extension of the household.[4] This understanding was true of city politics and extended right through to the management of the empire itself. Beginning with Augustus, the people regarded the emperor as the *pater patriae*, the "father of the fatherland." The empire itself could be and was described as the *domus Caesaris*, that is, "the house of Caesar" (Tacitus, *Hist.* I.11). Caesar's household, "a vast array of personal servants, imperial freedmen and slaves," quite literally ran imperial affairs.[5] Politics was inextricably tied up with kinship and patron-broker-client relations, as we have seen. Consequently, members of a ruler's personal household frequently handled matters that today lie under the jurisdiction of government bureaucracies. Where public offices existed, they were often based on household models, as in the case of "the ubiquitous *oikonomos* . . . who played a key part in the total *oikonomia* or management of household, club or state."[6]

Although Philo associates household management with women's roles, the title "steward" (*oikonomos*) was given most frequently to slaves or freedmen who administered the affairs of households and businesses, managed plantations, and acted as financial bursars.[7] The title was also given to officers of cities and/or political bodies such as the "tribe" (*phyle*) or "council" (*boule*). At various times and places, for example during the Hellenistic period in Asia Minor, such stewards were free persons, sometimes even holding citizenship (a privilege not granted to all free persons). By the Roman period, however, it seems that these civic officers were almost always slaves or ex-slaves, as were the household stewards who managed their masters' public and private affairs.[8]

[1] Malina, *The New Testament World*, 48.

[2] John Reumann, *Stewardship and the Economy of God* (Grand Rapids: Eerdmans, 1992), 11–12.

[3] Ibid., 13.

[4] Aristotle, *Politica* I.2.1252a, 3.10.2; see John H. Elliott, *A Home for the Homeless: A Sociological Exegesis of 1 Peter, Its Situation and Strategy* (Philadelphia: Fortress, 1981), 174.

[5] Elliott, *A Home for the Homeless*, 177.

[6] John Reumann, "'Stewards of God': Pre-Christian Religious Application of *Oikonomos* in Greek," *JBL* 77, no. 4 (1958): 339.

[7] Martin, *Slavery as Salvation*, 15.

[8] Ibid., 16–17.

Financial Management, Status, and Honor. The *oikonomos* is characteristically and even stereotypically associated with the management of financial resources, as we can see from the following assessment of the Egyptian king Ramses III, whom Diodorus of Sicily (ca. 56 B.C.E.) called Remphis:

> On the death of Proteus his son Remphis succeeded to the throne. This ruler spent his whole life looking after the revenues and amassing riches from every source, and because of his niggardly and miserly character spent nothing either on votive offerings to the gods or on benefactions to the inhabitants. Consequently, since he had been not so much a king as only an efficient steward, in the place of a fame based upon virtue he left a treasure larger than that of any king before him; for according to tradition he amassed some four hundred thousand talents of silver and gold. (*Bibliotheca Historica* I.62.5–6)

Not only does Diodorus associate efficient stewardship with administering and amassing wealth, he feels that it is an activity unbecoming to a king. In Diodorus' estimate, a virtuous king builds up his fame (honor) by acting as a benefactor (patron) to his subjects and brokering their relations with the gods. Diodorus clearly reflects the disdain of Greco-Roman elites for money-making occupations, a sentiment that the first-century Greek writer Plutarch also expresses.

In his *Aemilius Paulus* 12.6.5, Plutarch describes how Perseus abandoned an alliance against Rome upon being asked to pay each mercenary captain one thousand pieces of silver. Plutarch condemns Perseus for behaving like an *oikonomos* rather than a foe of the Romans. Acting like a steward, once again, is inappropriate behavior for an elite male. Indeed, for Plutarch, even associating with stewards is, at best, a deplorable necessity for those who inherit wealth. In another text, Plutarch complains that a father's death spells the end of a young man's pursuit of sports and learning. The young man must, henceforth, exchange these pleasant pastimes for the endlessly dreary "interrogation of servants, inspection of ledgers, *the casting up of accounts with stewards* and debtors, and occupation and worry that deny him his luncheon and drive him to the bath at night" (*Peri Philoploutias* 526.7.E–F, emphasis mine).[9]

In addition to giving us a glimpse of the life styles and expectations of elite males, Plutarch's remarks confirm that (1) *oikonomoi* functioned as accountants managing their masters' financial resources and (2) these managerial slaves or freedmen were not held in particularly high regard. This low regard is rooted in Greco-Roman notions that since all goods in life are limited, there are important

---

[9] A sumptuous luncheon and an afternoon at the baths were normal expectations for elite males.

consequences for how one might deal honorably in such a world. Malina and Rohrbaugh sum up the situation well:

> In the "limited good" world of the first century Mediterranean . . . seeking "more" was morally wrong. . . . Because the pie was "limited" and already all distributed, an increase in the share of one person automatically meant a loss for someone else. Honorable people, therefore, did not try to get more and those who did were automatically considered thieves. Noblemen avoided such accusations of getting rich at the expense of others by having their affairs handled by slaves. Such behavior was condoned in slaves since slaves were without honor anyway.[10]

Here we see one reason why the majority of private and public *oikonomoi* were of servile origin. Slaves were not only regarded by their elite masters as lacking the appropriate sensibilities for honorable activities, they were also actually encouraged to develop the money-grubbing attitudes and behaviors that their masters depised. Slaves and lower status persons (clients) were socialized to believe that their "well-being was completely wrapped up in the well-being and benevolence of the patron. Slaves and freedman who had been put in charge of their patron's wealth were proud when they were able to increase it, as their tombstones show."[11] A slave or freedman coveted such a position since it was one of the almost nonexistent avenues available for upward social mobility within an elite household, a social club, or even a municipality.[12] Yet such positions were inherently vulnerable. The elite needed stewards to maintain their public reputations while increasing their material resources, but looked down upon them. In soliciting access to potential patrons, high-status persons particularly resented having to deal with *oikonomoi* and saw their upward social mobility as a threat.[13] Peasants frequently did not deal willingly or happily with estate managers representing the demands of absentee landlords.

Stewards and Patronage: The Case of Arion. In his *Antiquities of the Jews,* Josephus recounts a series of events from the reign of Ptolemy Euergetes of Egypt (146–116 B.C.E.) that illustrate both the highs and lows of a steward's existence. The story begins with Ptolemy's marriage to Cleopatra, the daughter of the Seleucid monarch Antiochus. The transfer of her dowry that includes ownership of the provinces of Judea and Samaria necessitates the reallocation of tax revenues. The Judean high priest Onias, a man noted for his parsimony, refuses to pay the required twenty

---

[10] Malina and Rohrbaugh, *Social-Science Commentary on the Synoptic Gospels,* 124.

[11] Martin, *Slavery as Salvation,* 28.

[12] Ibid., 48.

[13] Ibid., 44; Saller, *Personal Patronage,* 64–66.

talents of silver to his new lord. An angry Ptolemy sends his friend Athenion as his ambassador to Jerusalem to lay out the choices for the recalcitrant high priest: either pay the tax or face a military invasion. When Onias stubbornly refuses to relent, his nephew Joseph comes forward and offers to negotiate a tax remission with the Egyptian king (*Ant.* 12.4.1–2).

Joseph must go to Ptolemy as a client to a patron but without any prior claim to the king's favor.[14] To ensure his success, he enlists Athenion, the Egyptian ambassador and friend of Ptolemy, to act as a broker for him (*Ant.* 12.4.3). Joseph secures his brokerage by wining and dining Athenion and presenting him "with rich gifts" (*Ant.* 12.4.2). This strategy works so well that Joseph is received at court and given a place of honor daily at the king's own table.

Joseph's arrival in Alexandria happens to coincide with the gathering of those who are bidding on the right to collect taxes totaling eight thousand talents from the regions of Coelesyria, Phoenicia, Judea, and Samaria. Normally, the king "farms" these contracts out to "the men of the greatest power in every city" (*Ant.* 12.4.3).[15] In this instance, Joseph claims that he can double the amount of taxes collected, and boldly declares that the favor of the king and queen are all the guarantees he needs to provide. That Ptolemy grants him the contracts out of "affection" (*Ant.* 12.4.3) illustrates the favoritism that characterizes patronage relationships.[16] Joseph returns to Judea not with a tax remission but with the tax farming rights to all the surrounding territories. He simply doubles the amount of taxes he collects in Phoenicia and Syria by killing anyone who refuses to pay the higher amounts and confiscating their property for the king. In this way, Joseph enriches himself (*Ant.* 12.4.5) and his Judean compatriots (*Ant.* 12.4.10). His indebtedness to Ptolemy's favor is acknowledged through his gifts to the king and queen and their friends, and later re-acknowledged by his son Hyrcanus, who refers to Ptolemy as his "father's benefactor" (*Ant.* 12.4.8).

This summary serves as an introduction to the incident involving the steward Arion. He is clearly identified as "the slave" (*ten doulen*). As such, Arion would have legally been a non-person, a "living implement" to be used for his master's benefit (see Plutarch, *Crassus* 2.8.1). He is also Joseph's "steward" (*oikonomos*). In this capacity he lives on his own with a wife in Alexandria, where he is responsible for

---

[14] Athenion's report to Ptolemy has Joseph recognizing him as the patron of the multitudes (*Ant.* 12.4.3).

[15] A more detailed discussion of taxation in first-century Mediterranean societies can be found in Ekkehard W. Stegemann and Wolfgang Stegemann, *The Jesus Movement: A Social History of Its First Century* (Minneapolis: Fortress, 1999), 49–50, 113–23.

[16] Pilch and Malina, *Biblical Social Values*, 89.

transferring the tax moneys to Ptolemy's treasury on specific dates. These taxes amount to no less than three thousand talents of silver—two hundred and twenty-five thousand pounds of precious metal—the equivalent of eighteen million dinarii.[17] Alongside managing these vast resources, Arion enjoys the respect and personal regard of the queen.

The birth of Ptolemy's son requires that Joseph send an appropriate gift to the king and queen. He sends his youngest and cleverest son, Hyrcanus, to Alexandria with a letter to Arion that instructs him to give Hyrcanus ten talents or a little more for the purchase of the gift. Hyrcanus, however, demands one thousand talents. Arion responds angrily and lectures the youth about how his master has worked too hard acquiring his wealth to have it squandered by his wastrel of a son. Hyrcanus has the steward thrown into prison. Arion's wife immediately goes to Cleopatra to inform her of Arion's situation. The queen, who holds Arion in great esteem, in turn tells her husband of Arion's predicament.

Ptolemy sends a message to Hyrcanus demanding explanations for both his failure to present himself at court and his treatment of Arion. Hyrcanus makes his excuses and explains that "He had punished the slave for disobeying his commands; for it mattered not whether a master was little or great . . . unless we punish such as these [the king himself could] expect to be despised by [his] subjects" (*Ant.* 12.4.8). Josephus tells us that the king laughs and is impressed by the young man's "soul." The king's response is reported back to Arion in his prison. Arion quickly realizes that "he had no way to help himself" (*Ant.* 12.4.9); therefore, he gives Hyrcanus the thousand talents and is let out of prison. Hyrcanus purchases one hundred boys and one hundred girls whom he gives to the king and queen respectively in a splendid procession in which each of these little slaves present a silver talent to the sovereigns. Hyrcanus disburses the remaining funds as monetary gifts (i.e., bribes) to the most important Egyptian officials, thus securing his family's favor in the Egyptian court (*Ant.* 12.4.1–9).

This narrative illustrates quite graphically the importance of kinship and patronage in political affairs, but what I find most striking about this incident is the complexity and ambiguity of Arion's position. The steward Arion can be classified as a managerial slave, a member of a small, highly visible cadre of slaves "whose informal social status was ambiguous and conflicted with their legal status."[18] Such managerial slaves functioned fairly independently from their owners'

---

[17] This calculation is based on information provided by Rousseau and Arav (*Jesus and His World*, 55–61), who also point out that "a dinarius was the wage for a day's work in the fields" (p. 59).

[18] Martin, *Slavery as Salvation*, 15.

day-to-day control, often exercising considerable authority and influence in relation to other slaves as well as to freeborn persons.[19] This independence is quite evident in Arion's case since he lives in Egypt, not Judea, where he enjoys entrée to the highest circles of the royal household. Usually, such a slave holding the title of "business agent" (*pragmateutes*) or "household manager" (*oikonomos*) was socially and legally recognized as an extension of the owner's own person. Insult or injury to such a slave represented a social affront to his owner and/or patron.[20] Ptolemy, for example, connects Arion's imprisonment with Hyrcanus' tardiness in paying his respects to himself (*Ant.* 12.4.8); the tardiness is a potential insult not only to the young man's father whom Arion represents but also to himself as Joseph's patron and benefactor.

Throughout the story the steward Arion plays the role of a faithful client to Joseph and to Ptolemy, scrupulously turning over the tax revenues to the royal treasury and endeavoring to fulfill his master's instructions in the face of Hyrcanus' extravagance. Secure in his owner's confidence and the king's esteem, he feels sure enough initially not only to refuse his master's son, but also to lecture him, that is, to take on a fatherly role in relation to his owner's son. After Arion is imprisoned, his wife seeks his release by turning to the queen who plays the role of broker by interceding for Arion with the king. Ptolemy responds by calling Hyrcanus to account for his actions; Hyrcanus then reminds Ptolemy of the right and necessity of all masters, whether great or small, to punish disobedient slaves. Because of Arion's legal status as a slave, even Ptolemy must give way before the claims of his owner, here represented by his freeborn son. Having failed to win his freedom and with it the affirmation of his decision-making powers through royal influence, Arion has no choice but to concede to Hyrcanus' demands, even though his master's son was "a child in age still" (*Ant.* 12.4.8). It should be noted that Hyrcanus could not just take the money, for he had to physically coerce his father's steward into giving it to him. What we can see in Arion's case is that in spite of their sometimes considerable responsibilities and authority, *oikonomoi* were personally vulnerable to physical abuse just like all other slaves.

Arion's situation as a managerial slave is exceptional with respect to the unusually large sums of money that he manages, but otherwise can be considered paradigmatic. As an *oikonomos*, Arion acted as the agent and representative of his master Joseph, who was not an official of either the Judean or Egyptian government, even though he was responsible for the collection of taxes throughout the

---

[19] Ibid., 15
[20] Ibid., 20.

region surrounding Judea. Joseph was a member of the high priestly household since he was the nephew of the high priest. He won the right to collect taxes as a favor, an act of patronage from Ptolemy. Arion's role as his master's agent and representative would have been similar to that of the managerial slaves who appear in the gospels. Momentarily we will turn to the gospels; but first, we need to look at some evidence for *oikonomoi* who functioned as civic officers.

Stewards as Officials in Municipal Government and Civic Organizations. As noted above, *oikonomos* was also the title of a civic official who may have been a free-born person, even a citizen, although in the Roman period most *oikonomoi* seem to have been slaves or freedmen. These stewards, like their domestic counterparts, functioned as accountants and registrars and were responsible for such things as "collecting fees, writing receipts, arranging for the erection of statues and inscriptions and the disbursement of funds."[21] Inscriptional evidence from the eastern Mediterranean indicates that such *oikonomoi* might also act as intermediaries and representatives of municipal governments in the rituals of political religion. At Ephesus (302 B.C.E.) a city steward or treasurer was instructed not only to pay for sacrifices on certain state occasions but also to offer sacrifices together with the priests and priestess of Artemis. At Priene, inscriptions from the fourth to first centuries B.C.E. instruct the city's *oikonomos* to provide the crowns and wreaths voted to be given to leading citizens at their funerals.[22] A second-century B.C.E. inscription from Magnesia-on-the-Meander directs the city's college of stewards to use the "revenues which they have for the financial administration of the city" to organize the monthly sacrifice of a bull to Zeus Sosipolis. The *oikonomoi* are to purchase a bull for the monthly rite, ensure it is fattened up on time, join with other city officials in prayer at the time of the sacrifice, and supervise the distribution of meat afterwards.[23] Instructions such as these raise intriguing questions about the role and duties of Erastus of Corinth, the one person identified in the New Testament (Rom 16:23) as an *oikonomos tes poleos,* a steward or treasurer of the city. These questions will be dealt with below.

Elective associations, including religious societies, also used the title *oikonomos* ("household steward" or "manager") to designate officers who carried out financial and other supervisory duties. A fragmentary inscription from the island of Lesbos provides instruction on choosing a properly qualified *oikonomos* who will ensure that no other men enter a building in which women celebrate a cultic

---

[21] Ibid., 19.
[22] Reumann, "Stewards of God," 342.
[23] Ibid., 343.

festival.[24] Papyrus fragments from Memphis, Egypt, name annually appointed stewards who were responsible for issuing supplies of bread to the priestesses at the Sarapeum in that city.[25] A steward, referred to as Hermias, is listed as an officer of a religious society associated with Hermes-Trismegistus at Ombos in Egypt.[26]

Summary. Stewards serving in households, cities, and elective associations all seem to be responsible for the management of financial and other resources. As slaves and freedmen, *oikonomoi* are the clients of their masters whose patronage and favor ensure their positions. They occupy an in-between status involving a sort of derivative or representative authority associated with their function of acting on behalf of superiors in economic and religious interactions that were embedded in their domestic or civic roles. As such, they can be seen as brokers for their patrons; their positions also enabled them to become patrons to other clients seeking benefits from their masters. When we turn to the literature of early Christ-followers, we find not only references to persons who act as stewards, but most significantly the adoption of the term *oikonomos* to characterize leadership roles within their assemblies.

Stewards and Managerial Slaves in the Gospels

Although several parables scattered throughout the Gospels feature slaves in managerial roles, only Luke explicitly uses the term *oikonomos* and its cognates.[27] These examples all occur within two parables: the faithful and prudent steward (Luke 12:41–48) and the allegedly "unjust" manager (Luke 16:1–8). Our examination of the two parables will begin with the former, move to a consideration of other parables that share the same theme of appropriate slave behavior in the absence of the master, and finally turn to the latter.

Luke 12:41–48. The parable of the faithful and prudent manager or steward is Jesus' response to Peter's question about an earlier parable. Both parables occur in a section containing a series of warnings to those who are unprepared for God's forthcoming rule. In the NRSV this section is entitled "watchful slaves" and is addressed to Jesus' disciples (Luke 12:22, 41), although crowds are present (12:1, 13, 54). Jesus urges his listeners to behave like slaves awaiting the return of their

---

[24] Ibid., 345.

[25] Ibid., 346.

[26] Ibid., 346–48.

[27] Harry Fledderman, "The Householder and the Servant Left in Charge," SBLSP 25 (1986): 21.

master from a wedding banquet. They are to be "dressed for action" (12:35) and "alert" (12:37). In a radical reversal of roles, the slave who is thus prepared will not only be "blessed" but will also be served a banquet by the master himself when he returns (12:37–38). The point of the parable is the need for alert vigilance in anticipation of the establishment of God's rule, an event signaled by the master's return.

The statement that follows makes the same point, but this time emphasizes the householder's perspective: "if the owner of the house had known at what hour the thief was coming, he would not have let his house be broken into" (12:39). The point of the parable is made clear in Jesus' final statement, "You also must be ready, for the Son of Man is coming at an unexpected hour" (12:40). Jesus' listeners, therefore, must be prepared for the sudden dawning of God's forthcoming reign. What is interesting is how that one event is presented differently in relation to slaves and householders. For the slaves, the establishment of God's rule will mean that their former masters will now serve them, whereas for the householder, the coming of the Son of Man will be like a thief breaking into his house. In other words, the new theocratic era will be good news for the slaves but bad news for the masters.

It is no surprise, then, that Peter immediately asks, "Lord, are you telling this parable for us or for everyone?" (12:41). Peter wants to know who are we—your inner circle of disciples—in this scenario? Are we slaves or householders? Will the coming of the Son of Man be good news or bad news for us? Jesus' responds by asking another question, "Who then is the faithful and prudent manager (*oikonomos*) whom his master will put in charge of his slaves, to give them their allowance of food at the proper time?" (12:42). Since Matthew 24:45–51 does not introduce this parable with any such question from Peter, the concern about whether the disciples are to identify with the slaves or the householders reflects a particular Lukan interest. Similarly in Matthew, the central character of the parable is identified only as a *doulos* ("slave"), a descriptor that Luke retains in verses 43, 45, and 46. By labeling this slave an *oikonomos*, Luke emphasizes his managerial role, thus setting him apart from the other slaves in a way that Matthew does not. This Lukan editing also points to his understanding that the disciples and their successors in the *ekklesia* of the late first century are neither householders nor ordinary slaves, but *oikonomoi* ("stewards") for the coming king.[28]

During his master's absence this slave-*oikonomos* has two choices. He may faithfully carry out the duties that his owner assigned to him before he left, in which

---

[28] Martin, *Slavery as Salvation*, 53; Reumann, *Stewardship*, 17.

case he will eventually be put in charge of all of his master's possessions (Luke 12:43–44). The slave manager's reward for faithful service is upward mobility.[29] Alternatively, the steward may use his owner's absence as an excuse for abusing the other slaves, self-indulgence, and drunkenness (12:45). Luke's word choices, once again, highlight the status difference between the *oikonomos* and other slaves in the household, in contrast to Matthew's, which describe the slave-manager as beating "his *fellow* slaves, and [who] eats and drinks *with drunkards*" (Matt 24:49, emphasis mine). The steward who chooses this path can expect that his master will "cut him in pieces and put him with the unfaithful when he returns" (Luke 12:46).

Jesus' (and Luke's) audiences would have recognized in these stories relatively common depictions of slave life that emphasize "acting properly in the absence of the slave owner."[30] Within the context of Jesus' ministry, the parable of the faithful and prudent steward speaks about the appropriate activity of the disciples in the present and temporary absence of God's reign in Israel.[31] Like the wise *oikonomos* who "provides on behalf of God," Peter and his fellow disciples will function as agents and brokers for God in Israel by healing, casting out demons, and proclaiming the good news of God's forthcoming rule.[32] In the Lukan rendering of the parable, the leaders of the *ekklesiai*, the successors to the disciples, are the ones who are reminded of their status as *oikonomoi*. In the context of Jesus' delayed return as the Messiah, congregational leaders are called to act as faithful and prudent stewards who manage on behalf of their absent master. Thus the parable functions not only to remind leaders of their duties and make them accountable for their actions, but also to provide criteria for affirming or rejecting the claims and authority of those who hold leading positions in the Christ-following assemblies.

Related Synoptic Parables. An independent parable about waiting slaves in Mark 13:33–37 also features the theme of appropriate slave behavior in the owner's absence. This parable, too, is addressed privately to the disciples, but concludes Jesus' final discourse to them in which he predicts and describes events that will culminate in the destruction of Jerusalem and the coming of the Son of Man.[33] Jesus' final words begin with an exhortation to the disciples to "Beware, keep alert;

---

[29] Martin, *Slavery as Salvation*, 53.

[30] Malina and Rohrbaugh, *Social-Science Commentary on the Synoptic Gospels*, 279.

[31] Arland J. Hultgren, *The Parables of Jesus: A Commentary* (Grand Rapids: Eerdmans, 2002), 160. Reumann, *Stewardship*, 17, sees here a critique of Judean leadership in the time of Jesus.

[32] Hultgren, *The Parables of Jesus*, 161.

[33] See detailed discussion in Malina and Rohrbaugh, *Social-Science Commentary on the Synoptic Gospels*, 204–7, 361–62.

for you do not know when the time will come" (13:33). He compares the situation to that of a householder going on a journey and leaving his slaves in charge, each with his or her assigned duties. The doorkeeper is specifically enjoined "to be on the watch" by staying awake throughout the four watches of the night—evening, midnight, cockcrow, and dawn—so that the master will not find him asleep when he returns unexpectedly (13:34–36). Jesus finishes with the injunction that all "Keep awake" (13:37). Diligence in carrying out one's duties and vigilant anticipation must characterize the disciple who awaits the sudden establishment of God's forthcoming rule. Although the parable is addressed specifically to the disciples, in Mark's context "all" (13:37) would include contemporary hearers of the gospel.[34]

The theme of a wealthy man leaving slaves in charge while going abroad also appears in the parables of the talents (Matt 25:14–30), the pounds (Luke 19:12–27), and the wicked tenants (Mark 12:1–12//Matt 21:33–46//Luke 20:9–19//Gos. Thom. 65). These parables do not contain the language of stewards and stewardship, nor do they depict the forthcoming "kingdom of God." Rather they seek to expose the inherent characteristics of a world that desperately needs God's rule and/or to illustrate the challenges faced in this world by those who wish to remain true to a vision of God's just reign. These parables also portray the roles that managerial slaves played and the vulnerabilities they endured as they were empowered to act as agents for their masters within these contexts.

In the parable of the allegedly "wicked tenants," which in fact concerns dispossessed peasants, slaves are sent to collect an absentee landowner's rents.[35] He assumes that the tenants will accord these slaves the same honor and respect that they would show him, for these slaves are his properly appointed agents. The tenants, instead, act out their resentment of the absentee landlord. By beating his slaves, sending them back empty-handed, insulting them, and finally killing them (Mark 12:3–5//Matt 21:35–36//Luke 20:10b–12), the tenants violently reject his claims to the products of their labor. In their eyes, the landowner's claims are illegitimate—he has forced them to go from subsistence agriculture to cash cropping by converting their ancestral lands into a vineyard. When the landowner sends his son as his most authoritative representative, expecting the tenants to show him respect, they see killing him as a way to reclaim what was once theirs. Such an action, however, only results in the destruction of the tenants (Mark

---

[34] Hultgren, *The Parables of Jesus*, 267.

[35] Stephen J. Patterson, *The God of Jesus: The Historical Jesus and the Search for Meaning* (Harrisburg: Trinity, 1998), 140.

12:9//Matt 21:40–41//Luke 20:16). This parable presents us not with a vision of what God's theocratic rule looks like, but with the reasons why it must be established and made real, and with the illusory nature of ancient Mediterranean societal claims to justice and fairness. Everyone in the parable acts appropriately and consistently with conventional expectations, "and yet, no one wins."[36] Although much more could be said about this parable, its present pertinence is its depiction of the vulnerability of slaves sent to represent their masters.[37] Presenting oneself as an agent of a person of high status did not necessarily guarantee a warm or even neutral reception; this agency, on occasion, could be downright dangerous.

The parables of the talents (Matt 25:14–30) and the parable of the pounds (Luke 19:12–27) illustrate the choices and consequences that faced a slave entrusted to act on his master's behalf in the ancient Mediterranean world.[38] As noted above, the "dishonorable" work of collecting rents, doing business, and investing money was relegated to slaves who were assumed to lack any sensibility for honor. In both of these parables, the master entrusted three slaves with sums of money. Two of the slaves behave as the master expects them to. They successfully "trade" with the money. In Matthew's version they double the amounts entrusted to them (25:20, 22), while in Luke's rendition these two slaves respectively earn ten and five times the amounts committed to their care (19:16, 18). When the master returns and learns of their success, he commends the two slaves and gives them charge of "many things" (Matt 25:21, 23) or of cities equaling the number of talents earned (Luke 19:17, 19). These slaves are well socialized into the patronal ideology of their master, perceiving that by promoting his interests they can attain a social mobility unavailable to non-elite persons in first-century Mediterranean societies.[39] Indeed, their master rewards them with positions of greater responsibility and authority.

The third slave, however, chooses to bury his master's funds in the ground (Matt 25:18) or to wrap up the money in a piece of cloth (Luke 19:20). Both of these responses would have been quite honorable if the slave had been a free person. Later rabbinic rulings, for example, teach that "burying a pledge or deposit was the safest way to care for someone else's money; if a loss occurred, the one

---

[36] Ibid., 141.

[37] For a more detailed discussion of this parable see Malina and Rohrbaugh, *Social-Science Commentary on the Synoptic Gospels*, 109–10, 199–200, 307–8; Hultgren, *The Parables of Jesus*, 351–82; Patterson, *The God of Jesus*, 138–41.

[38] I will treat these two parables together, despite their obvious differences (e.g., see Hultgren, *The Parables of Jesus*, 272–73), because what I am primarily interested in is the role of the slaves in relation to the master, which is identical in both.

[39] Martin, *Slavery as Salvation*, 26–30.

burying money had no responsibility. Tying up a deposit in a cloth . . . was riskier, however, and therefore left one responsible for any loss incurred."[40] In the societies of the ancient Mediterranean, in which goods were limited, an honorable person sought to maintain what he or she had.[41] Losing what was entrusted to one would entail loss of honor and status, while acquiring more necessitated depriving another of his or her possessions through some form of exploitation, such as theft or extortion. The third slave thus represents the situation of the "honorable slave" in the service of a rich man (Matt) or a claimant to a royal throne (Luke).[42] Even though he fears his master and knows that his master expects him to engage in exploitative trade (Matt 25:24//Luke 19:21), the third slave refuses to do so. In his own eyes the third slave has behaved appropriately, honorably, and successfully by preserving intact what he was given without causing harm or loss to any other person. But from his master's perspective, this slave is "wicked and lazy." At the very least, he ought to have invested the money with bankers who would have returned it with interest (Matt 25:26–27; see Luke 19:22–23). Regarding the third slave as either incompetent or insubordinate, the master punishes him by taking the money he had entrusted to him and giving it to another (Matt: 25:28//Luke 19:24).

For a peasant audience in first-century Galilee, these parables would have illustrated precisely the results that they could expect in dealings with the elites and their slave-managers: "to all those who have, more will be given, and they will have an abundance; but from those who have nothing, even what they have will be taken away" (Matt 25:29//Luke 19:26). We might say, "The rich get richer, and the poor get poorer." Once again, this parable is not unfolding a vision of God's forthcoming rule; rather, it exposes the inherently exploitative character of ancient Mediterranean elites as experienced in first-century Galilee and Judea. The rich man (Matt 25:24) and the royal throne claimant (Luke 19:21) are described as *skleros* and *austeros* respectively, words that carry the connotation of being hard or severe, even, "harsh, cruel, merciless, unyielding."[43] This master is accused of "reaping where [he] did not sow, and gathering where [he] did not scatter seed," an assessment that he himself affirms (Matt 25:24–26//Luke 19:21–22). Thus, by his own admission this aristocrat is a thief—taking what is not rightfully his. As Richard Ford has noted, "only western listeners, steeped in the mores of

---

[40] Malina and Rohrbaugh, *Social-Science Commentary on the Synoptic Gospels,* 385.

[41] Ibid., 385.

[42] While the phrase "honorable slave" would have been an oxymoron for high-status persons, it is attested in a funeral epitaph from Athens. See Martin, *Slavery as Salvation,* 46–47.

[43] BDAG, 930.

modern capitalism, could so thoroughly miss what was obvious to Jesus' original peasant audiences, namely, that the master's mode of operating is criminal."[44] The rich man or nobleman uses his power and position to exploit others, demanding that his slaves and servants similarly engage in rapacious pursuits.[45] Many slaves and freedmen were willing participants, having bought into the patronal ideology that ensuring their masters' success was in their own best interests. Jesus' parables present a challenge to that ideology.

Contrary to the dominant contemporary Western interpretation of this parable, it is, in fact, the third slave with whom the disciples and their successors are to identify, as the Nazorean version of this parable preserved by Eusebius suggests. In that "Hebrew" rendition, the first slave squanders his master's money with harlots and flute-girls and is cast into prison. The second multiplies his master's money and is rebuked by his master. The third slave hides the money and is accepted with joy. On the basis of this version of the parable, Eusebius proposes that Matt 25:30 ("As for this worthless slave, throw him into the outer darkness") may be an epanalepsis, a literary device that shifts focus back to the first two slaves and away from the third one (*Theophania* on Matt 25:14–15). As Malina and Rohrbaugh point out, "Eusebius cannot imagine the first two servants being commended by Jesus (in contrast to the wicked master who obviously commends these servants because they do his bidding), since they are little more than thieving accomplices."[46] Like the third slave, the disciple of Jesus in the real world of Mediterranean households, businesses, and cities must resist demands to imitate this kind of predatory behavior. Like the third slave, the Christ-follower must maintain his or her integrity and honor by refusing to exploit others regardless of the consequences.[47]

Luke 16:1–8. Perhaps the parable in Luke 16:1–8, of the so-called dishonest manager but more accurately entitled "the rich man and his manager," best illustrates the complexities and difficulties faced by managerial slaves. Scholars generally consider this as the most perplexing and difficult of Jesus' parables. Justin Ukpong asserts that the primary reason for its mystifying and puzzling character stems quite simply from contemporary Western readers' having been mistakenly "conditioned to identify with the rich man in the parable, who is then constructed

---

[44] Ford, *The Parables of Jesus*, 35.

[45] Luke's identification of the man as a throne claimant, probably Archelaus, together with the description of his ruthless nature, should mitigate against tendencies to see him or Matthew's rich man as an analogy for God (Malina and Rohrbaugh, *Social-Science Commentary on the Synoptic Gospels*, 305).

[46] Malina and Rohrbaugh, *Social-Science Commentary on the Synoptic Gospels*, 386.

[47] See the discussion in Ford, *The Parables of Jesus*, 32–46.

to stand for God."[48] As Ukpong demonstrates, a quick survey of Luke's use of the term "rich man" (*plousios*) indicates that it always carries a pejorative sense, consistently occurring in passages that critique material wealth. Examples include Jesus' curse on the rich (6:24), the parable of the rich fool (12:16), invitations to parties of rich people (14:12), the story of the rich man and Lazarus (16:19, 21, 22), the story of the rich noble man saddened by the prospect of selling all his property (18:23, 25), and the story of the rich but repentant tax-collector Zacchaeus (19:2).[49]

Comparing Luke 16:1–8 with the parables that precede and follow it further confirms Ukpong's assessment that the rich man should not be seen as a God figure. In chapter 15 Jesus introduces three characters—a shepherd (15:1–7), a woman (15:8–10), and a father (15:11–32)—who are "anxious about and search for what is lost."[50] The father welcomes back the son who has squandered his property in dissolute living (15:11–32), in sharp contrast to the rich man who dismisses the steward who has allegedly squandered his property (16:1–8). The steward's master is more similar to the rich man who ignores the plight of the beggar Lazarus lying before the rich man's gate (16:19–31). These contrasts and comparisons mean "that while it is reasonable to understand the main figures in chapter 15 as they are generally understood to stand for God, it is not reasonable to understand those in chapter 16 the same way."[51]

This analysis is consistent with both Jesus' and Luke's social location in ancient Mediterranean societies that considered all goods as limited and the acquisition of wealth as the result of theft, fraud, or extortion. As Malina and Rohrbaugh remind us:

> To be labeled "rich" was therefore a social and moral statement as much as an economic one. It meant the power or capacity to take from someone weaker what was rightfully not yours. Being rich was synonymous with being greedy.[52]

Although the rich (read "greedy") man in Luke 16:1–9 is not described quite as negatively as the landowner and the throne claimant in the previous set of par-

---

[48] Justin S. Ukpong, "The Parable of the Shrewd Manager (Luke 16:1–13): An Essay in Inculturation Biblical Hermeneutic," *Semeia* 73 (1996): 192, describes the traditional West African worldview as one quite similar to that which existed in the ancient Mediterranean: "there should be no exploitation of other human beings. Material wealth is regarded as God's gift to the whole community. Hoarding and profiteering at the expense of others are to be abhorred."

[49] Ibid., 197.

[50] Ibid., 198.

[51] Ibid.

[52] Malina and Rohrbaugh, *Social-Science Commentary on the Synoptic Gospels*, 400.

ables, he belongs in the same category. The rich man, therefore, is not a representative of God but an object of critique.[53] He is a member of the elite and the owner of a large estate. He has an *oikonomos*, a "steward" who is probably a slave, who was perhaps born in the household itself, and who has the authority to act on behalf of his master in arranging for the rental of his property, making loans, reducing and liquidating debts, and keeping the accounts of such transactions. He would have been paid a commission or fee on each transaction that he arranged.[54]

The story begins with unidentified persons approaching the rich man with accusations about the steward (16:1). The word that describes their action is the Greek word *diaballo*, the meaning of which is contested. It can mean "to accuse," "deceive by false accounts," "slander," "calumniate"[55] or to "bring charges, inform either justly or unjustly."[56] Therefore, we cannot rule out the possibility that persons motivated by jealousy, retribution, or greed may have unjustly accused the steward.[57] The unnamed informants allege that the steward is "squandering" his master's property (16:1). The Greek verb *diaskorpizo*, which means to "scatter, disperse" or "squander, waste," is the same one that is used to describe the activity of the prodigal son who fritters away his inheritance in dissolute living (15:13).[58] The steward is known for activities that are inappropriately dissipating his master's resources, or has been suspected of them.[59]

The rich man summons the steward and demands from him an accounting of his stewardship, not because he wants to determine whether the charges are true, but because he has already decided to remove the slave from his managerial position (16:2). Surprisingly, the master does not demand repayment of the squandered resources, which may signal that he is a merciful man, willing to acknowledge an interpersonal obligation to a slave whom he has entrusted to represent him.[60] It might also suggest that he is not particularly concerned about the loss of the money or other material goods. Rather, he is more intent on repairing

---

[53] Ukpong, "The Parable of the Shrewd Manager," 198, 201.

[54] Malina and Rohrbaugh, *Social-Science Commentary on the Synoptic Gospels*, 292; Ukpong, "The Parable of the Shrewd Manager," 201.

[55] LSJ, 389–90.

[56] BDAG, 226.

[57] See discussion in of *diaballo* in John G. Lygre, "Of What Charges? (Luke 16:1–2)," *BTB* 32, no. 1 (2002): 23; David Landry and Ben May, "Honor Restored: New Light on the Parable of the Prudent Steward (Luke 16:1–8a)," *JBL* 119:2 (2000): 297; Mary Ann Beavis, "Ancient Slavery as an Interpretive Context for the New Testament Servant Parables with Special Reference to the Unjust Steward (Luke 16:1–8)," *JBL* 111 (1992): 48.

[58] BDAG, 236.

[59] Landry and May, "Honor Restored," 298; Lygre, "Of What Charges?" 23–24.

[60] Malina and Rohrbaugh, *Social-Science Commentary on the Synoptic Gospels*, 292.

any damage to his honor that may result from the steward's activities. Public reputation is at least as important as wealth, if not more so, in establishing social status
and prestige in ancient Mediterranean societies. The rich man will be judged on
the basis of his ability to control the behavior of his subordinates. If his steward
carelessly wastes his master's resources by engaging in inappropriate behaviors,
then it is the master who will lose prestige and status among his peers. To prevent
such a disaster, the master unilaterally dismisses the steward without giving him an
opportunity to defend himself.[61]

Like the prodigal son, who also scatters and wastes the resources entrusted to
him, the steward devises a plan. Unlike his counterpart in the former story who
admits that he "sinned" and is "no longer worthy" (15:17–19), the manager acknowledges no wrongdoing (see 16:3–4 with 15:17–19). The tone of his solilo-
quy instead suggests a lack of control over his situation.[62] Particularly if he is a
slave, and to a somewhat lesser degree if he is a freedman, he is quite dependent on
his master's good will and favor.[63] So he contemplates his prospects. Removed
from his position as manager, he will be reduced either to "digging," that is, working in the fields, or running away and becoming a beggar (16:3). He acknowledges
that he is not physically strong enough to do the former and is ashamed to do the
latter (16:3). Unable to countenance these degrading options, he concludes that
"he must do something that will allow him to keep his position as a steward." [64]
He understands that he is being dismissed because of allegations that his actions
dishonor his master. He therefore comes up with a plan that he hopes will enable
him to retain his managerial position and/or to gain a new circle of patrons.[65]

The steward's plan involves granting favors to his master's debtors in anticipation of their future hospitality and good will toward him once word gets out that
he has been removed from his position. He summons them individually and has
them rewrite their contracts. The first owes the rich man "a hundred jugs of olive

---

[61] Landry and May, "Honor Restored," 298–300.

[62] Lygre, "Of What Charges?" 25.

[63] Ukpong, "The Parable of the Shrewd Manager," 204, regards the steward as an employee who
is poor, and so without rights.

[64] Landry and May, "Honor Restored," 300. Many scholars (e.g., Ukpong, "The Parable of the
Shrewd Manager," 205) assume the steward is trying to devise a way to secure new employment.
since he is a slave, that move is highly unlikely. His only realistic option is to try to clear his name
and prove his loyalty and continued usefulness to his master.

[65] Malina and Rohrbaugh, Social-Science Commentary on the Synoptic Gospels, 293. See also Martin, Slavery as Salvation, 25, who uses inscriptional evidence to demonstrate that slaves could have patrons
who were not their owners.

oil" (16:6), the equivalent of approximately nine hundred gallons of oil.[66] The steward reduces the amount owed by fifty percent. The second debtor owes his master "a hundred containers of wheat" (16:7), the equivalent of about one hundred and fifty bushels.[67] In this instance, the steward reduces the debt by twenty percent. The debtors have not yet been informed of the rich man's decision to remove the steward from his position, and so believe that he is acting legitimately in his capacity as the rich man's agent. They do not know what motivates him to rewrite their contracts in this favorable way. Yet having accepted these favors, the debtors, if they are honorable men, are now morally obligated to him. Not only will they receive him into their homes, they will publicly praise him and his master for relieving their burden of debt.

The steward has thus placed his master in a serious predicament. The rich man knows that the steward acted after being informed of his dismissal; therefore, the redrawn contracts are not legally binding on his master.[68] The rich man must decide if he will honor them or not. On the one hand, if he nullifies them, he risks alienating his clients, whose debts are large enough that they may, in fact, represent the rent or tax debts of an entire village.[69] Not only will his reputation suffer, but he could even find himself in the same sort of position vis-à-vis his tenants as the landowner in the parable of the "wicked" tenants. On the other hand, if he "allows the reductions to stand, he will be praised far and wide (as will the manager for having made the "arrangement") as a noble and generous man."[70] His honor will have been enhanced, as will the standing of the steward. By honoring the rewritten debt contracts, the rich man indicates that he stands behind the steward despite the allegations—perhaps unfounded—of his wastefulness. Indeed, the steward is counting on his master to accept his actions as proof that he knows quite well how to use his master's material resources in the most appropriate way.

The parable concludes with the master's commending, or more accurately, expressing "his admiration for or approval of," the steward.[71] The rich man approves of his manager because he has demonstrated that he is *phronimos*, which means "sensible, thoughtful, prudent, or wise."[72] The steward has acted in his master's behalf with the loyalty and prudence that is expected of a managerial slave (see Luke

---

[66] Malina and Rohrbaugh, *Social-Science Commentary on the Synoptic Gospels*, 293.

[67] Ibid.

[68] Ibid., 292.

[69] Ibid., 293.

[70] Ibid.

[71] See *epaineo* in BDAG, 357.

[72] BDAG, 1066.

12:42). As Landry and May put it so succinctly, "The master commends the steward because he knows how well the manager's recent actions will reflect on him."[73]

Yet in spite of his approval and praise, the rich man still views the steward as *ton oikonomon tes adikias* (16:8), a phrase which can mean either "the unjust or unrighteous steward" or "the steward of unrighteousness or injustice." If translated as the "unjust steward," then it seems to refer to some quality or action of the slave himself. The master's judgment of his steward reflects "the exploitative economic system's concept of justice, which is giving to everyone their dues."[74] From the master's perspective, his wealth is due to him and should be given to him regardless of the extent of exploitation involved. In this instance, the injustice consists in the fact of the steward's depriving his master of rents contractually and legally due him.[75] In the eyes of his master, the steward has cleverly enacted an injustice against him that is ironically beneficial to his public reputation. It also benefits both the steward by securing his future and the tenants by significantly reducing their debts.

If we translate *ton oikonomon tes adikias* as "the steward of unrighteousness," then it is possible to see him as an agent charged with handling the fruits of his master's unjust economic pursuits.[76] Remember that the man was "rich," that is, by definition a greedy man who accumulates wealth at the expense of the peasants who are his tenants. The steward has participated willingly in his master's exploitative economics until he himself becomes a victim of this man's "justice." Confronted by immediate dismissal based on anonymous, perhaps even spurious allegations, the steward suddenly finds himself in a position where standing in solidarity with his master's debtors is the best way to secure some sort of future for himself. By reducing their debts, he may even be consciously trying to make up for the exploitation that the tenant farmers had previously suffered through him (like Zacchaeus in Luke 19:1–10). If so, then his actions can be seen as a critique of his "master as an exploiter, and of his former self as an agent of the oppressive system."[77] By calling the manager "unjust in the very act of praising his ingenuity (v. 8a), the master acknowledges the manager's critique."[78]

In the parable of the rich man and his steward, Jesus "raises questions about personal identity and survival, attitudes to wealth and possessions, integrity and

---

[73] Landry and May, "Honor Restored," 305.

[74] Ukpong, "The Parable of the Shrewd Manager," 203.

[75] Ibid., 204.

[76] Colin Brown, "The Unjust Steward: A New Twist?" in *Worship, Theology and Ministry in the Early Church: Essays in Honor of Ralph P. Martin* (ed. Michael J. Wilkins and Terence Paige; JSNTSup 87; Sheffield: Sheffield Academic Press, 1992), 141.

[77] Ukpong, "The Parable of the Shrewd Manager," 205–6.

[78] Ibid., 207.

service to God."[79] How can a disciple survive in the real world of ancient Mediterranean societies? What is the appropriate behavior of a disciple who finds him or herself in a position of responsibility within a household, a business, an association, or a city? Does one collaborate in the rapacious economics of the rich who are one's earthly masters, employers, or supervisors? Or does one seek to enact as well as one can an alternative concept of justice in which material resources are seen as gifts from God to be shared equitably so that no one does without, in which it is a crime to exploit another human being, and in which the rich use their wealth to benefit others.[80] The "prudent" steward of Luke 16:1–8 comes to the realization that he must do the latter.

Summary. Although a number of parables feature slaves acting as agents for their masters, only Luke actually uses the term *oikonomos* to describe these characters and to set them up as examples for the inner circle of Jesus' disciples and their successors in the *ekklesiai*. In Luke 12:41–48 the most important qualities of the steward are faithfulness and prudence or wisdom. These are demonstrated by the way that the steward uses his master's absence as a time to pursue his assigned duties with diligence, ensuring that the "other slaves" (i.e., members of the group) are properly cared for. Here the steward is seen as God's or Jesus' agent within the community. Similar parables urging a stance of vigilant anticipation of the forthcoming reign of God are found in Luke 12:35–40 and Mark 13:33–37. Those parables appear to be addressed to disciples in general rather than to those invested with responsibility for the group.

Luke 16:1–8 highlights the quality of prudence or wisdom in bringing about restitutive justice in a world where one's superiors regard the equitable sharing of material resources as "unjust." The steward's wisdom is demonstrated by the fact that everyone wins: the debtors are given some relief, the master thereby retains or gains honor, and the steward is praised by both master, albeit ambivalently, and tenants for whom he is a hero.[81] Although the steward is formally the agent of the rich man, his brokering of better conditions for the debtors demonstrates his loyalty to an even higher master. His prudence ameliorates a situation that could easily deteriorate into the sort of relations illustrated in the parable of the "dispossessed peasants," better known as the "wicked tenants" (Mark 12:1–12// Matt 21:38–46//Luke 20:9–19). The steward's decision to reduce the debts of his master's tenant farmers places him in a position of vulnerability and risk not

---

[79] C. Brown, "The Unjust Steward," 142.
[80] Ukpong, "The Parable of the Shrewd Manager," 206.
[81] Ibid., 207.

unlike that of the third slave in the parables of the talents (Matt 25:14–30) and
pounds (Luke 19:12–27). A refusal to participate in the exploitative business affairs of one's master will predictably result in punishment, not praise. Although
the third slave remains true to his vision of what constitutes honor and justice, he
loses any opportunity to enact that vision in the world in which he lives. Again,
the prudence of the steward in Luke 16:1–8 makes him a better choice as a
potential model for early church leadership.

In Luke's view, then, a leader in the *ekklesia* is to see him or herself as a steward,
an agent for God and Christ. Faithfulness, as demonstrated through diligence in
carrying out one's duties, is a desirable quality. Also desirable are prudence and
wisdom, perhaps even shrewdness, especially in the risky business of promoting
and actualizing God's alternative vision of justice. The Lukan *oikonomos* thus is a
potentially subversive figure.

As we shall see below, Paul describes himself as a steward of Christ both to
claim authority and to subvert the culturally dominant ideology of benevolent
patriarchalism by insisting that faithful stewardship is characterized by an imitation of Christ's self-emptying solidarity with humanity. In the pseudo-Pauline
epistles, stewardship language is retained, but the focus turns to "Paul's" role in
the divine *oikonomia*, with an emphasis on the favor or grace shown to him. "Paul"
becomes a proponent of the very ideology that he seeks to counteract in I Corinthians. In Titus and in the letters of Ignatius, stewardship language is used to affirm the authority of bishops unmitigated by Paul's theology of the cross.

Stewards in Pauline and Other Early Jesus-Group Texts

Paul's Undisputed Letters. In a list of greetings that he sends from Corinth to the congregation in Rome, Paul identifies a man named Erastus as the *oikonomos tes poleos,*
"the city treasurer" or "steward" (Rom 16:23).[82] Although Paul tells us nothing
else about Erastus, we can infer a few things about him.[83] Like the majority of municipal *oikonomoi* in the Roman period, Erastus probably would have been of servile

---

[82] The Erastus named in Acts 19:22 is probably not the same person as the one mentioned in
2 Tim 4:20.

[83] An inscription from Corinth identifies a man named Erastus as an *aedile,* or commissioner of
public works. *Oikonomos* and *aedile,* however, are not equivalent offices. Any connection between the
two, therefore, is purely hypothetical, and is dependent on the possibility that the Erastus mentioned in Rom 16:23 was later elected to the office of *aedile* (see discussion in Meeks, *The First Urban
Christians,* 58–59; Stegemann and Stegemann, *The Jesus Movement,* 293). While an interesting hypothesis, it is not significant to the present discussion.

status, either a slave or a freedman.[84] His position within the city administration would have resulted from his education, talents, and the influence of his patron(s). If his responsibilities were similar to those of the *oikonomoi* mentioned in the various inscriptions above, then Erastus may have been required to play a role in the political religion of Corinth. Consequently, he could well have been one of those whom "others see . . . eating in the temple of an idol" (I Cor 8:10). Would he have been one of those who argued in his own defense that "no idol in the world really exists" (I Cor 8:4), and that "food will not bring us close to God" (I Cor 8:8)? Would he have been able to "flee from the worship of idols" (I Cor 10:14), as Paul suggests, and still retain his position? We can only speculate.

Paul's opening remarks in Galatians 4 also provide some insights into the role of stewards and the perceptions of them in the ancient world. Paul asserts that "heirs, as long as they are minors, are no better than slaves" (Gal 4:1). Even though they are property owners, they remain under the authority of guardians and trustees (*epitropous . . . oikonomous*) until the date set by their fathers (Gal 4:2). Paul compares the situation of his Galatian congregants to such minors who previously were enslaved to the "elemental spirits of the world" (4:3) and to "beings that by nature are not gods (4:8). In Christ, however, they are now fully children and heirs (4:7). Paul's comments indicate that a minor heir might well resent the *oikonomos* whom his father appointed to administer his estate. Once again, we see that the position of steward was beset with ambiguities and vulnerabilities.

Most intriguing is Paul's decision to describe himself explicitly as "a slave" (*doulos*) of Christ (Rom 1:1; Phil 1:1; Gal 1:10) and to liken his ministry to that of "a managerial slave" (*oikonomos*). In a context of rivalry and competition over the relative status of the apostles known to the *ekklesia* in Corinth, Paul urges his audience to think of himself, Apollos, and Cephas as "servants [*hyperetas*] of Christ and stewards [*oikonomous*] of God's mysteries" (Gal 4:1). For Paul, the term steward describes the peculiar nature of the apostleship to which he and the other apostles are called, not a general function or role within the *ekklesia*.[85] Paul understands his apostolic role to be like that of a slave appointed to manage his master's resources. Here those resources are identified as the "mysteries of God," that is, God's secrets made known to the apostle through revelation.[86] Paul's conception

---

[84] Stegemann and Stegemann, *The Jesus Movement*, 293; Meeks, *The First Urban Christians*, 58–59.

[85] The word *oikonomos* does not occur in the list of general roles and functions in the church either at I Cor 12:27–31 or I Cor 14 (see John Reumann, "*OIKONOMIA*: Terms in Paul in Comparison with Lucan *Heilsgeschichte*," *NTS* 12 (Jan 1967): 161.

[86] Reumann, "*OIKONOMIA*," 161; Ben Witherington III, *Conflict & Community in Corinth: A Socio-Rhetorical Commentary on 1 and 2 Corinthians* (Grand Rapids: Eerdmans, 1995), 139.

of his apostleship finds its closest parallels, not in the Greek mystery cults, but in Epictetus' discourse on the fundamental nature of the Cynic's calling (ca. 60–140 C.E.).[87] Epictetus argues that one cannot become a Cynic without God anymore than one can claim for himself the role of *oikonomos;* in a well-managed household one must be assigned to his post by the master of the house (Diatr. 3.22.2–3). The true Cynic, a "servant (*hyperetes*) of Zeus who is Father of us all," participates in his rule (Diatr. 3.22.82). The apostle of Christ and the Cynic preacher thus both claim a paradoxical and even counter-cultural sort of honor and status as servants and slave-agents of God.

The managerial slaves of high status persons are figures to be reckoned with in the patron-broker-client system of social relations that dominate the ancient world. Members of the elite resent their positions, but lower status persons covet them.[88] We ought to understand Paul's claim that he is a slave or servant of Christ and a steward of God within this context where his claim functions as a "title of authority and power by association."[89] While Paul, Apollos, and Cephas may be personally quite insignificant, as slaves and servants of one who is much greater they command the respect and honor due to their master. This respect becomes clear in the argumentation that follows Paul's initial claim to be regarded as Christ's servant and God's steward.

Paul acknowledges the truism that it is necessary for stewards to be found faithful or trustworthy (1 Cor 4:2). Yet neither the members of the congregation nor, indeed, any other human can judge how faithful Paul and his fellow apostles really are. Paul insists, "It is the Lord who judges me" (4:4). In other words, Paul is directly responsible to the Lord and not to his congregants! Paul's argument here clearly reflects the hierarchical nature of social relations in the ancient eastern Mediterranean. Within elite households, stewards receive their appointments from their owners and are accountable only to them.[90] To the extent that municipal and imperial stewardships are patronage appointments, similar notions of responsibility would apply. The master's or patron's resources are the ones that the *oikonomos* must administer faithfully and for which he must give an accounting. In Paul's case, the Lord will determine at his coming whether Paul and the other apostles have been faithful administrators of God's mysteries (4:5). There is no

---

[87] In the Greek world, *oikonomos* is a not title given to temple administrators or those who administer the mysteries at Eleusis or Delphi; but Epictetus does use it (see Reumann, "Stewards of God," 340–42).

[88] Martin, *Slavery as Salvation,* 56.

[89] Ibid., 55.

[90] Ibid., 59–60.

reason, therefore, for anyone in the church to be "puffed up in favor of one" apostle over the other (4:6). Paul uses the notion of being God's steward to deny the legitimacy of any attempts of congregational members to judge him by comparing him with other apostles—he is answerable ultimately only to God.

Although Paul's insistence that his congregants have no right to judge him may sound arrogant in our ears, we need to remember that Paul's remarks are directed particularly at those members who, according to Greco-Roman standards, enjoy or aspire to high social status.[91] These members are the ones most critical of Paul and are the ones whom he describes as being "filled," "rich," and "reigning like kings" (4:8). They are "wise," "strong," and "held in honor" (4:10). These are congregational members who enjoy a certain amount of status and honor within Corinthian society, and expect to receive the same within the *ekklesia*. Paul challenges their perceptions of social status, power, and wisdom and offers them an alternative model.[92]

In contrast to the honorable members whom he is seeking to correct, Paul admits that he is regarded as foolish, weak, and disreputable (4:10). The apostle regularly experiences hunger and thirst, and is poorly clothed, beaten, homeless, and weary from manual labor (4:11–12). The source of his weariness is particularly important, for Greco-Roman literary sources consistently regard manual labor as despicable, slavish, and degrading to both body and mind.[93] No true teacher or philosopher would engage in such demeaning activity (Epictetus, *Diatr.* 3.22.45–47). Yet Paul readily admits that he works with his hands.[94] Paul does not deny the servile nature of his position; instead, he accepts it and turns it around. He is a servant, but a servant of Christ; he is "a slave-agent" (*oikonomos*), but a slave-agent of God. Here Paul speaks in solidarity with the vast majority of people in his society for whom such claims would not have been shameful at all, but were, in fact, the only kinds of claims to authority and power that they could make. In this society, "being connected to someone in power, even if only as a slave, was the next best thing to being in power oneself."[95]

As Christ's servant and God's steward, Paul is responsible not for his own resources, but for God's. Precisely in the process of making divine mysteries known through the preaching of the gospel, Paul fathered, or perhaps "gave birth to" (*egennesa*), the church in Corinth (4:15). Hence, its members are his "beloved

---

[91] Ibid., 121–22; Witherington, *Conflict & Community*, 137.

[92] Witherington, *Conflict & Community*, 149.

[93] Martin, *Slavery as Salvation*, 44.

[94] Paul's manual labor clearly distinguishes him from a Cynic preacher.

[95] Martin, *Slavery as Salvation.*, 30.

children" (4:14). As God's agent (broker), therefore, Paul can claim the status and honor of being the father (patron) of even the highest status person in the congregation. Speaking in the name of God, Paul calls these high status persons to imitate him (4:16). He challenges these upper-echelon persons to see in his own practice of poverty, homelessness, and manual labor for the sake of the gospel a faithful "Christian" model for how they are to conduct themselves as "leaders" within the *ekklesia*.

Paul uses this same subversive rhetorical strategy in his response to those Christ-followers who are attempting to justify their attendance at temple rituals and meals where meat sacrificed to idols is served (1 Cor 8:1–11:1). This issue points to the presence within the Corinthian congregation of relatively high status persons, such as Erastus, who hold positions within the wider society that require participation in Corinthian political religion. Paul's argument is directed specifically to these persons. In the discussion that follows, I will focus on chapters 8 and 9, where the issue of eating sacrificed meat is introduced and an initial answer is given, which Paul illustrates with the example of his own missionary practice.

The explicit topic of this section of Paul's letter is "food offered to idols" (8:1), that is, eating meat that comes from sacrificial rites in the context of banquets and/or other ceremonies or rituals that might occur in the temple of an idol (8:10). Based on Paul's running dialogue with the high status members, it appears that these persons defend their behavior by claiming to know that "there are no such things as idols, and food is irrelevant so far as our standing with God is concerned."[96] Paul appears to concede that they have some legitimate arguments (8:1–8), but then warns them to "take care that this right (*exousia*) of yours does not somehow become a stumbling block to the weak" (8:9). One of the central questions, then, that Paul seeks to address is the appropriate use of one's *exousia*— "authority, right, liberty or freedom."[97] Should one insist on exercising one's rights even if it harms another church member? Paul's answer is an unequivocal "no." He asserts, "I will never eat meat, so that I may not cause one of them to fall" (8:13).

Although chapter 9 appears to be a digression defending Paul's apostolic rights and freedom, it functions within the context of 1 Corinthians as an example of the kind of behavior advocated at the end of chapter 8.[98] Paul argues that, as a free man and an apostle, he has a "right" (*exousia*) to receive support from his

---

[96] Witherington, *Conflict & Community*, 186.

[97] Martin, *Slavery as Salvation*, 69.

[98] Ibid., 77–78.

congregations and to be accompanied by a wife (9:4–5). He has a right *not* to work for a living (9:6). Yet Paul has not made use of these rights; indeed, he would rather die than do so (9:15). Paul's practice of refusing or giving up his apostolic right to receive support from his congregations is intended to be analogous to a high status member of the *ekklesia* giving up his or her right to eat meat offered to idols. Both actions require that a person forgo receiving his or her due, behavior that elite persons in Paul's society would disdain.[99]

Paul explains his refusal to exercise his right to support by asserting that preaching the gospel is a necessity and an obligation laid upon him as an apostle (9:16). Were it a role that he had chosen of his own free will, he would receive pay, but since against his will he has been entrusted with an *oikonomia*—a stewardship or perhaps an assignment as a steward—he does not (9:17).[100] Here Paul contrasts "receiving a wage" with "being entrusted with an *oikonomia*," both of which are ambivalent situations in the ancient world. From the perspective of the elites, only low status persons work for a wage.[101] The truly free and wise man accepts neither gifts nor wages (Xenophon, *Apology* 16). Paul refuses to preach for a wage, but apparently other apostles do. Is he, therefore, more honorable, more free, and wiser than they? Yet Paul's refusal to make his living from the gospel puts him in a position where he must engage in manual labor in order to feed, clothe, and shelter himself. Isn't manual labor even more degrading than being paid to preach? It may be; then again, it may not. Although Paul argues that he preaches involuntarily, like a slave, he is not just any average slave; he is a managerial slave whose master is none other than Christ himself.[102]

As Christ's slave-agent, Paul shares and participates in his master's honor and status. Indeed, it is Christ who defines what constitutes honorable behavior for his representatives. It is Christ's behavior that Paul believes he is modeling for his congregants in Corinth, for he concludes with the exhortation, "Be imitators of me, as I am of Christ" (11:1). The heart of what that modeling means may be summed up in the Christ hymn of Phil 2:5–11, where Christ is described as one "who, though he was in the form of God, did not regard equality with God as something to be exploited, but emptied himself, taking the form of a slave (*doulos*)."[103] Paul exemplifies this behavior by not exploiting his rights as an apostle; indeed, he refuses to accept the support that is due to him as an apostle. This refusal in turn

---

[99] Ibid., 79.

[100] Ibid., 71–74; Reumann, "*OIKONOMIA*," 159.

[101] Martin, *Slavery as Salvation*, 81.

[102] Ibid., 80.

[103] See discussion in Witherington, *Conflict & Community*, 212; Martin, *Slavery as Salvation*, 135.

necessitates that in order to survive he become a manual laborer, that is, that he lower himself socially.

Consequently, Paul can claim to be free with respect to all, yet a slave to all, for the sake of winning more to the gospel (9:19). He specifically identifies "those under the law," "those without the law," and "the weak" as persons whom he seeks to save (9:20–23). As Martin points out, "By mentioning the weak last, Paul emphasizes that and makes his submission to the weak the rhetorical goal of the list."[104] It should be noted that there is no mention of "the strong," "the wise," "those who live like kings" or even "the knowing," that is, those upper-status persons in the congregation to whom the list is addressed. Thus it is the weak, that is, non-elite residents of Corinth, with whom Paul identifies himself by engaging in manual labor and by characterizing himself as a managerial slave.[105] To benefit them he does not demand payment for his preaching. Out of sensitivity to their scruples, Paul urges the higher status members to refrain from exercising their right to eat meat sacrificed to idols. In this way he bears a resemblance to the demagogic or populist leader frequently condemned in the literature of the Greco-Roman elites.[106]

Paul's use of *oikonomos* and *oikonomia* functions to affirm and solidify his claim to the status, honor, rights, and authority of an apostle. As Christ's slave/servant and a steward of divine mysteries, Paul participates in the status and honor of his master. He represents Christ, acts in Christ's behalf, and speaks in Christ's name. Thus he can command a very high status and honor within the Christ-confessing community.[107] Yet, it is precisely as Christ's slave and God's steward that he is enslaved to all (19:19). Socially locating himself alongside manual laborers and slaves, Paul thus leads from a "position among the lower class."[108] This leadership from below represents a stark contrast to the dominant Greco-Roman ideology of benevolent patriarchalism assumed by the more well-to-do members of the Corinthian congregation. According to that model, a good leader acted "like a kind father" whose compassionate care and concern for his social inferiors were never permitted to undermine his social superiority, which was manifested in "the traditional badges of high social status: sufficient income, leisure, education, avoidance of manual

---

[104] Martin, *Slavery as Salvation,* 118–19.

[105] See discussion in ibid., 118–24.

[106] Ibid., 86–116.

[107] Of course, the title "slave of Christ" will not carry this connotation outside of the *ekklesia;* in the wider first-century Mediterranean world, the term would have been meaningless or perhaps even carried a negative meaning.

[108] Martin, *Slavery as Salvation,* 134.

labor, education, and appropriate dress and demeanor."[109] Paul displays none of these "badges." He argues for forms of leadership in which high status and rights are exchanged for low status and slavery, and in which authority ought to be granted to those who in this way faithfully represent the crucified Christ.

Other Texts. Paul is not alone in using slave terminology to identify himself in relation to Christ, as we can see from the opening lines of a number of New Testament epistles: "James, a slave of God and of the Lord Jesus Christ" (Jas 1:1), "Simon Peter, a slave and apostle of Jesus Christ" (2 Pet 1:1), "Jude, a slave of Jesus Christ" (Jude 1). According to the author of Colossians, Epaphras and Tychicus are his fellow-slaves (*syndoulos*) and servants (*diakonos*) of Christ (1:7; 4:7). The recipients of prophecies are identified as slaves of Christ and/or God in the book of Revelation. This reference includes both John the seer (1:1) and the believers to whom Revelation is addressed (1:1; 2:20; 19:5; 22:6). The author of I Pet 4:10–11 interestingly uses the term *oikonomos* not to describe congregational leaders but to refer to all Christ-followers, urging them to behave like *kaloi oikonomoi poikiles charitos theou* ("good stewards of God's manifold grace"). Here all believers are slave managers of the particular gifts which have been bestowed on them and which they are to use in service to one another. Later Pauline trajectories (e.g., Titus 1:7 and Ign. *Eph.* 5.2) retain the term as characterizing leaders and, in particular, bishops, a subject to which we will return below.

The fairly widespread use of slave terminology testifies to the social location of these early Jesus groups among persons of servile origins and/or relatively low status, that is, the majority of the population of the eastern Mediterranean. From the perspective of the dominant elites these Jesus groups and their leaders would be marginal.[110] While the rhetoric of slavery would be offensive to high status persons, it could function quite differently within the *ekklesia* to emphasize solidarity between leaders and congregational members. Both *oikonomos* and *doulos* serve the same master and belong to the same household, thus serving one another. Even when the leader functions as a steward, he remains a slave, as we see in Paul's self-designation as slave of Christ and steward of God's mysteries. In the *ekklesia* the slave-manager imitates Christ, not the benevolent patriarch of Greco-Roman patronal ideology, at least in the early literature of Christ-confessing groups. In some ways, then, slave terminology can function similarly to and perhaps synonymously with brother-sister language in establishing the boundaries and nature of relationships within the fictive kinship group that comprises the *ekklesia.*

---

[109] Ibid., 114–15, 125.
[110] Ibid., 57.

Pauline Trajectories. In the pseudo-Pauline texts the language of stewards and stewardship seems to take a somewhat different turn. The author of Colossians has Paul describe himself as becoming a "servant" or "minister" (*diakonos*) of the church "according to the *oikonomian tou theou ten dotheisan moi*" (1:24–25).[111] There are several possibilities for understanding this phrase. MacDonald suggests that *tou theou* is a genitive of origin; hence, we should read the entire phrase as "the stewardship or commission God gave me."[112] In this case the phrase is analogous to Paul's own self-description of having been "entrusted with a stewardship" (1 Cor 9:17), and would mean that he is a steward responsible for making known and revealing to the saints the word and mystery of God (Col 1:25–26). Placed in a different syntax, its meaning is basically the same as in the undisputed letter, even though the emphasis is no longer on the counter-cultural nature of the apostle's authority but on his role in the revelation of God's mysteries. Yet that tradition may not be entirely forgotten, for the author labels both Epaphras and Tychicus as a *syndoulos* ("fellow slave") and a minister of Christ (Col 1:7; 4:7).

Alternatively, *oikonomia tou theou* was a common phrase denoting God's administration of the universe in popular Hellenistic philosophical discourse.[113] Here again we see how the household provides the basic metaphor for all other forms of social organization—civic, political, imperial, and cosmic. In particular, Stoics often depicted the divine administration of the world as operating through subordinates like Fate, Providence, heavenly bodies, nature, or *logos*.[114] The literature of Hellenistic Judaism similarly uses *oikonomia* and related terms such as *dioikesis* and cognates to describe YHWH's rule in nature and history.[115] Philo, for example, portrays the world as governed by God's *oikonomia* with the *logos* acting as God's *oikonomos* (*QG* 4.110 and *QE* 2.39). If the author of Colossians is operating within a similar tradition, then it might be better to understand *oikonomian tou theou* as referring to God's plan, that is, the mystery which is now being revealed to the saints (Col 1:26). Paul's ministry within that plan is to make known the word of God (1:25). Such a reading definitely moves away from the subversive use of slave terminology and images that

---

[111] Margaret Y. MacDonald, *Colossians and Ephesians*, Sacra Pagina Series, Vol. 17 (Collegeville, Minn.: Liturgical, 2000), notes that "this precise phrase is not found in the undisputed letters" (p. 80). Paul does describe himself and others as *diakonoi*, through whom his readers came to believe (1 Cor 3:5), as servants of a new covenant (2 Cor 3:6), servants of God (2 Cor 6:4), or servants of Christ (2 Cor 11:23). Even Satan has *diakonoi* who disguise themselves as ministers of righteousness (2 Cor 11:15)! And Christ himself might be misconstrued as a servant of sin (Gal 2:17).

[112] Ibid.

[113] Reumann, "*OIKONOMIA*," 162.

[114] Ibid., 150.

[115] Ibid., 152.

we see in the Gospels and the undisputed Pauline Letters. What is emphasized in Colossians is Paul's role within the divine *oikonomia*.

This development is clearer in Ephesians. The author of Ephesians begins by praising "the God and Father of our Lord Jesus Christ" (Eph 1:3) for making known "to us the mystery of his will" (1:9). As set forth in Christ, God's will consists of an *oikonomian tou pleromatos ton kairon* ("an economy" or "plan for the fullness of time") to gather up all things in the Christ (1:10). Here *oikonomia* clearly refers to God's direction of the cosmos, and has no servile connotations whatsoever.[116]

Later the author, speaking as Paul, reminds his readers that they have heard of the *oikonomian tes charitos tou theou* that was given to him for them (3:2). The phrasing is similar to Col 1:25 and might be translated as "the stewardship of the grace of God."[117] Thus it seems that Paul is responsible for managing God's grace or favors, once again described as a mystery—a divine secret revealed to Paul as well as to the holy apostles and prophets—that concerns the inclusion of the Gentiles in the body of Christ (Eph 3:3–6). By God's grace he is a servant or minister (*diakonos*) for this gospel (3:7). Specifically, he has been given the grace or favor of bringing the "riches of Christ" to the Gentiles, of making everyone see the plan of the mystery hidden for ages in God, *he oikonomia tou musteriou tou apokekrummenou apo ten aionon en to theo* (3:9). The description of Paul's stewardship as a grace or favor given to him reflects the favoritism that underlay such appointments in households, cities, and the empire. Again, the author is uninterested in examining the counter-cultural implications of Paul's role as *oikonomos* for church leadership, but instead concentrates on how that role "brings God's plan to fruition."[118] This emphasis is consistent with the deutero-Pauline authors' endorsement of the dominant ideology of benevolent patriarchalism (cf. Col 3:18–4:1; Eph 5:21–6:9).

The trends that we see emerging in the deutero-Pauline epistles continue in later Pauline trajectories. For example, the notion of a divine plan (*oikonomian theou*) reappears in 1 Timothy as the proper content of teaching and faith, while the "myths and endless genealogies" that "certain people" are wont to promote (1:4), count as improper content. Ignatius of Antioch, writing about 108 C.E., also refers to the divine plan (*oikonomian theou*) according to which Mary conceived Jesus from the seed of David and the Holy Spirit (Ign. *Eph.* 18.2). He promises to explain more of this plan (*oikonomias*) to his readers as it is revealed to him (Ign. *Eph.* 20.1–2). As John Reumann has observed, this notion of a divine *oikonomia*

---

[116] MacDonald, *Colossians and Ephesians*, 202.

[117] Ibid.

[118] Ibid., 261.

becomes increasingly common in the writings of the church fathers from the second century onwards.[119]

Oikonomos is retained in still later Pauline trajectories, but is used to affirm the authority of local congregational leaders, who are titled *episkopos* ("overseer" or "bishop"), rather than that of the apostle. While the pseudo-Pauline author of Titus concentrates on the personal attributes of the man selected for this role, Ignatius of Antioch highlights his role as a broker of God's resources.

Paul describes himself as Christ's slave (hence, slave to all) and a steward of God's mysteries; however, the pseudo-Pauline author has Paul introduce himself as God's slave (*doulos theou;* Titus 1:1). He addresses "Titus" as his "loyal child" (1:4), thus highlighting the fictive-kin (patronal) nature of their relationship. As a father/patron he directs "Titus" to put things in order on the island of Crete by appointing elders for each/every town (1:5). Whoever is to serve in this capacity ought to be blameless, not accused of debauchery, not rebellious, the husband of one wife, and the father of children who are believers (1:6). These qualifications resemble those given for bishops and deacons in 1 Tim 3:1–3 and 3:8–9. What the pseudo-Pauline author adds in the letter to Titus is a reason for these qualifications: the *episkopos* ("overseer" or "bishop") must be blameless because he is "like God's steward" (*hos theou oikonomon* [1:7], author's translation). The elders together, or perhaps one of the elders in each town, assumes the role of overseer, and then functions like God's *oikonomos*—a managerial slave who represents, speaks, and acts on behalf of his master. Hence, his personal characteristics must adequately reflect those of his master. He must not be arrogant, quick-tempered, addicted to wine, violent, or greedy but must be hospitable, a lover of goodness, prudent, upright, devout, and self-controlled (1:7–8). In other words, the bishop must be a proper Greco-Roman gentleman. Additionally, he must also "be able both to preach with sound doctrine and to refute those who contradict it" (1:9). Paul's emphasis on imitating Christ is nowhere mentioned as a necessity or even a possibility for these local congregational leaders. Instead, the pseudo-Pauline author seeks to affirm the authority of those men with particular high status attributes as the ones most appropriately capable of functioning as leaders—God's stewards—in the household of faith.

Ignatius of Antioch. Ignatius of Antioch, writing to the church in Ephesus about the year 108 C.E., also speaks of bishops as exercising stewardship, but derives his language from the Gospels. He asserts:

---

[119] John Reumann, "*Oikonomia* = 'Covenant'; Terms for *Heilsgeschichte* in Early Christian Usage," *NovT* 3 (1959): 282. See also Reumann, *Stewardship*, 27–42.

And the more anyone sees the bishop keeping silent, the more that person should respect him. For everyone whom the householder (*oikodespotes*) sends into his stewardship (*eis idian oikonomian*) we must receive in the same way as the one who sent him. So
it is clear that one must look upon the bishop as the Lord himself (Ign. *Eph.* 6.1).[120]

The situation here implies some sort of deficiency on the part of the bishop, described here as "keeping silent." Given the paucity of Ignatius' remarks, we cannot
determine whether this silence refers to the Ephesian bishop's retiring nature, lack
of eloquence, inability to pray and preach extemporaneously, or inadequacy in
countering false teaching.[121] Whatever it may entail, the bishop's silence is probably something that Ignatius feels must be defended because some saw it as a reason to disregard and/or oppose the bishop.

Ignatius argues that the bishop's silence should result in more, rather than less,
respect; indeed, the bishop should be looked upon as the Lord himself. Ignatius
justifies this position by alluding to and combining two sayings of Jesus. The
statement about a householder sending someone to take care of his affairs seems
to be drawn from Matthew's version of the parable of the "wicked tenants," in
which a landowner sends slaves to collect his rents (21:33–43). Only Matthew
describes the owner of the vineyard as a "householder" (*oikodespotes*). Ignatius' reference to householders and stewardship evokes the social institutions of absentee
ownership and the habit of entrusting country estates, urban properties, and
urban businesses to slave-managers. For Ignatius, then, the bishop is like such a
slave who manages a household in the absence of the householder.

The notion of receiving or welcoming the one who is sent as the "one who sent
him" is preserved with variations in a number of early Jesus-group writings where
it seems to have been applied to itinerant disciples, apostles, prophets, and the
like. In Matt 10:40, whoever welcomes Jesus welcomes the one who sent him.
Jesus asserts in John 13:20 that "whoever receives one whom I send receives me;
and whoever receives me receives him who sent me." Paul applies the saying to
himself, for example, when he commends the Galatians for receiving him as Christ
Jesus (Gal 4:14). The *Didache* instructs its readers to receive teachers, apostles/
prophets (11:1–3), and visitors as the Lord (12:1). The *Didache* also directs its audience to honor those who preach God's word as the Lord (4.1), suggesting a
movement in the direction of recognizing a ministry of the word.

In marked contrast, Ignatius uses the saying about receiving the one whom
the householder sends to argue that a silent bishop must be regarded as the Lord

---

[120] Translation published by Schoedel, *Ignatius of Antioch*
[121] Ibid., 56

himself. For him, episcopal prestige and authority have nothing to do with skill, competency or capacity for speaking God's or anyone else's words; rather a bishop is to be obeyed simply because he is the Lord's steward sent or appointed to manage God's household on earth. In other words, Ignatius conceives of the bishop occupying a status and role which confers authority in and of itself regardless of the individual's personal skills or accomplishments. That status and role are sufficient for recognizing the bishop as an authoritative person in the Christ-following community.

For Ignatius, then, the local congregation is analogous to a household whose owner is absent. The bishop functions as a steward put in charge during the master's absence. Throughout his letter to the church in Ephesus, Ignatius exhorts his audience to be "joined in one obedience, subject to the bishop" (Ign. *Eph.* 2.2). Obedience and submission are, of course, acts of commitment, confirming and validating the authority of the bishop.[122] Such commitment is the appropriate way to honor and glorify Christ, according to Ignatius, and has the added consequence of making the Ephesian congregants holy in every respect (Ign. *Eph.* 2.2). Obedience to the bishop, as Ignatius understands it, demonstrates one's piety, one's proper attitude toward the divine authorities who sent him. His readers can be assured of acting in harmony with God's purpose when they are in harmony with the purpose of the bishop, who is in harmony with the purpose of Jesus Christ, who in turn is in harmony with the purpose of God (Ign. *Eph.* 3.2–4.1). What Ignatius spells out here is a hierarchy of mediators. God's purpose is made known through Jesus Christ (broker #1), whose purpose includes God's and is articulated by the bishop (broker #2). Solidarity with the bishop is a symptom or a proof of unity with the divine authorities whose purposes he represents and expresses.

Using musical imagery, Ignatius spells out the benefits of being in harmony with the bishop. He begins by urging the Ephesian congregants to follow the example of their council of elders who are "attuned to the bishop like strings to a cithara." Through such concord and harmonious love, Jesus Christ is made present or, as the Syrian bishop puts it, "is sung" in the midst of their congregation (Ign. *Eph.* 4.1). He assures his readers that when they "sing with one voice through Jesus Christ," the Father hears and recognizes them (Ign. *Eph.* 4.2). Again, the hierarchy of mediation is stressed. In order to be recognized and heard by the divine patron, church members must approach him through Christ by joining their

---

[122] See discussion of authority and its validation in Thomas W. Overholt, *Channels of Prophecy: The Social Dynamics of Prophetic Activity* (Minneapolis: Fortress, 1988), 71–72.

voices together with that of the bishop. Access to the heavenly patron and his favors is available through a very specific chain of mediators. Participation in the corporate rituals and ceremonies led by the bishop is the only proper means of approaching Christ, who ensures access to God, as Ignatius makes even clearer in the next passage.

The Syrian bishop warns his readers, "Let no one deceive himself; if anyone is not within the altar, he lacks the bread of God" (Ign. *Eph.* 5.2). In Greco-Roman religions the altar symbolized the principal point of mediation between the earthly and heavenly realms.[123] Ignatius uses the term altar figuratively to symbolize the venue in which the "bread of God" is made available to humans, that is, in the Eucharistic gathering of the church over which the bishop presides.[124] He refers to the "bread of God" again in his final remarks to the Ephesians, where he describes it as "the medicine of immortality, the antidote preventing death" (Ign. *Eph.* 20.2).[125] Thus, the "bread of God" turns out to be potent stuff, indeed, which is obtainable only at the bishop's table. It represents a resource that the divine patron alone controls and dispenses through the mediation of Christ and his earthly agent and broker, the bishop.

In the Greco-Roman world, requests put to a powerful patron were much more likely to succeed when they came from and/or received support from those closest to the patron—members of his immediate family, friends, or employees.[126] This aspect of daily life is reflected in Ignatius' assertion that the Father hears and recognizes those who approach him in unity with the bishop (Ign. *Eph.* 4.2). It is also evident in his insistence that the corporate prayers of the "bishop and the whole church" are more powerful than those said by "one or two" (Ign. *Eph.* 5.2). The Eucharistic gathering is an occasion not only for receiving goods from the heavenly Father, but also for making one's petitions

---

[123] Richard Gordon, "The Veil of Power: Emperors, Sacrificers and Benefactors," in *Pagan Priests: Religion and Power in the Ancient World* (ed. Mary Beard and John North; Ithaca, N.Y.: Cornell University Press, 1990), 202.

[124] Schoedel, *Ignatius of Antioch*, 55.

[125] Ignatius combines Johannine, Didachist, and Hellenistic terminology to describe the Eucharist. "Bread of God" is used as a synonym for the "bread of life" in John 6:33. There, too, the one who eats this bread will not die, but will live forever (John 6:50–51). The same notion occurs in *Did.* 4.8, where the Eucharist is described as immortal food. Similarly, "medicine of immortality" is the name of a legendary drug referred to in Hellenistic medical and religious literature. For further discussion, see Clayton N. Jefford, "Did Ignatius of Antioch Know the *Didache?*" in *The* Didache *in Context: Essays on Its Text, History, and Transmission* (ed. Clayton N. Jefford; NovTSup 77; Leiden: Brill, 1995), 330–51; David E. Aune, *The Cultic Setting of Realized Eschatology in Early Christianity* (NovTSup 28; Leiden: Brill, 1972), 147 n. 4; Schoedel, *Ignatius of Antioch*, 97.

[126] Saller, *Personal Patronage*, 108–9, 152–53.

known to him. Privileged access to the divine patron and those resources that he controls are the benefits of being "within the altar," of taking part in the gathering about the bishop's table.[127]

Another benefit is indicated several paragraphs later, where Ignatius urges his readers to come together more frequently for "thanksgiving" and glorifying God. The Syrian bishop asserts that when the congregation comes together in this way, the "powers of Satan are swept away and his destructiveness is brought to an end" (Ign. *Eph.* 13.1). Peace in the Christ-confessing community abolishes warfare both in the heavenly and earthly realms (Ign. *Eph.* 13.2). Similar notions are present in Ignatius' explanation of the meaning of the incarnation in Ign. *Eph.* 19.2–3. There he asserts that the revelation of God in human form heralds the "newness of eternal life" and the destruction of the old dominion that is characterized by death, evil, bondage, and magic. Ignatius seems to conceive of the Eucharistic gathering as a collective means of tapping into this power, which became active in the world at the time of Christ's birth. In doing so, the church and its members are empowered and protected against the forces of evil. God's patronage, thus, includes access to protection as well as to heavenly goods.

What Ignatius is describing here in his flowery and effusive style is a system of mediation in which the bishop plays the role of broker or mediator between the heavenly and earthly realms. The bishop presides at the "altar" at the point in time and space where communication between earth and heaven takes place. God is represented as the Father, the divine patron, who hears and recognizes those who approach him through the agency of his son Jesus Christ and with one voice in unity with the bishop (Ign. *Eph.* 4.1–2). The bishop's intermediary status is a position of power associated with his role as the steward sent to manage access to God and to divine goods and services.

Summary. Just as Paul used the image of the steward to buttress his own apostolic authority, Ignatius uses the notion of stewardship to affirm the authority of a bishop who "keeps silence." Both situations appear to presuppose a challenge to authority. In Paul's case, high-status members of the congregation see his missionary practices as too servile to enable him to act as a leader. If the bishop's silence in Ign. *Eph.* 6.1 is related to the rhetorical skills of the Ephesian bishop, or rather the lack thereof, then Ignatius may be dealing with a similar situation. The differences between the two are, however, dramatic. For Paul, his downward social mobility and lifestyle of manual labor are demonstrations that he is fulfilling his role as Christ's agent and representative. Ignatius is more concerned about establishing

---

[127] See Aune, *The Cultic Setting,* 165.

a clearly delineated chain of command that limits and controls access to divine resources. For Ignatius, the bishop is a broker mediating between the divine realm and the congregation. The language of stewardship is one way, but not the only way, that he expresses this notion. He can be much more explicit, for instance, when he commends the Magnesian elders for not taking advantage of the youthful appearance of their bishop Damas, and for recognizing that when they deal with him they are interacting with "the Father of Jesus Christ, the bishop of all" (Ign. *Mag.* 3.1). Later in the same letter, Ignatius asserts that the bishop presides "in the place (*eis topon*) of God," while the elders stand "in the place (*eis topon*) of the council of apostles and the deacons . . . [who] have been entrusted with the ministry of Jesus Christ" (Ign. *Mag.* 6.1). In the letter to the Trallians (3.1), Ignatius goes even farther and calls the bishop a "type" or "image" (*typos*) of the Father. Very little about the Ignatian conception of episcopal authority is servile. Rather, Ignatius emphasizes the authority that accrues from being God's agent and representative in the congregation, an authority unmitigated by Paul's insistence that faithful stewardship is measured by how well one models the self-emptying solidarity of Christ with lowly humanity.[128]

Conclusion

In this chapter we have examined the role of the *oikonomos* in ancient households as well as in civic government and associations. As the appointed agent of his elite master, the steward was able to carry out many important economic and religious functions both in the private domestic and public political domains. In the figure of the steward we see a leadership role rooted in and emerging from the ancient household that enabled those who normally could not aspire to positions of authority, such as slaves, to do so. Since the early churches were composed primarily of non-elite members of society it is not surprising that they found the image of the steward useful for affirming the status and authority of leaders within congregations. Having done so, the question then became how to measure faithful stewardship. Does it consist in unquestioning obedience to human masters (e.g., the model of the two "successful" slaves in the parables of the talents and of the pounds), or does it necessitate a subversive critique of culturally dominant forms of leadership (e.g., the shrewd steward in Luke 16:1–8)? For the Apostle Paul, faithful stewardship required taking a stance in solidarity with the weak in

---

[128] This discussion of Ignatius of Antioch is a summary of my article "Bishops as Brokers of Heavenly Goods: Ignatius to the *Ephesians*," *Life and Culture in the Ancient Near East* (ed. Richard E. Averbeck, Mark Chavalas, and David Weisberg; Bethesda, Md.: CDL, 2000), 389–98.

imitation of Christ's self-emptying that functioned to subvert the dominant cultural ideology of benevolent patriarchalism. The deutero-Pauline and pseudo-
Pauline authors and Ignatius focus more on the steward as a figure to be honored
and obeyed because of the divine grace and favor he enjoys. These authors seem to
answer the question about what constitutes faithful stewardship by adopting the
culturally dominant values of benevolent patriarchy. In Ignatius' writings especially, we see the bishop as steward functioning as a broker mediating divine goods
to human congregations. In the next chapter we will explore this dimension of
leadership more fully by examining the role of prophets in bringing about change
and innovation in a world that prized the venerable past and traditional ways.

3
PROPHETS

Prelude

"WE HAVE VISITORS TONIGHT," was the message that greeted each person. As they entered the room, they were directed toward their appropriate places. Men and boys filled one side of the room: the few householders perched on benches along the front wall, their sons and other free men sat before them on mats, freedmen and slaves squatted behind them on the floor. The women and girls were organized similarly on the other side of the room, but widows shared the benches with the householders. A group of virgins sitting near the front was singing softly, "Holy, holy, holy. . . ." One of the male householders was reading a letter to the men beside him. Scattered throughout the room, a half dozen persons—men and women—were standing, praying with arms outstretched, and were swaying gently. Fragments of a lively discussion of a Scripture passage going on in the middle of the women's section rose above the general hubbub. The host stood to acknowledge the three visitors who were making their way through the crowd to the front. He explained to the gathering that their visitors this evening included an eminent apostle charged with taking the gospel to the Diaspora, together with representatives of the Greek assemblies he had founded.

Accepting the host's invitation to speak, the apostle immediately launched into an impassioned description of how the Holy Spirit had manifested itself, time and time again, among the Greeks. Those near the front of the room responded to his stories with enthusiastic applause and cries of "hallelujah!" Toward the back of the room, a man tried unsuccessfully to shush the group around him, so that he could hear. Suddenly, the visitor's body went stiff, his knees bent slightly forward, his spine arched backward, and his arms extended stiffly from his sides. With his eyes closed he opened his mouth and began to call out, "el-la-ja, el-la-ja, el-la-ja," over and over again, his voice rising on the third note as his hands clenched and unclenched in time with this chant.[1] Sitting near the middle of the crowd, two women picked up the same pulsing chant, their vocalizations accompanied by the pumping motions of their tightly clasped hands. Several people began chanting, "come, Spirit, come," and clapping rhythmically. A group of men at the back of the room began a circle dance. Suddenly, the visitor opened his eyes. Looking bemused, he shrugged slightly and turned to his companions, asking if any of them wished to speak.

As the women at the front of the room began another song, a thin elderly man jumped up. Hair standing on end, purple-faced, and wild-eyed, he made his way up to the visitor in a frenzy of uncoordinated, jerky steps.[2] Swaying slightly on his feet, the old man pulled the visitor's leather belt from about his waist. While the visitor watched in wonder, the old man used it to tie his own feet and hands together and shouted, "This is the way the authorities in the city will bind the man who owns this belt." Cries of dismay from the visitor's entourage were drowned out as a baby began to cry; the mother's attempts to soothe the infant resulted only in ear-piercing wails. The host launched into his closing blessing as the virgins and widows added a musical benediction. As the crowd rose and began to struggle toward the door, the host stayed behind, explaining to the visitors where they would be staying for the night.

Introduction

The scene that I have just described is an imaginative reconstruction of a gathering at Philip's house during Paul's stopover in Caesarea en route to Jerusalem (Acts 21:7–11). I have deliberately highlighted aspects of early Jesus-group practice that are quite alien to many, if not most, Western Christians today—the experiences of speaking in tongues and prophetic revelation. My descriptions of the practitioners of these activities are drawn from the work of ancient and modern observers of these phenomena. Both are manifestations of altered states of consciousness.

Winkelman describes an altered state of consciousness (ASC) as "a biologically based mode of consciousness" that is widely referred to as transcendent,

---

[1] This description of *glossolalia* is based on Felicitas D. Goodman, *Where the Spirits Ride the Wind: Trance Journeys and Other Ecstatic Experiences* (Bloomington & Indianapolis: Indiana University Press, 1990), 14–15.

[2] This description of spirit possession is based on Lucian, *Juppiter tragoedus* 30, and discussion in Aune, *Prophecy in Early Christianity*, 33.

transpersonal, and/or mystical.[3] Such states of consciousness are marked by a "greater predominance of brain activity from the right hemisphere and nonfrontal parts of the brain" in contrast to "ordinary waking" consciousness that is "dominated by the left hemisphere's rational, linear, verbal modes of experience."[4] ASCs can be induced by a wide variety of activities, such as drumming or chanting; dancing; fasting; exposure to extreme cold, heat or other physical or emotional stressors; induced dream or sleep states; meditation; hallucinogens; alcohol; community rituals; and/or temporal lobe syndrome.[5] In addition, Goodman has documented the effectiveness of certain ritualized body-postures for inducing ASCs.[6]

Winkelman identifies three major ASC traditions in human cultures: the soul flight or journey of the shaman, the possession trance of the medium, and the meditative/mystical traditions. Each of these categories includes a range of behaviors that appear to be linked. For example, shamanic soul flight is associated with excessive motor behavior (e.g., dancing), sleep states, unconsciousness, out-of-body experiences, astral projection, and near-death experiences.[7] Possession ASC is linked with temporal lobe syndrome (amnesia, spontaneous seizures, rapid onset of illness, tremors or convulsions, and compulsive motor behavior) and involves alterations in consciousness, awareness, personality, or psychological functioning that are accounted for by the occupation of the body by a spirit entity. Possession ASCs are found most frequently in social situations characterized by stratification, hierarchy, and/or nutritional deprivation.[8] Meditative or mystical ASCs tend to be associated with sleep deprivation, auditory driving, fasting, social isolation, and other practices designed to heighten awareness and lead to an awakening, liberation, or enlightenment.[9]

An extensive study of 488 societies undertaken in the late 1970s found that 90 percent of them had one or more institutionalized forms of this experience. Eighty-eight percent of circum-Mediterranean societies, past and present, had culturally patterned ASCs. Contemporary Western secularized society appears to be an exception to this almost universal experience.[10] Not only are we contemporary

---

[3] Michael J. Winkelman, "Altered States of Consciousness and Religious Behavior," in *Anthropology of Religion: A Handbook* (ed. S. D. Glazier; Westport & London: Praeger, 1997), 402.

[4] Ibid., 404.

[5] Ibid., 398–401.

[6] Goodman's book, *Where the Spirits Ride the Wind*, is devoted to exploring different postures depicted in Paleolithic and early native American artwork.

[7] Winkelman, "Altered States of Consciousness," 411–12.

[8] Ibid., 412–15.

[9] Ibid., 410–11; 415–19.

[10] Summarized in Pilch, "Visions in Revelation," 232–33.

Western readers for the most part unfamiliar with ASCs, we have been socialized to view such experiences negatively. Western psychology, in particular, has tended to label these experiences as pathological or infantile.[11] This opinion is only exacerbated by the marginalization of ASC experiences in our culture to charismatic religious movements, Eastern cults, and the illegal drug sub-culture. Winkelman asserts that the only mainstream American ASC experience involves the bar scene and similar contexts that result in intoxication, which he sees as a non-constructive, and even destructive, form of ASC. [12]

The intensely subjective and socially conditioned nature of the ASC experience is an additional barrier for many Western, scientifically oriented persons. While it is possible to record the physiological changes that occur in the human body during an ASC experience, the content of the experience—what the person sees and hears—cannot be captured. Indeed, the content of an ASC appears to be quite ambiguous, for it seems to consist of light, geometric shapes, and/or other vague images that must be interpreted within a belief system in order for the ASC to make sense.[13] From a "cognitive neuroscientific perspective," the experience "has no meaning until the one who has the experience gives meaning and interpretation to it."[14] This will inevitably be socially and culturally determined.

Despite our cultural biases, neurophysiological studies demonstrate that ASCs provide optimal brain conditions for learning, memory, and attention, all mechanisms responsible for self-realization, feelings of conviction and authenticity, and a more objective perspective on reality.[15] An understanding of ASC is especially important for contemporary readers of early Christian texts because those texts were written by persons socialized in circum-Mediterranean societies that had culturally patterned ASC. We cannot simply dismiss narratives of visions, angels, and so forth as imaginary when they were regarded by the original writers and their audiences as greatly significant. Despite the fact that these experiences seem strange to us, having an appreciation for the significance of ASCs can expand our understanding of early Christ-followers and how they made sense of the world in which they lived.

To understand the importance of ASC experiences among the early followers of Jesus, we need to recall that the peoples of the Greco-Roman world conceived of their universe as populated by both human and nonhuman (divine and de-

---

[11] Winkelman, "Altered States of Consciousness," 404.
[12] Ibid., 421.
[13] Pilch, "Visions in Revelation," 239; Pilch, "Paul's Ecstatic Trance Experience," 13.
[14] Conversation with Pilch, March 14–17, 2002.
[15] Winkelman, "Altered States of Consciousness," 402–4.

monic) beings. Gods, goddesses, demigods, angels, spirits, daimons, and other phenomena, that contemporary westerners either dismiss or think of as supernatural, were regarded as part of the created world.[16] They perceived this world to be organized hierarchically according to a system of vertical stratification that placed the ordinary person far below the level of the human and nonhuman rulers of his or her world. Regardless of whether they were dealing with gods or mortals, first-century individuals and households faced the same difficulty: how to gain access to universally limited resources that were controlled by a tiny but disproportionately powerful elite.[17] As Lightstone puts it, the "religious problematic was one of mediation, the transportation, as it were, of goods and services" between the human and divine arenas.[18] Mediators were needed who could communicate between the two spheres and attract to human communities the necessary blessings of God or gods. Prosperity, good fortune, and the like were conceptualized as favors that the deity or deities granted in exchange for human gratitude and praise, and that humans obtained through the mediation of others.[19] In other words, the gods and goddesses of the Greco-Roman world were conceived of as divine patrons, whose favors were mediated to their human clients by a variety of persons that included priests, diviners, and prophets.

As Aune reminds us, the common Greek word *prophetes*, transliterated in English as "prophet," meant quite simply a spokesperson or announcer. It was one of the titles that might be given to the person at an oracle shrine who transmitted the deity's response to a particular inquiry. As such, the word *prophetes* took on the technical meaning of "one who speaks on behalf of the god." In the Greek context, Aune points out, this specialist was neither divinely inspired nor a predictor of future events. The Greek-speaking Israelites who produced the Septuagint used the word *prophetes* to designate persons who mediated to humanity divine revelations received in visions, auditions, or dreams. In Jesus groups, the term referred to those who were regarded as inspired spokespersons for God.[20] In the discussion that follows, "prophecy" and "prophets" will be used in this broad sense, and will include persons and roles that functioned to mediate divine revelations and other blessings.

In the ancient world, then, prophets were one category of mediator or broker between the divine and the human, and may be classified either as central or

---

[16] Pilch, "Visions in Revelation," 134.

[17] Garnsey and Saller, *The Roman Empire*, 12–25; Malina, *The New Testament World*, 81–107; Crossan, *The Historical Jesus*, 45.

[18] Lightstone, "Christian Anti-Judaism," 111–12. See also discussion of patronage in chapter 1.

[19] Saller, *Personal Patronage*, 23.

[20] Aune, *Prophecy in Early Christianity*, 195.

peripheral intermediaries on the basis of their social location.[21] Central intermediaries played official roles in the political religion of the day, legitimating and
maintaining the existing social order. Examples of prophets with links to the
central cult in the Israelite tradition would be Samuel, Jeremiah, Haggai, and
Zechariah; Nathan, who functioned as King David's court prophet, would be a
similar figure.[22] Judean writers in the Hellenistic and Roman periods linked prophetic gifts with priestly status (e.g., I Macc 4:45b–46; 14:41; Josephus, *J.W.*
3.351–354). The sage or philosopher with the gift of prophecy might also be included here.[23] In the Greek world, central intermediary prophets may be identified
with figures connected with local shrines of gods and heroes, such as the Pythia at
Delphi, the priestesses at Dodona, and other givers of oracles. Governments and
their military wings employed technical diviners, trained in interpreting omens,
signs, sacrifices, dreams, and unusual events thought to reveal the will of the
gods.[24] These skills were often the restricted specialties of designated groups (e.g.,
the sacerdotal college of Rome) or of particular families.[25]

Peripheral intermediaries operated outside the structures of the dominant and
central religious cults. They were not personnel attached to temple or shrine, government or military. Freelance prophets and diviners practiced their arts in more
private settings at the request of individual persons, sometimes as retainers in the
households of the elite.[26] Prophecy and divination were integral aspects of normal
social and religious life in the Greco-Roman world, assisting individuals and families to determine life choices, understand the causes of misfortune, and, in general,
reduce the risks inherent in a number of human enterprises such as love and war.[27]

The revelatory arts, together with miracle working, exorcism, and faith healing,
were not only commonplace, but were also potential sources of prestige, importance, and wealth for the practitioners.[28] While most ancient Greeks and Romans
firmly believed that the gods really did communicate with humans through lots,
signs, dreams, and prophecies, they could be, and often were, wary and skeptical

---

[21] Ibid., 20.

[22] Ibid., 83–84.

[23] Ibid., 141–52.

[24] Aune, *Prophecy in Early Christianity*, 35. See also John North, "Diviners and Divination at Rome,"
in *Pagan Priests: Religion and Power in the Ancient World* (ed. Mary Beard and John North; Ithaca, N.Y.:
Cornell University Press, 1990), 52–53.

[25] North, "Diviners and Divination," 66–67.

[26] Ibid., 69–70; Aune, *Prophecy in Early Christianity*, 41.

[27] Aune, *Prophecy in Early Christianity*, 47.

[28] Robert Garland, "Priests and Power in Classical Athens," in *Pagan Priests: Religion and Power in the
Ancient World* (ed. Mary Beard and John North; Ithaca, N.Y.: Cornell University Press, 1990), 85.

of their human messengers. Prophets and diviners who sold their services in the marketplace were suspected of being motivated by self-interest.[29] Those who came from low status backgrounds were frequently regarded with disapproval, suspicion, and hostility. Their activities were seen as a potential threat to the established order, as indicated by charges of witchcraft and sorcery that led to intolerance and persecution.[30]

In Israelite traditions, prophetic gifts were also a potential source of social status. More importantly, prophets operating at the peripheries of society advocated social change or helped maintain social stability in times of crisis.[31] Amos and Hosea stand out as such peripheral intermediaries calling for social reform. Apocalyptic prophecy, which flourished from about 200 B.C.E. to 100 C.E., arose as a form of resistance to Hellenization and later, to Roman domination.[32] The Qumran sect that produced the Dead Sea Scrolls seems to have been a resistance movement that produced such literature. Among the peasants of first-and second-century Judea, a number of apocalyptic prophets emerged at fairly regular intervals, attracting large crowds of followers in the expectation of experiencing the "tokens" or "signs" of God's imminent deliverance. In imitation of Joshua (Josh 3), or perhaps Elijah (2 Kgs 2:6–8), Theudas (44–46 C.E.) promised to part the Jordan to enable his followers to re-enter the holy land from the wilderness. An unnamed Egyptian prophet planned to lead his followers from the wilderness east of the Jordan to Jerusalem, where the walls would collapse at his command, thereby recapitulating Joshua's conquest of Jericho (Josh 6:1–21). John the Baptist seems to have been a prophet of this type, and Jesus at least began his career following in his footsteps.[33]

At first glance it may seem that prophecy functioned differently in Israelite and non-Israelite contexts. Prophecy, divination, and revelatory arts were commonplace in the Greco-Roman cities and countryside, a part of normal everyday life. Among Israelites divination, augury, soothsaying, sorcery, casting spells, consulting ghosts and spirits, and necromancy were condemned in Scripture (Deut 18:10). This condemnation does not mean, however, that Israelites were uninterested in determining God's will in advance, if they could. Casting lots and dreams

---

[29] Aune, *Prophecy in Early Christianity*, 32–36.

[30] North, "Diviners and Divination," 58–59; Richard Gordon, "Religion in the Roman Empire: The Civic Compromise and Its Limits," in *Pagan Priests: Religion and Power in the Ancient World* (ed. Mary Beard and John North; Ithaca, N.Y.: Cornell University Press, 1990), 252–55.

[31] Aune, *Prophecy in Early Christianity*, 20.

[32] Ibid., 110.

[33] Crossan, *The Historical Jesus*, 46.

were approved means of divination. Indeed, as Aune asserts, the frequent condemnation of other forms of divination in the Hebrew Bible points to their persistence.[34] The Galilee in which Jesus grew up was also the home of Honi the Circle Drawer, famous for his ability to pray for rain, and of Hanina ben Dosa, renowned for healing through prayer. Both of these figures would have been perceived by their contemporaries as persons favored by God and hence able to intercede or broker divine favors on the behalf of others.

Prophecy, whether practiced by Greeks, Romans, Israelites, or Christ-followers, always involved the common element of some sort of revelatory trance experience, that is, altered states of consciousness.[35] Sometimes this experience took the form of possession in which a god, spirit, or other external power was believed to enter and take control of the intermediary's personality. Typical signs of divine possession included sudden onset, use of a loud voice, abnormal tones and rhythms of speech, physical manifestations of excitement or ecstasy, or trance.[36] The result would be oracles presented as the direct speech of the possessing divinity or spirit.[37] Communication with gods and spirits could also occur in meditative or mystic states or in the temporary flight or absence of the soul. Here, the result would be a vision in which the intermediary saw and/or heard things imperceptible to others, or even a journey through the spirit world that would occur during the shaman's voyage.[38] Such altered states of consciousness could be involuntary, uncontrolled, and initially unpredictable, but with practice, specialists learned to control these experiences.[39] The ancient Israelite prophets and Greco-Roman priestesses, such as the Pythia, engaged in controlled states of altered consciousness.[40] Uncontrolled altered states of consciousness may have been experienced within the context of the mystery cults.[41]

As we turn to the writings of post-Jesus groups for information about prophets, we will pay close attention to three different aspects of the phenomenon of prophecy. (1) We will examine the importance and types of altered states of consciousness that form the basis of prophecy among Christ-followers. (2) We will examine the social locations of those regarded as prophets. Were they central or peripheral in relation to the texts and/or communities with which they are associ-

---

[34] Aune, *Prophecy in Early Christianity*, 42.

[35] Ibid., 22, 86.

[36] Ibid., 47–48.

[37] Ibid., 33.

[38] Pilch, "ASC: A Kitbashed Model," 134.

[39] Aune, *Prophecy in Early Christianity*, 86.

[40] Ibid., 14.

[41] Ibid., 42–43.

ated? Did they hold positions of honor, status, and leadership? (3) We will in-
quire about the social and religious function of their prophecy. To what sorts of
questions and issues were the prophets responding?

Jesus

Jesus regarded himself as a prophet, as did his contemporaries. The New Testament Gospels record two instances in which Jesus referred to himself as a prophet.
He is reported to have shrugged off the less than enthusiastic reception that folks in
Nazareth gave him by noting that, "Prophets are not without honor, except in their
hometown, and among their own kin, and in their own house" (Mark 6:4//Matt
13:57//Luke 4:24; John 4:44). In response to a warning to flee Galilee because
Herod Antipas wished to kill him, Jesus is said to have quipped, "it is impossible for
a prophet to be killed outside of Jerusalem" (Luke 13:33).

As reported to Herod Antipas, public opinion in Galilee claimed that Jesus was
either Elijah or a "prophet, like one of the prophets of old" (Mark 6:15//Luke
9:8; Matt 14:5). The disciples provided a similar recital to Jesus himself (Mark
8:28//Matt 16:14[42]//Luke 9:19). Jesus' entry into Jerusalem stirred the crowds
to announce that, "This is the prophet Jesus from Nazareth in Galilee" (Matt
21:11). Observers responded to Jesus' raising of the widow's son at Nain by proclaiming, "A great prophet has risen among us!" (Luke 7:16). The Samaritan
woman at the well (John 4:19), the crowds who participated in the feeding of the
five thousand (John 6:14), and the blind man whose sight Jesus restored (John
9:17), made similar responses. On one occasion it was Jesus' teaching about the
Spirit that elicited the exclamation, "This is really the prophet" (John 7:40). The
disciples on the road to Emmaus described their master as a prophet to the risen
Jesus himself (Luke 24:19). Simon the Pharisee questioned Jesus' status as a
prophet in light of Jesus' apparent failure to recognize the woman who washes his
feet with her tears as a sinner (Luke 7:39). The chief priests and Pharisees denied
Jesus' status as a prophet on the grounds that Scripture does not predict the emergence of a prophet from Galilee (John 7:52). The view that Jesus' contemporaries
regarded him as prophet is, thus, widely attested in both early and later gospel narratives. To those who witnessed his healings and heard him speak, he appeared to
be a prophet, similar to the biblical figure of Elijah, whom Aune describes as a
"shamanistic prophet," combining the roles of holy man, sage, miracle worker,
and soothsayer.[43]

---

[42] Matthew's version includes Jeremiah.

[43] Aune, *Prophecy in Early Christianity*, 84.

Was Jesus a shaman then? Craffert and Pilch have recently argued that this social type might help us understand Jesus.[44] As defined by Craffert, shamanism or
the "shamanic complex" is a regularly occurring, cross-cultural "family of traditions" in which social functions such as healing, mediating, prophecy, exorcism,
and spirit possession flow out of ASC experiences.[45] Often through an involuntary ASC, the spirit(s) choose the shaman (or holy man/woman in the Israelite
context). A period of initiation and tutelage by both the spirit and a real-life
teacher must follow the initial unbidden call, during which the shaman-to-be acquires the necessary ritual skills to manage his or her ongoing ACS experiences
that may take the form of soul flight, possession, or vision.[46] Through these
means the shaman acts as an intermediary or broker between the human community and spirit beings that occasionally cause problems for humans.

Pilch argues that events in Jesus' life may be understood in terms of a shamanic
call and initiation.[47] Jesus first meets John the Baptist, his teacher and guide. His
baptism by John is the occasion for an altered state of consciousness experience
in which Jesus sees the spirit of God descending upon him and hears a voice de-
claring that he is God's beloved son (Mark 1:9–11//Matt 3:13–17//Luke
3:21–22). Pilch interprets this scene as Jesus' call to be "a shaman, a holy man, a
broker on behalf of the patron/God."[48] According to the Gospel narratives, Satan
tested Jesus after his baptism (Mark 1:12–13//Matt 4:1–11//Luke 4:1–13). In
Pilch's interpretation this scene is where "Jesus demonstrates that he has acquired
the necessary ritual skills to deal with and control the spirit world."[49] Pilch identifies the incidents of walking on the sea (Mark 6:45–52//Matt 14:22–33//
John 6:16–21) and the transfiguration (Mark 9:2–10//Matt 17:1–9//Luke
9:28–36) as evidence of continuing ASC experiences in Jesus' life.[50] Jesus' healings and exorcisms are typical activities of shamans, and derive from his ability
to communicate with and master the spirits that were believed to influence hu-

---

[44] Peter Craffert, "Jesus and the Shamanic Complex: First Steps in Utilizing a Social Type
Model," *Neotestamentica* 33, no. 2 (1999): 321–42; Pilch, "Altered States of Consciousness Events,"
103–15.

[45] Craffert, "Jesus and the Shamanic Complex," 324.

[46] Craffert, "Jesus and the Shamanic Complex," 326–27; Pilch, "Altered States of Consciousness
Events," 107–8.

[47] Pilch prefers to use the terms "holy man," *saddiq*, or *hasid* as the appropriate biblical terms for the
shamanic complex as it occurred in the Israelite context in which Jesus operated (conversation
March 4–17, 2002).

[48] Pilch, "Altered States of Consciousness Events," 108.

[49] Ibid., 109.

[50] Ibid., 109–10.

man life.[51] In the world in which Jesus' lived, these activities caused some observers to proclaim that he was a "prophet," an intermediary between God and humanity.

Not everyone regarded Jesus in this way. As we have seen, Simon the Pharisee, the chief priests, and the Pharisees in Jerusalem questioned Jesus' status as a prophet. These persons close to or at the center of power in first-century Judea attempted to deny Jesus this status by pointing to his lifestyle and origins. In the eyes of his society's elites, Jesus was a peasant or artisan from the cultural backwater of Galilee who had a habit of hanging out with "sinners." For them, Jesus' healings, exorcisms, and teaching were insufficient evidence of his claim to be a prophet who spoke and acted for God. The judgment of the chief priests and Pharisees seems to reflect the prejudice of ancient elites against persons of lower status and provides a clear indicator of Jesus' own social location. He may be described as a peripheral prophet emerging and operating outside the official structures of first-century Judean political religion. Jesus' healings and teachings about the forthcoming reign of God were intended to demonstrate practically and theoretically how Israel ought to, can, and will function with God as its father or patron. Jesus recruited disciples whom he sent out to do the same (Mark 3:16–19; 6:7–13; Matt 10:1–42; Luke 6:12–16; 9:1–6). In this way, Jesus acted as the initiator of a movement whose goal was to prepare fellow Israelites for the religious, political, economic, and social changes accompanying the establishment of God's rule. In this theocracy, God would act as a father or a patron to all of Israel, replicating Jesus' visionary experience of a God who interacted with him as a father/patron to a son/favored client.[52]

ASC experience was thus foundational for Jesus, providing inspiration and what we might call spiritual resources for his ministry. As we shall see, ASCs continued to be an important base in the development and evolution of Jesus groups in the years following Jesus' death and resurrection. In many of these groups, especially those that produced our canonical texts, prophets and prophetic figures were seen as intermediaries or brokers for the resurrected Christ rather than God. For these groups, Jesus the prophet and holy man came to occupy a unique

---

[51] Two similar understandings of Jesus are presented by Marcus J. Borg and Stevan L. Davies. Borg, "Jesus Before and After Easter: Jewish Mystic and Christian Messiah," in *The Meaning of Jesus: Two Visions* (ed. Marcus J. Borg and N. T. Wright; San Francisco: HarperSanFrancisco, 1999), 53–76, describes Jesus as a "spirit person" whose mystical experience of God was the foundation of his ministry as a healer, wisdom teacher, social prophet, and movement initiator. In *Jesus the Healer: Possession, Trance, and the Origins of Christianity* (New York: Continuum, 1995), Davies attributes Jesus' ability to heal and exorcise to spirit possession, i.e., Jesus was possessed by the Spirit of God.

[52] Malina, *The Social Gospel of Jesus*, 141–49.

position as the only or primary intermediary agent of the one God. This notion is expressed in a number of different ways, ranging from Paul's assertion that "for us there is one God, the Father . . . and one Lord Jesus Christ, through whom are all things and through whom we exist (I Cor 8:6), to John's description of Jesus as "the Father's only son" (1:14), to the declaration in I Tim 2:5 that there is "one mediator between God and humankind, Christ Jesus, himself a human." Our examination of prophets and ASCs in the early churches will therefore focus on persons who were seen as representing or mediating Christ's presence, with one exception. In the *Gospel of Thomas* it appears that ASC experience was regarded as making one equal to Christ. But first, let us turn to an apostle who never called himself a prophet, even though he was one.

Paul

Paul never called himself a prophet, insisting that he was an "apostle" or messenger of Christ (Rom 1:1; I Cor 1:1; 2 Cor 1:1; Gal 1:1). Yet revelatory experiences significantly determined the direction of Paul's life and ministry. He started out with a fairly high status since he was born in Tarsus, a city of some repute. His education as a Pharisee put him close to the center of Israelite religious life, close enough that he could persecute and harass the followers of Jesus. It was an ASC experience that caused his radical change from persecutor to promoter of the Jesus movement. In language reminiscent of the prophetic calls of Isaiah (Isa 49:1–6) and Jeremiah (Jer 1:5), Paul claimed that he had been set apart and called by God through a revelation of Jesus Christ for the specific purpose of proclaiming the gospel among the Gentiles (Gal 1:15–16, 12). A revelation prompted him to visit Jerusalem fourteen years later and lay out before the acknowledged leaders of the Jesus Messiah group the gospel he was preaching (Gal 2:2).[53] Paul shared information gained in ASCs with the members of the house churches as we can see from his letters.

Paul explicitly grounds his call to be an apostle and his decision to go to Jerusalem in "revelations." What he means by this can be discerned from his comments in 2 Cor 12:1–11, where he describes how he had been "caught up into the third heaven . . . in Paradise and heard things that are not to be told" (2 Cor 12:2–4). Such experiences characterize a sky journey or shamanic voyage, a non-possession

---

[53] I have adopted Malina's distinction between *Jesus Messiah groups* based in Jerusalem (cf Acts), *Messianic Jesus groups* that remained faithful to Torah (so-called Jewish Christians like Matthew's community), and *Resurrected Jesus groups* such as those founded by Paul in the Greek east; see *The Social Gospel of Jesus*, 154–59.

form of ASC.[54] A little later in the same passage, Paul indicates that, in response
to his repeated prayer to have the thorn in his flesh removed, the Lord had informed him that divine grace would be sufficient for him and that power is made
perfect in weakness (2 Cor 12:8–9). Since prayer was one of the accepted prepa-
ratory techniques for receiving revelations, it is quite likely that Paul received this
divine oracle while in an altered state of consciousness.[55] It seems then, that like
many of his contemporaries, Paul turned to ASCs for information about and so-
lutions to life's dilemmas. As Pilch indicates, this is the normal function of ASCs
in Mediterranean cultures.[56]

As Christ's apostle in the non-Israelite world Paul was a peripheral figure. Not
only was he not a member of the inner circle of Jesus' original disciples, he was an
outsider, a stranger in the cities where he labored. Although he was the founder of
house churches in a number of places, he never settled in any one of them. Thus
he remained outside and somewhat peripheral to the everyday life of the Christ-
confessors that he recruited. This may account, at least in part, for the fact that
Paul's references to his ASC experiences are all made in the context of defending
his apostolic status. They serve together with his claims to be a trustworthy steward
of the gospel as evidenced in his self-emptying lifestyle to validate his position of
authority among the members of the house churches he established in the cities of
the eastern Mediterranean.

From Paul's other remarks, we can discern that ASC experiences were a source
of honor and status as well as a cause of conflict within Paul's congregations. At
the end of a discussion of marriage and celibacy in 1 Cor 7:40, he quips, "and I
think that I too have the Spirit of God," suggesting that the opposition also
claimed to be inspired by God's Spirit. Paul's evaluation of speaking in tongues (a
form of ASC) in relation to prophecy (another type of ASC) clearly indicates rivalry between congregational members adept at different forms of ASC. Paul
notes that he speaks in tongues more than any of them (1 Cor 14:18), signaling
his spiritual superiority over them. But Paul places a higher value on prophecy because it builds up, encourages, and consoles the entire community and not just the
one speaking (1 Cor 14:3–4). He asserts that he can benefit the congregation
more by speaking in revelation, knowledge, prophecy, or teaching (1 Cor 14:6).
Paul insists that any spiritually empowered person will recognize his instructions
as "a command of the Lord" (1 Cor 14:37). Yet some continued to doubt that

---

[54] Pilch, "ASC: A Kitbashed Model," 134.

[55] Aune, *Prophecy in Early Christianity*, 266.

[56] Pilch, "ASC: A Kitbashed Model," 137.

Christ really was speaking in or through Paul and desired proof (2 Cor 13:3). In Paul's letters, ASC experiences turn out to be desirable, even necessary, but ambiguous and ambivalent means of acquiring and legitimating status and leadership.

The focus of Paul's ministry differed rather markedly from that of Jesus. Jesus demonstrated in word and deed what the forthcoming reign of God would look like. He recruited disciples to go out and do the same, creating a social movement oriented to changing society and paving the way for a new theocracy. Paul's gospel was not the message of Jesus, but a message about the resurrected Christ who would soon return as Lord. Paul's goal was to invite non-Israelites to change their allegiance and their lifestyles. By accepting the resurrected Christ as their Lord, non-Israelites could participate in the impending reign of the God of Israel over the entire cosmos. This new allegiance required some significant lifestyle changes, such as dissociating from Greco-Roman domestic and political religion. To nurture and support their new way of life "in Christ," Paul organized his recruits into fictive kinship groups, modeled on Diaspora Israelite synagogues and Greco-Roman elective associations. Altered states of consciousness experiences were regarded as "the first fruits of the Spirit" given in anticipation of the salvation that Christ was soon to bring (see Rom 8:23–25). Prophets and speakers in tongues played central roles in the worship lives of these groups and were involved in competition and conflict with one another.

Given the centrality of prophecy in Paul's personal life story and in the practice of the Resurrected Jesus groups that he formed, it is not surprising that Paul's letters contain prophetic statements. To the congregation in Thessalonica, Paul gave instructions "through the Lord Jesus" about appropriate sexual behavior.[57] These new followers of Christ were to avoid fornication, to treat their sexual partners with "holiness and honor, not with lustful passion like the Gentiles," and were not to sexually exploit church members (1 Thess 4:2–6). To fail to live up to these ethical standards would be to invite God's eschatological vengeance (1 Thess 4:6–8). To those who are worried about the fate of their deceased loved ones, Paul declares again "by the word of the Lord"[58] that the dead in Christ will rise first to meet their coming Lord in the air (1 Thess 4:15–17). Neither instructive response is a teaching of the historical Jesus; they are prophetic oracles uttered or transmitted by Paul. He and his audiences presumably accepted them as authentic

---

[57] Aune, *Prophecy in Early Christianity*, 260, considers this phrase as a functional equivalent of the OT prophetic messenger formula.

[58] Ibid., 255. This is a common introduction to prophetic oracles (see 1 Kgs 20:25; 2 Kgs 13:1ff.; 21:35; Sir 48:3).

teachings of the resurrected Christ.[59] Paul identifies a similar oracle in I Cor 15:51–52 as a "mystery," that is, a divine secret. Paul discloses the secret that when Christ returns everyone will be changed: the dead will be raised imperishable, and those who are living will be transformed. Another eschatological secret that Paul shares with his readers is that once "the full number of the Gentiles has come in . . . all Israel will be saved" (Rom 11:25–26). In all four examples given here, Paul introduces new teaching and material into the nascent Resurrected Jesus tradition by labeling each a "word of the Lord" or a "mystery," that is, a prophetic oracle or a divine secret revealed. In doing so, Paul turns his followers' attention not to scenarios of how God's reign will operate in human society once established (the focus of Jesus' teaching), but to end-time scenes of cosmic rescue and vengeance.

It seems fair to say that Paul placed a high value on ASC experiences as a source of personal authority and innovation, but insisted that they needed to be evaluated in terms of their ability to build community and encourage and console church members. We might add that in Paul's eyes an authentic apostle and prophet would be one who could be seen as a faithful steward, representing the crucified Christ's solidarity with alienated humanity.

Luke-Acts

Although Paul himself never explicitly claimed the status of a prophet, the author of Luke-Acts identified him as such (Acts 13:1). This two-volume work reflects the perspectives of non-Israelite Resurrected Jesus groups toward the end of the first century in the cities of the eastern Mediterranean basin where Paul had been active. Distinctive emphases of Luke-Acts include worship and prayer, and food and meals that are explicitly linked (Acts 2:42, 46). This is a reflection of the location of post-Jesus-group worship in household meal contexts. Women and other disadvantaged, excluded, or oppressed persons also figure prominently in the work of this evangelist. But most importantly, Luke-Acts highlights both the work of the Holy Spirit and of those who mediate the Spirit's knowledge and blessings to others.[60]

Luke-Acts is filled with revelatory phenomena. The angel Gabriel appears first to Zechariah and then to Mary to announce the births of their sons (Luke 1:5–28). The pregnant women are filled with the Holy Spirit and prophesy

---

[59] Ibid., 235–37, provides Greco-Roman parallels of instances where post-mortem oracular sayings were accorded the same status as teachings delivered during a poet or holy man's life time.

[60] Mark Allen Powell, *Fortress Introduction to the Gospels* (Minneapolis: Fortress, 1998), 92–94.

(Luke 1:39–55), as does Zechariah after the birth of his son, John (1:67–79). Angels appear to shepherds to announce the birth of Jesus (2:8–20); Simeon and Anna are led by the Spirit in proclaiming Jesus' birth (2:25–38). Jesus' vocation is marked by ASC experiences at his baptism (3:21–22), his testing in the wilderness (4:1–13), and his transfiguration (9:28–36). He heals and casts out demons by drawing upon the power of God (11:20). In every way Jesus fits the image of the shamanic prophet discussed above.

Jesus predicts that the Wisdom of God will send "prophets and apostles" (11:49). Prophets and apostles thus appear to be the leadership figures that Luke and his audience are most interested in. Yet very little is said about them in the gospel. Jesus does give the twelve "power and authority over all demons and to cure diseases" (9:1). In imitation of Jesus their mission is to proclaim the forthcoming reign of God and to heal (9:2). Later Jesus sends "seventy others" to every town and place where he intends to go; they too are charged with healing the sick and proclaiming the nearness of God's reign (Luke 10:9). Neither the twelve nor the seventy are called prophets in the gospel, though as we shall see, that changes in Acts.

As Minear points out, Luke presented Jesus as a prophet whose "vocation presupposed that of John and predetermined that of his apostles."[61] He argues that in the gospel the disciples acted as Jesus' apprentices who through a series of visions beginning with the transfiguration (Luke 9:28–36) and the resurrection (Luke 24) and culminating in Acts, are initiated and empowered to become prophets like their resurrected master and apostles on his behalf.[62] At the end of Acts 1, for example, we learn that Matthias has been chosen by lot (a process of divination) to replace Judas in his ministry and apostleship, and so was added to the eleven apostles (1:21–26). This selection is immediately followed by the statement that on the day of Pentecost "they"—the apostles—were all together (2:1). They are next described as filled with the Spirit and speaking in tongues, phenomena that fulfill Joel's oracle that in the last days God's Spirit will be poured out so that men and women will prophesy (2:17–18). The twelve, therefore, were endowed with the gift of prophecy through what Minear calls a "vision," that is, an ASC experience.[63] They are empowered to heal (Acts 3:1–10) and to preach boldly (Acts 3:1–11; 4:1–22). In other words, the apostles become shamanic prophets like their master, Jesus.

---

[61] Paul S. Minear, *To Heal and to Reveal: The Prophetic Vocation according to Luke* (New York: Crossroad, 1976), 8; see also Aune, *Prophecy in Early Christianity* , 192.

[62] Minear, *To Heal and to Reveal,* 122–36.

[63] Ibid., 133–40.

This transition is even more dramatic in the case of Paul, who goes from persecutor to promoter of the Jesus movement as a result of an ASC experienced while traveling to Damascus to arrest Christ-followers (Acts 9:1–9). His vision of the resurrected Christ is followed by three days of blindness and fasting, then instruction and baptism at the hands of Ananias, who is himself directed to Paul in a dream vision (Acts 9:10–19). These events can be interpreted as the initial steps in becoming a shaman. A spirit has contacted Paul, identified itself, and provided him with a real-life teacher.[64] Paul's early preaching in Damascus, Jerusalem, Tarsus (Acts 9:19–30), and Antioch (Acts 11:25–26) can be understood as representing his years in training when he acquired the necessary skills to mediate between the human and divine spheres.[65] That he had succeeded is signaled in the explicit mention that he was a prophet in Antioch who had been set apart by the Holy Spirit for the special task of taking the gospel to the Gentiles (Acts 13:1–3). The rest of the narrative chronicles Paul's prophetic career. Filled with the Holy Spirit, he unmasks and blinds a false prophet (Acts 13:4–12), heals a crippled man (14:8–20), exorcises an unclean spirit of divination from a slave girl (16:16–18), heals and exorcises many in Ephesus (19:11–12), and even raises the dead (20:7–12). Paul receives visions (Acts 16:9–10) and falls into trances during which he sees Jesus (22:17–21). All of these experiences mark him as a shamanic-type prophet like Jesus.

In Acts the roles of apostle and prophet are not identical, but they are closely linked. Initially, the twelve apostles primarily function as witnesses to Jesus' resurrection (1:22). After Pentecost they become prophetic figures engaged in preaching and healing in Jerusalem. Conversely, Barnabas and Paul, are initially identified as two of the prophets active in Antioch (13:1), but are not called apostles until after they had been set aside for the special task of taking the gospel about Jesus to non-Israelites (14:4, 14). For Luke, then, it seems that apostles were by definition prophets; however, not every prophet was an apostle, for example, Agabus (11:27–28; 21:10–11), Judas and Silas (15:32), Simeon Niger, Lucius of Cyrene or Manaen (13:1), and the four virgin daughters of Philip (21:8–9).

Not only are the apostles, that is, the twelve and others, described as prophetic figures transformed by ASC experiences, every significant step in spreading the

---

[64] See Pilch's discussion of the call and initiation of a shaman in "Altered States of Consciousness Events," 107–8.

[65] Although Acts 9:30 simply states that Paul was sent to Tarsus, we can safely assume that he preached there based on his own statement that he proclaimed the faith in Syria and Cilicia, the capital of which was Tarsus (Gal 1:21–22).

good news of Jesus' resurrection is the result of some form of ASC. Unbelievers hear the gospel preached by persons "filled with the Holy Spirit" (4:8; 7:55–56; 13:9–11); in other words, the preachers are perceived to be possessed by or in direct contact with a divine spirit. Persecutors of Jesus' followers and foreigners become Christ-confessors as a result of visionary experiences (9:1–9; 10:3–6). Community leaders make decisions based on information received in visions (10:10–16; 16:9–10; 18:9–10; 22:17–21; 27:23–24) and/or uttered by prophets (11:27–28; 13:1–3; 15:28; 20:23; 21:4, 10–11). New groups of believers manifest all the signs of spirit possession, speaking in tongues, praising God, and prophesying (8:14–17; 10:44–46; 19:1–6).[66]

Aune notes that the proliferation of oracles and revelations in Luke-Acts has a literary function. He asserts, "the copious references to prophecies, visions, miracles, and persons 'filled with the Holy Spirit' that punctuate the narrative at critical junctures provide an exciting force which controls the movement of the plot."[67] In this respect, he contends, Luke-Acts resembles other Hellenistic and Roman epics and tragedies in which divination and oracles are used to direct and develop the plot. Aune concedes, quite rightly, that simply because prophetic revelations serve literary purposes in these texts this does not mean that they are unhistorical. He does not, however, explain how the texts might be historical.[68] Knowledge of ASCs helps the reader find those explanations. There is a high degree of probability that these texts are indeed accounts of how early Christ-confessors in the Greco-Roman cities of the eastern Mediterranean went about their everyday business. Stories of prophecies, visions, and the like certainly would not have functioned as persuasive rhetoric for the evangelist's first-century audience unless they reflected common Greco-Roman practices of consulting deities and spirits for assistance in making decisions in life.

The apostles endowed with the gift of prophecy and the prophet commissioned as an apostle are central figures in the development of "the Way," as Luke calls the movement that arose after Jesus' resurrection (Acts 9:2). Information gained in ASCs directs the apostles in establishing Resurrected Jesus groups; prophecy and other ASC experiences continue to play a central role in the communal lives of these groups. They stand in continuity, therefore with the Pauline *ekklesiai.* Like Paul, this evangelist legitimates innovation and change by presenting them as divinely inspired through ASC experiences. In contrast to Paul's open ad-

---

[66] Aune, *Prophecy in Early Christianity,* 193.

[67] Ibid., 192.

[68] Ibid.

mission that prophecy was a cause for intramural rivalry and conflict, Luke gives few signals that it was problematic. The only false prophets who appear in the book of Acts are quickly detected and successfully neutralized by the Apostle Paul (13:4–12; 16:16–18). Luke's unqualified positive assessment of prophets and ASC was not shared by others in the early churches, as we shall see in our examinations of the *Didache* and the Gospel of Matthew.

Didache

Didache is the common title for a text called *The Teaching of the (Twelve) Apostles: The Lord's Teaching through the Twelve Apostles to the Gentiles.* Originating in Syria during the second half of the first century, perhaps as early as 50–70 C.E.,[69] it reflects the perspectives of an Israelite Messianic Jesus group addressing non-Israelites. Although the *Didache* is frequently described as a rudimentary manual of church order, an overview of its contents reveals that it is intended not as a universal or comprehensive church order but as a selective one that provides guidance on a limited number of specific issues related to the initiation and inclusion of non-Israelite members.[70] It contains instructions for catechesis (1.1–6.2), baptism, fasting, prayer, the Eucharist (6.3–11.2), tithing, leadership (11.3–15.4) and a concluding apocalyptic appeal (16.1–8). The non-Israelite audience is encouraged to abandon their previous way of life (5.1–2) and to become as Torah-observant as possible (6.2–3). At the same time they are encouraged to adopt practices that will clearly distinguish them from their Israelite neighbors (e.g., 8.1–3). The text displays numerous contacts with the Matthean tradition and forms the basis of third- and fourth-century Syrian church orders.[71]

The *Didache* first mentions prophets in connection with the conduct of the Eucharist. The author sets out the specific prayers to be said at the beginning and end of the meal, introducing them with the phrase, "give thanks in this way" (9.1, 10.1). The instructions concerning the Eucharist conclude with the injunction, "but allow the prophets to give thanks as much as they like" (10.7). These directions simply imply that the prophets are not limited to the prayer format laid out

---

[69] Aaron Milavec, *The Didache: Faith, Hope, and Life of the Earliest Christian Communities, 50–70 C.E.* (New York: Newman, 2003), vii.

[70] Ibid., vii; Jonathan A. Draper, "Ritual Process and Ritual Symbol in Didache 7–10," *VC* 54 (2000): 123.

[71] Tugwell, *The Apostolic Fathers,* 1; Jonathan A. Draper, "Torah and Troublesome Apostles in the *Didache* Community," *NovT* 33 (1991): 347–72; Jonathan A. Draper, "Christian Self-Definition Against the 'Hypocrites' in *Didache* 8," *SBLSP* (1992), 362–78; Clayton N. Jefford, *The Sayings of Jesus in the Teaching of the Twelve Apostles* (VCSup 11; Leiden: Brill, 1989), 4–16.

in the text, but may offer an unlimited number of spontaneous prayers. However, the text does not tell us when these prophetic prayers occur in the Eucharist. Were they limited to the conclusion of the event?[72] Could a prophet offer spontaneous prayers throughout the eucharistic meal? More importantly, could the prophet replace the prayers in the text with his or her own extemporaneous ones?[73] Although it is not possible to fill in these details, prophets clearly have a special role to play in the eucharistic liturgy.

Directions concerning the reception of teachers (11.1–2) and apostles who are also prophets (11.3–6) follow these liturgical instructions.[74] The latter are prophets temporarily engaged as emissaries and envoys of Jesus groups. By definition they are persons in transit. The *Didache* instructs its audience to provide hospitality without question to any such person, in accordance with the commandment of the gospel (11.3–4). However, this hospitality is strictly limited to food and lodging for two days, and provisions for the next leg of the journey. Any apostle-prophet who stays longer or who asks for money must be regarded as a "false prophet" (11.5, 6). It seems unlikely that these apostle-prophets would have had much opportunity to participate in the community's worship services. They are outsiders on the way to somewhere else who are given little or no opportunity to claim any status or leadership in the communities addressed by the *Didache*. In this respect they are distinguished from those prophets who "speak in spirit" (11.7).

Prophets who "speak in spirit" have far greater opportunities to acquire the status and honor of leadership, yet they are to be treated with caution. That they "speak in spirit" points to some sort of ASC experience as the basis of their speech. Although the ASC experience may include glossolalia, it is probably not limited to that phenomenon, for it is expected to result in quite comprehensible teaching, orders, and requests (11.9–12).[75] Whatever the content or style of such prophetic speech, it is not to be tested or examined; to do so is to commit the sin that will not be forgiven (11.7). Although no assessment of the prophet's speech is to be made, the author warns them:

---

[72] See Aaron Milavec, "Distinguishing True and False Prophets: The Protective Wisdom of the *Didache*," in *Journal for Early Christian Studies* 2, no. 2 (1994): 121.

[73] Jonathan A. Draper, "Social Ambiguity and the Production of Texts: Prophets, Teachers, Bishops and Deacons in the Development of the Jesus Tradition in the Community of the *Didache*," in *The* Didache *in Context: Essays on Its Text, History and Transmission* (ed. Clayton N. Jefford; NovTSup 77; Leiden: Brill, 1995), 298.

[74] Milavec, "Distinguishing True and False Prophets," 125–26.

[75] Draper, "Social Ambiguity and the Production of Texts," 296; Milavec, "Distinguishing True and False Prophets," 129.

Not everyone who speaks in spirit is a prophet, but only if he has the Lord's way of life. So the false prophet and the prophet will be known by their way of life. (11.8)

It is possible, therefore, to test and evaluate a prophet's conduct, if not his or her pronouncements. Specifically, a true prophet displays the Lord's way of life or behavior.

There follow four examples of prophetic behavior that may be assessed. A prophet "in spirit" may give an order for a table, that is, a meal, but may not eat of it. If he does, he proves himself to be a "false prophet" (11.9). The meal in question here is probably not eucharistic; Aune provides evidence from the Greek magical papyri that revelations were on occasion used to provide food and banquets for the practitioner.[76] This evidence coheres with the instruction in 11.12 not to listen to a prophet who asks, while in spirit, for "money or something" to be given to him. It is acceptable, however, for a prophet to request "money or something" for others who are in need (11.12). The Didachist thus makes it clear that true prophets, even when speaking "in spirit," may legitimately request things for others, but not for themselves. These instructions serve to reinforce the rules of hospitality set out in 11.3–6. True prophets do not use their prophetic gifts for self-enrichment or to exceed the limits of normal hospitality offered to itinerant Jesus-group members. These instructions are not unlike Paul's insistence that the most valuable ASC experiences are those that build up the community rather than the individual and that faithful stewardship is marked by solidarity with the weak.

A false prophet may also be identified by the fact that although he teaches the truth, he "does not do what he teaches" (11.10). No doubt, "truth" is to be measured against the authoritative standard set out in the *Didache*.[77] True prophets will not only affirm and augment its ethical, practical, and liturgical guidelines, but will also practice its teachings. The true prophet, therefore, would be expected to avoid food offered to idols (6.3), fast on Wednesday and Friday (8.1), and recite the Lord's Prayer three times daily (8.2–3). A true prophet would not practice astrology (3.4), tell lies (3.5), use obscene language (3.3), or do any of the other activities listed as contrary to "the way of life" in the *Didache*. Careful observation of a visiting prophet's habits and conduct would quickly determine whether he or she was true or false.

A prophet who has been examined and found to be true might do things that he does not teach others to do, such as enacting "the earthly mystery of the church" (11.11). Exactly what this phrase means is not spelled out in the text, nor

---

[76] Aune, *Prophecy in Early Christianity*, 225 n. 211.
[77] Milavec, "Distinguishing True and False Prophets," 129.

does it have any close parallel in any other writings of the period. Traditionally, scholars have interpreted this phrase as a euphemism for spiritual marriage between a prophet and prophetess. Others have considered it a reference to the celibate lifestyle of the prophet who sacrificed home and family for vocation.[78] The text itself supports neither interpretation. Whatever these mysterious acts may be, the author the *Didache* justifies them "because the prophets of old did exactly the same" (11.11). A quick glance at the Hebrew Bible reveals that Isaiah walked naked and barefoot for three years (Isa 20:1–6). Jeremiah wore a yoke around his neck (Jer 27:1ff.). Ezekiel lay before a model of Jerusalem, alternating from his left to right side according to a divinely laid out agenda (Ezek 4:1–8). Hosea married a prostitute (Hos 1:4–9). The "earthly mystery of the church" might refer, then, to any bizarre or potentially scandalous behavior that the prophetic vocation necessitated. The prophet is not to be judged or condemned for these, but neither should others be encouraged to imitate the prophet's strange activities.

The Didachist instructs his readers to welcome and materially support "every true prophet" who wishes to settle permanently in their community (13.1). These prophets are not engaged in apostolic missions (11.3–6) and their conduct has been tested and proven according to the instructions given in 11.7–12. In the churches that the *Didache* addresses, these resident prophets have the status of high priests (13.3) and act as their chief mediators with God. As high priests, they are to be the recipients of the "first-fruits," a portion of everything that community members produce or own (13.1–7). If a community does not have such a resident prophet, they are to give these first-fruits to the poor (13.4). The prophet-high priests are described as performing religious and ritual services (*leitourgousi . . . ten leitourgian*), such as offering prayers during Eucharist (10.7) for the community alongside teachers, bishops, and deacons (15.1–2).

Prophets, thus, turn out to be the most significant figures in the *Didache*. Not only do they receive more attention than any other group mentioned in the text, the instructions concerning their high status are quite explicit.[79] The basis for the prophet's prominence is his or her "speaking in spirit," a personal capacity to mediate spiritual or divine information received in altered states of consciousness directly to their human audiences. Although this ability is highly valued, it is also regarded with deep ambivalence. As the Didachist warns, "not everyone who speaks in spirit is a prophet" (11.8). ASCs should not lead to an immediate grant

---

[78] Milavec, "Distinguishing True and False Prophets," 132–34; Draper, "Social Ambiguity and the Production of Texts," 397 n. 6.

[79] Prophets are mentioned fifteen times, apostles three times, teachers twice, bishops and deacons once.

of authority. Only those prophets whose spirit-inspired speech is not self-serving and whose conduct matches the "truth" they teach are the prophets to be listened to and heeded. The *Didache* thus provides a mechanism whereby "certified," that is, tested and approved, prophets can assume positions of permanent leadership in some Messianic Jesus groups.[80] By requiring that all prophets be tested, the *Didache* effectively undermines their potential authority by subordinating them to the judgments of local community leaders (i.e., householders able to act as patrons to Jesus groups).[81]

In spite of the high honor and material support accorded to resident prophets in the *Didache*, Aune notes that they "appear curiously irrelevant for the ongoing life" of the communities.[82] Not every house church has a prophet, and in these situations life goes on, with the first fruits being given to the poor (13.4). Bishops and deacons who "also perform for you the services of the prophets and teachers" can just as easily provide church leadership (15.1). Those chosen or elected to these offices should be "worthy of the Lord, gentle men, not lovers of money, truthful and approved" (15.1). The writer warns his audience not to despise these figures, "for they are your honored ones with the prophets and teachers" (15.2). This last instruction suggests that, in the communities addressed by the *Didache*, there were some who did not think much of these appointed officials preferring instead the leadership of divinely inspired prophets and teachers. The *Didache* reflects a more complex and nuanced situation, and displays much more ambivalence toward prophets than do either Paul or Luke, a stance which was shared with the Gospel of Matthew.

Matthew

The Gospel of Matthew reflects the perspective of a Messianic Jesus group located in Syria or northern Palestine. No longer part of the larger Israelite community, its members are engaged in a process of self-definition over against its parent.[83] Matthew's gospel purports to be a book about the life and activities of Jesus, yet it is shaped by and reflects the needs and concerns of the author and his

---

[80] Aune, *Prophecy in Early Christianity*, 225–26.

[81] Draper, "Social Ambiguity and the Production of Texts," 292–93.

[82] Aune, *Prophecy in Early Christianity*, 209.

[83] J. Andrew Overman, *Matthew's Gospel and Formative Judaism: The Social World of the Matthean Community* (Minneapolis: Fortress, 1990), 141–47; Anthony J. Saldarini, "The Gospel of Matthew and Jewish-Christian Conflict," in *Social History of the Matthean Community* (ed. David Balch; Minneapolis: Fortress, 1990), 38–61; Stephen G. Wilson, *Related Strangers: Jews and Christians 70–170 C.E.* (Minneapolis: Fortress, 1995), 55.

immediate audience. Matthew relates events and teachings of Jesus that he believes will be particularly useful to the members of the community for whom he writes, focusing, for example, on Jesus' interpretation and application of Torah (Matt 5–7). Such special emphases provide insights into the social situation of the gospel writer and his Messianic Jesus group. Among passages that are distinctive to Matthew, three refer to prophets.

In Matt 23:29–26 the gospel writer reconfigures a saying from the Q source, in which Jesus condemns the Pharisees for building the tombs of the prophets whom their ancestors killed, while claiming that they would not have behaved as their forebears did. They demonstrate their hypocrisy by their treatment of the messengers whom Jesus sends: prophets, sages, and scribes (23:34). Comparing this statement to Luke's version in which Jesus reports that Wisdom will send prophets *and apostles* easily demonstrates that these figures particularly interest this evangelist (Luke 11:49).[84] Matthew's rendition suggests that prophets, sages, and scribes could potentially lead the Messianic Jesus groups that produced and/or used the Gospel of Matthew. Our interest here concerns the "prophets" who are also the subjects of two other distinctively Matthean passages.

The gospel writer warns his readers and hearers to beware of "false prophets," who come to the community in sheep's clothing but are really wolves (Matt 7:15).[85] These prophets are outsiders who seek entry into Matthean house churches because they prophesy, cast out demons, and do deeds of power in Jesus' name (7:22).[86] Such activities by themselves are insufficient to merit the Lord's commendation or participation in God's reign (7:23). According to the evangelist, false prophets are identifiable by "their fruits" (7:16), their failure to do the will of Jesus' Father in heaven (7:21), and their deeds of lawlessness (7:23). Although Matthew provides no specifics, these statements all point to conduct and lifestyle. It is likely that he expects prophets to be judged on the basis of their keeping Torah, as interpreted by Jesus and taught in the Matthean community.[87] Overall, this passage casts doubt on the sincerity and integrity of these prophets who come

---

[84] A discussion of Luke 11:49 follows in the next section.

[85] Matthew 24:11, 24 also contain warnings against false prophets in the context of his expansion of Mark's "little apocalypse" (Mark 13//Luke 21). In that passage the false prophets appear to be similar to the figures that are described by Josephus as proclaiming signs of deliverance from Roman domination. They are not relevant to our discussion of leadership within the Matthean circle of messianic Jesus groups.

[86] Francis Wright Beare, *The Gospel according to Matthew: Translation, Introduction, and Commentary* (San Francisco: Harper & Row, 1982), 195.

[87] Overman, *Matthew's Gospel and Formative Judaism*, 117–19.

from outside.[88] It effectively undermines any potential that they might have to act as leaders in the Matthean Jesus groups.

Not only is Matthew leery of visiting prophets, in his own community there seems to be a shortage of persons willing to engage in prophetic ministries. Overman has shown how the gospel writer's arrangement of the sending of the twelve disciples in chapter ten points to the situation of the Matthean community. Overman notes that Matthew introduces this account with Jesus' plea concerning the need for more "laborers" who are willing to minister to the people in the cities and towns (9:35–38). Chapter ten provides a set of instructions and a description of the mission that awaits them. Like the original twelve, these laborers will engage in proclamation, healing, exorcism, and raising the dead (10:7–8). They will wander from village to town, carrying no provisions with them and giving their services without expectation of payment aside from food (10:9–11). They are told how to deal with persecution from Israelite community leaders and Roman officials (10:17–19) as well as how to deal with conflict with members of their own families (10:21, 35–37). These itinerant envoys of Jesus are referred to as "prophets," "righteous ones," and "little ones" (10:40–42),[89] and appear to be similar to the apostle-prophets referred to in the *Didache.*

These "missionaries," as Overman calls them, are to be welcomed and assisted "in the name of a disciple" (10:42), suggesting that "the disciples or their successors" in authority in Matthew's community have sent them out or commissioned them. There appears to be a greater demand for such prophets than there are individuals willing and able to undertake such ministries. Overman argues, moreover, that the commissioning of such "laborers" is no longer the central focus of the Matthean community.[90]

In Matthew's presentation, then, prophets are associated with wandering ministries involving proclamation, exorcism, healing, and other deeds of power. On the one hand, there are few home-grown prophets, and those who do arise from within the community are sent out. As commissioned disciples they are, therefore, subordinate to the "disciples" or their representatives in Matthew's Messianic Jesus group. These prophets do not remain in the community to mediate divine goods and services to its members; they go elsewhere. However, prophets from outside the Matthean circle may seek a reception in this community. These

---

[88] Aune, *Prophecy in Early Christianity*, 223–24; Robert H. Smith, "Matthew's Message for Insiders: Charisma and Commandments in a First-Century Community," *Interpretation* 46, no. 3 (1992): 229–39.

[89] Overman, *Matthew's Gospel and Formative Judaism*, 121.

[90] Ibid. See also Jefford, *The Sayings of Jesus*, 122–23.

strangers are viewed with suspicion. Their prophetic gifts and wonder working power do not automatically legitimate them in the eyes of the gospel writer. Adherence to Matthean standards of conduct must accompany the ability to mediate between God and humanity. In this way itinerant prophets are subordinated to the authority of local community leaders who are the articulators and arbiters of Torah-according-to-Jesus. Clearly for Matthew, both groups of prophets—those sent out by the community as well as those seeking admission into it—are peripheral figures. Matthew's gospel does not contain provisions such as we find in the *Didache* for setting up a tested and certified prophet as the community's high priest. There is little room, therefore, for prophets to achieve leadership positions within the community.

The Gospel of Matthew reflects the situation of a community that has moved away from the leadership of prophets and toward scribal leadership, a situation reflected in Jesus' promise to send "prophets, sages, and *scribes*" (23:34; see 13:52 and Luke 11:49). Jesus' final commandment to "disciple" and teach all nations (Matt 28:19–20) overshadows the earlier prophetic commission. This emphasis does not mean, however, that Matthew is uninterested in prophetic or other revelatory phenomena. The gospel begins with a narrative containing three dream-vision experiences that are crucial for ensuring the survival of the infant Jesus. Each step of Jesus' life is explicitly identified as fulfilling oracles spoken by the ancient prophets of Israel. Peter, Matthew's ideal leader, is invested with scribal authority *because he is the recipient of a revelation.* In response to Peter's confession that Jesus is the Messiah, the son of the living God (16:16), Jesus replies, "Blessed are you, Simon son of Jonah! For flesh and blood has not revealed this to you, but my Father in heaven" (16:17). Consequently, Jesus gives Simon a new name, the keys of the kingdom, and the authority to bind and loose (16:18–20). The authority to bind and loose could refer to authoritative teaching (28:20), forgiveness of sin (26:28), exorcisms (12:29), or excommunication (18:17–18). Matthew's Peter is no prophet, yet divine revelation remains a necessary qualification for legitimate scribal leadership among Matthew's Messianic Jesus groups. This qualification may be symptomatic of a gradual transition from one form of leadership to another, or it may simply point to Matthew's social location in a time and place where some evidence of divine favor or sanction was a necessary aspect of all legitimate authority.

Matthew shares with the *Didache* a concern for distinguishing authentic prophets from false ones and for subordinating them to the judgment of local community leaders. Both see proficiency in ASC experiences as an insufficient criterion for leadership, Matthew even more so than the *Didache.* Both of these texts emerge from Israelite Messianic Jesus groups that are concerned about distinguishing themselves from other Israelite groups and are oriented toward recruiting non-Israelites into their midst. It might be tempting at this point to conclude that Israelite based Messianic Jesus groups were less open to prophetic activity and viewed ASCs as more problematic than the non-Israelite Resurrected Jesus groups established by Paul and addressed by Luke. To do so would necessitate over generalizing about Messianic Jesus groups. The picture is much more complicated, as will be demonstrated by the following explorations of the Johannine literature and the *Gospel of Thomas.*

The Gospel of John and 1 John

The Gospel and Epistles of John reflect the perspective of a sectarian[91] or anti-society Messianic Jesus group[92] that originated in Palestine but had relocated elsewhere by the time of writing. While Ephesus in Asia Minor is the site proposed by tradition, Syria or Egypt, in particular Alexandria, are also possible. Although some scholars posit a traumatic separation from the synagogue as the basis for the Johannine community's anti-societal stance,[93] the evidence is inconclusive.[94] Relocation following the Jewish War (66–73 C.E.) into an area where the group was unwelcome or only partly integrated into the established society is also possible. This relocation would also account quite adequately for the development of the Gospel's distinctive vocabulary that has been described as "immigrant" Greek and "anti-language."[95]

John's narrative of Jesus differs markedly from the stories that the other New Testament evangelists tell. Jesus' ministry transpires over a three-year time span, including several trips between Galilee and Jerusalem. Jesus performs no exorcisms,

---

[91] David Rensberger, "Sectarianism and Theological Interpretation in John," in *What is John? Volume II, Literary and Social Readings of the Fourth Gospel* (ed. Fernando F. Segovia; SBLSymS; Atlanta: Scholars Press, 1998), 139–56; Wayne A. Meeks, "The Man from Heaven in Johannine Sectarianism," *JBL* 91 (1972): 44–72.

[92] Bruce J. Malina and Richard L. Rohrbaugh, *Social-Science Commentary on the Gospel of John* (Minneapolis: Fortress, 1998).

[93] Rensberger, "Sectarianism and Theological Interpretation in John," 139.

[94] Adele Reinhartz, "The Johannine Community and its Jewish Neighbors: A Reappraisal," in *What is John? Volume II, Literary and Social Readings of the Fourth Gospel* (ed. Fernando F. Segovia; SBLSymS; Atlanta: Scholars Press, 1998), 112.

[95] Sharon H. Ringe, *Wisdom's Friends: Community and Christology in the Fourth Gospel* (Louisville, Ky.: Westminster John Knox, 1999), 12; Malina and Rohrbaugh, *Social-Science Commentary on the Gospel of John,* 9.

although he does perform seven "signs."[96] Jesus tells no parables about the forth-coming reign of God but does engage in long discourses that focus on his own identity. There is no sending of the twelve in Jesus' name to heal and to proclaim God's reign. The Johannine Jesus does not promise that he or Wisdom will send prophets, apostles, sages, scribes, or other leaders to the community; he does not warn anyone about false prophets. Instead, he promises to remain with them in the form of the Paraclete, who is the Spirit of Truth or the Holy Spirit (14:16–17, 26).

In the Gospel of John, Jesus is identified as a prophet more frequently than in the Synoptics. The Samaritan woman at the well concludes that Jesus is a prophet because of his perceptive insight about her marital situation (4:19). The five thousand whom Jesus feeds declare, "This indeed is the prophet who is to come" (6:14). The blind man whose sight Jesus restores is quite sure that his healer is a prophet (9:17). For these persons Jesus is a prophet because he is able to mediate to them knowledge, food, and sight. Those who witnessed Jesus' proclamation during the festival of booths also concluded that he "is really the prophet" (7:40). Why? The text (7:37–38) is very brief and sparse on details:

> On the last day of the festival, the great day, while Jesus was standing there, he cried out, "Let anyone who is thirsty come to me, and let the one who believes in me drink. As the scripture has said, 'Out of the believer's heart shall flow rivers of living water.'"

The most obvious answer is that Jesus displayed recognizable signs of spirit-possession, such as crying out in a loud voice suddenly without warning.[97]

The Fourth Gospel characteristically peppers Jesus' monologues with sayings that bear a remarkable resemblance to ancient oracles of self-commendation. Prophets uttering such oracles frequently began with the formula "I am" or "I came" and followed it with a claim to divine status or to be a vehicle for divinity, which could be used to introduce expository or dialogical oracles.[98] The Johan-nine Jesus uses the "I am" formula to identify himself as the bread of life (6:35, 48, 51); the light of the world (8:12; 9:5); the gate for the sheep (10:7, 9); the way, truth, and life (14:6–7); and the true vine (15:1). Through these terms Jesus claims to be (or at least speak for) divine Wisdom herself.[99] Jesus' prophetic cry,

---

[96] These include changing water in to wine (2:1–12), healing the official's son at Capernaum (4:46–54), healing the paralyzed man at Bethesda (5:1–18), feeding the five thousand (6:1–15), walking on water (6:16–21), restoring a blind man's sight (9:1–7), and raising Lazarus (11:1–44).

[97] See above, n. 36.

[98] Aune, *Prophecy in Early Christianity*, 40, 70–71.

[99] Ringe, *Wisdom's Friends*, 61.

"Let anyone who is thirsty come to me" (7:37), further identifies him as one who speaks as or for divine Wisdom.[100] Jesus' declarations that "I am from above" (8:23) and "I came from the Father" (16:28) also resemble self-commendation oracles revealing Jesus' status as God's intermediary on earth. That these speeches are unique to this gospel suggests that such prophetic utterances were important features of communal life for members of John's Messianic Jesus group.

Although it is common among scholars to regard the Johannine discourses as the work of later prophets, Davies argues that some of these peculiar sayings may, in fact, be utterances of the prophet Jesus.[101] Davies' case rests on two points. First, it has been demonstrated that much of the Johannine discourse material derived from oral or written sources first produced in a Semitic language. "The likelihood that much of the Johannine sayings material was early and Aramaic in origin" increases the probability that it may have originated directly from Jesus.[102] More important, however, is Davies' realization that Jesus was a spirit-possessed prophet and healer, that is, one who sometimes spoke and acted while in altered states of consciousness. For him this realization means that the Spirit that possessed and spoke through Jesus actually made statements that hearers attributed to Jesus. It is this Spirit of God, that identified itself as "the Son," who asserted, "I have come down from heaven, not to do my own will, but the will of him who sent me" (6:38) and other similar claims (e.g., 8:23; 9:5; 10:30; 14:6–7; 16:28). The evangelist later attributed these oracular statements directly to Jesus rather than the divine one who spoke through him, making a move similar to Matthew's treatment of the Q oracle about God's Wisdom sending prophets (Matt 23:34; Luke 11:49).[103]

The centrality of prophecy in the Johannine community is affirmed by the Gospel's emphasis on the Spirit. John the Baptist testifies that he saw (in an ASC) the Holy Spirit descend from heaven and remain on Jesus (1:32). A heavenly voice informed him that Jesus was the one who would baptize "with the Holy Spirit" (1:33). Later Jesus describes himself as one whom God has sent, speaking the very words of God because he has been given the "Spirit without measure" (3:34). This Johannine Jesus insists that seeing and/or entering the reign of God depends on being born from above, from water and the Spirit (3:3, 5). True worshippers must worship God "in spirit" because God is in fact Spirit (4:23–24). It is the Spirit who gives life, but the words of Jesus are the source of both (6:63). Jesus is

---

[100] Ringe, *Wisdom's Friends*, 61. See also Catherine Cory, "Wisdom's Rescue: A New Reading of the Tabernacles Discourse (John 7:1–8:59)," *JBL* 116 (1997): 95–116.

[101] Davies, *Jesus the Healer*, 152, 197.

[102] Ibid., 160–61.

[103] Ibid., 151–69, 195.

the one who promises to send the Holy Spirit, the Paraclete (14:26), which his disciples receive from him in a resurrection appearance, that is, during an ASC experience (20:19–23). Only then are they empowered to believe and understand the events of Jesus' ministry (2:22; 7:39; 12:16). Indeed, it seems as if a primary purpose of Jesus' ministry in the Fourth Gospel was the giving of the Spirit.[104] Since Spirit-inspired or induced speech and knowledge are central to John's story of Jesus, it is likely that the ASC experiences that are the basis of both were also central to the life of the Messianic Jesus group for whom the Fourth Gospel was written. Davies has even argued that the Johannine discourses were actually designed to motivate and facilitate entry into trance, a form of ASC.[105]

Although ASCs and prophetic activity were central to the life of the Johannine community, the gospel intimates that they were also a source of conflict. On one hand, they led to a sense of superiority over non-Johannine followers of Jesus that may be discernible in the Gospel's depiction of the "disciple whom Jesus loved" and Peter. Wherever these two characters appear in each other's company, the beloved disciple always comes out on top. At the Last Supper (13:1–38), the beloved disciple is portrayed as enjoying a direct, intimate relationship with Jesus that parallels that of Jesus with the Father. Just as Jesus resides close to the bosom of the Father (1:18), so the beloved disciple reclines against the bosom of Jesus (13:23). Peter must appeal to the beloved disciple to relay questions and answers to and from Jesus. Later, the beloved disciple facilitates Peter's entry into the high priest's courtyard following Jesus' arrest (John 18:15–18). In contrast to Peter, who denies Jesus and disappears, he continues to follow Jesus to the place of crucifixion. Jesus confers on the beloved disciple special status by placing in his hands the welfare of his mother (19:25–27). The beloved disciple reaches the empty tomb first and rightly concludes that Jesus has been resurrected, while Peter is left puzzled by the evidence (20:1–10). In a post-resurrection ASC, the beloved disciple recognizes Jesus on the beach by the Sea of Galilee (21:7). Even Peter's elevation to the role and status of shepherd in an ASC encounter with Jesus is legitimated by the testimony of the beloved disciple (21:15–24).

The centrality of prophetic activity also led to intramural conflict within the Johannine Messianic Jesus group itself. Woll's analysis of the first farewell dis-

---

[104] Urban C. von Wahlde, *The Johannine Commandments: 1 John and the Struggle for the Johannine Tradition* (New York: Paulist, 1990), 117; Jerome H. Neyrey, *An Ideology of Revolt: John's Christology in Social-Science Perspective* (Philadelphia: Fortress, 1988), 182–215; Bruce J. Malina, "The Maverick Christian Group—The Evidence of Sociolinguistics," *BTB* 24, no. 4 (1994): 173.

[105] Davies, *Jesus the Healer*, 200; see also Malina and Rohrbaugh, *The Social Science Commentary on the Gospel of John*, introduction.

course shows that two primary issues are in question: the disciples' access to heaven (13:31–14:11) and the conditions of their agency on earth (14:12–26).[106] He asserts that in the first part of the discourse (13:31–14:11) the evangelist makes it quite clear that Jesus goes first to heaven because he is *from* there; and so, he belongs there. The ascent of the disciples, on the other hand, depends upon Jesus' prior return and preparation of a place for them in heaven. Jesus' place in heaven is original, while that of the disciples is secondary, derived from and dependent upon Jesus.[107] This point is made emphatically in 14:4–11, where Jesus declares that he is the exclusive agent of access to God. Woll argues that this passage reflects a conflict within the Johannine community about the status and authority of its prophetic leaders. The gospel writer understands these figures to be subordinate to Jesus, while some of them at least see themselves as equal to Jesus.[108]

The second half of the discourse (14:12–26) presents the disciples as successors to the powers and place of Jesus on earth, whose authority derives from the indwelling Paraclete or Spirit of truth.[109] These disciples are reminded that the Spirit is given at Jesus' request to those who love Jesus and keep his commandments (14:15–16). In this way the evangelist identifies the Spirit with the figure of Jesus, thus turning spirit possession into evidence for the subordination and dependence of the disciples upon Jesus. This dependence is reinforced by the gospel writer's insistence that the Paraclete primarily functions to remind them of the words of Jesus (14:26). Woll sees here an effort by the gospel writer to effectively limit the scope of Spirit-inspired prophecy by subordinating it to the Jesus of history, while legitimating the beloved disciple's interpretation of Jesus' words by implying that it is the product of the Paraclete's role of remembrance and recollection.[110]

Von Wahlde reaches a similar conclusion after examining the Paraclete sayings sprinkled throughout the farewell discourse. In the first of these (14:16–17), Jesus asserts that he will ask the Father to send *another* Paraclete to the soon-to-be-bereft disciples. This Spirit of truth will replace its prototype, Jesus. In the second Paraclete passage (14:26), Jesus explains that the Paraclete or Holy Spirit sent by God in Jesus' name will function to remind the disciples of all that Jesus has said. In the third saying (15:26–27) it is Jesus who will send the Paraclete or Spirit of

---

[106] Woll, *Johannine Christianity in Conflict,* 33.
[107] Ibid., 38.
[108] Ibid., 66.
[109] Ibid., 89–91.
[110] Ibid., 96–105.

truth to testify on his behalf. The fourth saying (16:7–11) describes the Paraclete convincing the world about sin, justice, and judgement. In the final Paraclete saying (16:12–15) we discover that the Spirit of truth speaks only what it has heard; in particular it glorifies Jesus, who possesses all that the Father has. Von Wahlde concludes that in these texts the gospel writer firmly anchors the activity of the Spirit in the words of Jesus.[111] Why? To answer this question we need to read 1 John:

> Beloved, do not believe every spirit, but test the spirits to see whether they are from God; for many false prophets have gone out into the world. By this you know the Spirit of God: every spirit that confesses that Jesus Christ has come in the flesh is from God, and every spirit that does not confess Jesus (or that dissolves or does away with Jesus) is not from God . . . this is the spirit of the antichrist. (1 John 4:1–3)

Von Wahlde has reconstructed the prophetic conflict reflected in 1 John by classifying and analyzing the various statements that the author makes about and against his opponents.[112] He identifies three types of statements: (1) claims to special status; (2) convictions about the identity, meaning, and purpose of Jesus; and (3) ethical concerns. These statements point to the major issues of contention between the author and his opponents.

With regard to their special status, both the author and his opponents claim to have "fellowship with the Father" (1:3, 6), "know God" (2:3–4, 13–14; 4:6–8a), "abide" in God (2:5–6, 24, 28; 3:6, 24; 4:12, 13, 15, 16), and "love God" (4:20). Both profess to be "in the light" (1:7; 2:9–10) and to be "from the truth" or to "know the truth" (3:19; 2:21–22). Each group lays claim to an "anointing" by the Spirit (2:20; 3:24; 4:1–6, 13) as well as to possession of the Spirit (4:1, 13; 5:6). Both groups insist that they are God's children (3:1–3, 10; 4:7; 5:1) who have "passed from death to life" (3:14).[113] These claims are the language of religious experience and point to the source of the assertions of status.[114] Both the author and his opponents are claiming to be directly and immediately linked with the divine realm. Both groups regard themselves as particularly favored and gifted by God. What emerges is a picture of a community in which two groups appear to be

---

[111] Von Wahlde, *The Johannine Commandments*, 121–22.

[112] See also Judith M. Lieu, *The Theology of the Johannine Epistles* (Cambridge: Cambridge University Press, 1991), 3, 16; Kenneth Grayston, *The Johannine Epistles* (Grand Rapids: Eerdmans, 1984), 4, 37–38; Raymond E. Brown, *The Epistles of John: Translated with Introduction, Notes, and Commentary* (AB 29–29A; Garden City, N.Y.: Doubleday, 1982), 87.

[113] Von Wahlde, *The Johannine Commandments*, 109–10.

[114] Lieu, *Theology of the Johannine Epistles*, 31.

claiming the same inspired prophetic status along with the authority derived from that status.

The three claims to status that seem unique to the author and his group reflect an important difference between these rivals. They claim to have communion with God's Son, Jesus Christ (1:3), to possess the Son along with the Father (2:23; 5:11–13), and to abide in the Son and the Father (2:24, 28). For the writer of I John, Jesus appears to be a divine being alongside God/Father and Spirit. The author's opponents appear to make no such assertions.[115] An analysis of the christological statements shows that the author's prophetic rivals do not believe that Jesus is the Christ or the Son of God who came in the flesh (2:22; 2:23–24; 4:2; 2 John 7). They do not believe in Jesus' name (3:23) or his ability to atone for sins (1:7–10), and are accused of ignoring Jesus' teaching that they have had from the beginning (1:1–3; 2:7, 24; 3:6, 11; 2 John 8, 9). The opponents are also charged with a failure to keep the commandments (2:4), especially the command-ment to love one another (3:17–18). Their sinful actions (3:4, 8, 10) belie their boasts of being free from sin (1:8, 10).

As von Wahlde himself states, the christological and ethical statements function primarily as "tests" to determine which claims to status are valid and authentic. This testing suggests that we are not dealing with a theological crisis as von Wahlde as-serts, but with a social conflict that has theological overtones and implications. The conflict is concerned less with *what* the correct content of the Johannine tradition is than it is about *who* its authentic representatives and interpreters are. In this situation of prophetic rivalry, the Johannine writer insists that the content of prophetic speech must be tested for conformity to a particular christological confession and to a particular code of behavior defined as "love." First and foremost concerned to re-fute his opponents' claims to prophetic status, the writer of I John tries to convince his readers that his rivals are liars, deceivers, and antichrists.[116]

Among members of the Johannine Jesus group, then, prophetic activity was quite central. It formed the core of their understanding of Jesus and served as the basis for the content of the gospel that they produced and used. Prophetic figures like the beloved disciple enjoyed much higher status than characters like Peter. This is a Messianic Jesus group that is quite different from communities of the *Didache* or Matthew, with their emphasis on Torah observance and preference for household and/or scribal leadership. ASC experiences, perhaps not unlike the

---

[115] Von Wahlde, *The Johannine Commandments*, 109–10.

[116] "Antichrist" is the term coined by the writer of I John to label those people who deny that Jesus is uniquely the Christ, and who, perhaps, claim to stand in his place (see von Wahlde, *The Johannine Commandments*, 160, 186 n. 6, 191 n. 43).

glossolalia and prophecy experienced in the Pauline *ekklesiai*, were core features of the Johannine assemblies. As we saw in the Pauline groups, ASC activity became a source of conflict over status. In the Johannine case those honor contests were intimately linked to increasingly divergent understandings of the role and status of Jesus in relation to God and to the disciples. That conflict resulted in the breaking away of part of the community and may have been one of the factors that eventually paved the way for the acceptance of a pastoral leadership model associated with Peter and validated by Johannine prophets. But what about those who left or were pushed out of the Johannine Messianic Jesus groups? Far too many times in Christian history the voices of dissenters have been lost. In this instance, however, a serendipitous find in the sands of Egypt enables us to get a sense of what the opponents of the Johannine authors were about.[117] To that text we will turn now.

Gospel of Thomas

The *Gospel of Thomas* is perhaps the most famous document recovered from the desert sands near Nag Hammadi, Egypt in 1945, meriting mention in the popular film "Stigmata." It was known and quoted by a number of church fathers, most notably Hippolytus (170–239 C.E.) who associated it with deviant and unacceptable teaching. The extant fourth-century manuscript is a Coptic translation of an earlier Greek version, only fragments of which have been preserved. The *Gospel of Thomas* was probably compiled toward the end of the first or the beginning of the second century C.E. in Syria.[118]

Unlike the New Testament Gospels, the *Gospel of Thomas* contains no narrative; it does not tell the story of Jesus' life and deeds but simply records "the secret sayings that the living Jesus spoke" (*Gos. Thom.* Incipit). The hearer is challenged to uncover the interpretation of the Gospel's secret sayings in order to achieve immortality (Saying 1). The text seems to emerge from and reflect the concerns of a scattered and loosely structured movement of ascetics who live solitary lives marked by detachment from the world as crystallized in the command to "be

---

[117] For a more detailed discussion of the John-Thomas conflict see Elaine H. Pagels, *Beyond Belief: The Secret Gospel of Thomas* (New York: Random House, 2003), especially chapter 2.

[118] Richard Valantasis, *The Gospel of Thomas* (New York: Routledge, 1997), 13–20; John S. Kloppenborg, et al., eds., *The Q Thomas Reader* (Sonoma, Calif.: Polebridge, 1990) 391–92; Stephen J. Patterson, *The Gospel of Thomas and Jesus* (Sonoma, Calif.: Polebridge, 1993), 113–20; Stevan L. Davies, *The Gospel of Thomas and Christian Wisdom* (New York: Seabury, 1983) 3, 16–21; James M. Robinson, Paul Hoffmann, and John S. Kloppenborg, eds., *The Critical Edition of Q* (Minneapolis: Fortress, 2000), lxxvii–lxxviii.

passersby" (Saying 42), or even homeless itinerancy (Saying 86).[119] Having set aside family ties, property, conventional economic activities, and even traditional religious disciplines, such as fasting, prayer, almsgiving, dietary and purity obser-vances, they are instructed to walk about the countryside, healing and eating what-ever is served to them (Saying 13).[120] Amazing powers over the physical world (Saying 106), an intimate relationship with Jesus (Sayings 75, 108), and immor-tality (Sayings 1, 11, 18, 19, 111) follow. Here we will concentrate on those sayings most directly related to the topic of prophets and ASC experiences.

In Saying 13, Jesus asks his disciples to compare him to someone and to de-scribe who he is like. Simon Peter replies that Jesus is like a "righteous angel" or a "righteous messenger," while Matthew identifies him as a "wise philosopher" or a "wise lover of wisdom." Thomas tells his "master" that he is incapable of comparing Jesus. This answer is the correct one, as Jesus' response indicates. He tells Thomas:

> I am not your master. Because you have drunk, you have become intoxicated from the bubbling spring which I have measured out. (Saying 13.5)

Affirming Thomas' position, Jesus declares that Thomas is not subordinate to him, apparently since Thomas has "drunk" and "become intoxicated." These last two terms may serve as metaphors for some sort of ecstatic or visionary experi-ence. This phenomenon of "intoxicated" access to divine knowledge resembles the "natural divination" in the ancient world that arose from the deity's direct pos-session of the diviner.[121] It appears to be the equivalent of ASCs experienced among other Jesus groups.[122]

One aspect of the Thomasine Jesus group suggests that they may have been the forerunners of, if not the actual, prophetic rivals of the Johannine writers. Thomas' "intoxication" means that Jesus is no longer his master (Saying 13.5). He is not subordinate to Jesus, but in fact claims to enjoy both parity and identity with Jesus. This is made explicit in Saying 108, where Jesus says,

> He who will drink from my mouth will become like me. I myself shall become he, and the things that are hidden will be revealed to him.

---

[119] Valantasis, *Gospel of Thomas*, 11; Patterson, *Gospel of Thomas and Jesus*, 128–31.

[120] Patterson, *Gospel of Thomas and Jesus*, 126–48.

[121] Aune, *Prophecy in Early Christianity*, 23.

[122] Stevan L. Davies, "The Christology and Protology of the *Gospel of Thomas*," *JBL* 111 (1992): 675, asserts on the basis of a parallel concept in John 7:37b–39a that the motif of drinking from Jesus refers to the reception of the Holy Spirit and that Thomas receives both the Spirit and words of wisdom from Jesus.

The Thomasine follower of Jesus becomes an agent of revelation, equivalent to or identified with Jesus.[123] Even the name of the Gospel's hero, Didymos Judas Thomas, points to this sense of identity when we realize that he is Jesus' twin not because of birth[124] but because in an altered state of consciousness, he is one with or perhaps possessed by Jesus.

In the *Gospel of Thomas*, the character of Thomas epitomizes that community's ideal disciple, an "intoxicated," that is, Jesus-possessed, mediator of divine secrets, a prophetic or shamanic figure. Jesus and Paul were similar figures themselves. Prophetic activity caused conflict in the congregations established by Paul, since some members saw ASC experience as a basis for achieving honor and status. Spirit-inspired prophets and apostles were central figures in the development of the early church according to the writer of Luke-Acts. In the *Didache* and in Matthew, however, itinerant prophets were regarded with suspicion and hostility, and are subordinated to the local community leaders. While the *Didache* allowed for the possibility of a central leadership position for a certified prophet, in the Matthean communities there appears to be a preference for scribal leadership. Within the Johannine community prophecy was central in legitimating the community's anti-societal stance, but ultimately led to a conflict that necessitated the testing of prophetic figures, and eventually to their replacement by pastoral leaders.

It is quite likely, therefore, that in the *Gospel of Thomas* we meet the very sort of prophetic figures whose influence may have been welcomed warmly, cautiously, or not all in many of the early churches. Even some who welcomed prophetic activity were concerned to control the phenomenon. References to itinerant prophets as "ravenous wolves" (Matt 7:15), "liars" (I John 2:4, 22), "antichrists" (I John 2:18, 22), and "children of the devil" (I John 3:10) point to the level of animosity they could arouse. Saying 13 explicitly addresses the hostility and even potential violence that a prophet might meet. Thomas refuses to share what Jesus has revealed to him because Peter and Matthew would respond by stoning him, and in doing so, would destroy themselves (*Gos. Thom.* 13.6–8). Thomas, thus, acknowledges that its message may be offensive, perhaps even blasphemous, in the ears of other followers of Jesus, even rousing them to violent actions.[125] Yet, it is claimed that the power of these words is such that any attempt to punish or harm the speaker will turn out to be self-destructive.

---

[123] Patterson, *Gospel of Thomas and Jesus*, 169–70; Davies, "Christology and Protology," 675–76.

[124] See Kloppenborg et al., *Q Thomas Reader*, 90–91, on various theories about the identity of Thomas as Jesus' twin brother.

[125] Davies, "Christology and Protology," 676.

The text reflects a context in which local church leaders are deciding to grant or deny hospitality to itinerant prophets on the basis of testing and examining the itinerant's conformity to social customs (e.g., *Did.* 11:1–12; Matt 7:15–21) and/or to specific statements of belief (2 John 7–10). In this situation Thomasine followers of Jesus are advised to keep their mouths shut in order to protect themselves from the potential violence of their hosts. Thomas' refusal to share his special knowledge is not just a strategy of self-defense; it is also intended to protect the uncomprehending disciples. In the interests of securing the safety of both the itinerant prophet and his or her potential audience, that special knowledge must be kept secret. Jesus reveals these "mysteries" only to those who are worthy (Sayings 62, 93). Those who guard and mediate the interpretation of the secret sayings of Jesus hold the key to life and death (Saying 1). By implying that the teachings of the local church leaders are in some way deficient, this secrecy also functions to undergird the authority of these prophets and to enhance the appeal of their message.[126]

The Jesus-possessed itinerants that we meet in the *Gospel of Thomas* are clearly peripheral figures who, nevertheless, seek to claim a status equal to that of Jesus as the keepers and revealers of divine secrets. As we have seen, this seems to be precisely the phenomenon that is opposed in the Johannine literature. In the first farewell discourse, the Johannine evangelist seeks to counter the idea that the Spirit-possessed disciples are equal to Jesus by reminding them that Jesus alone is originally from heaven and that the Spirit is given to those who love Jesus (John 13:31–14:26). Similarly, the writer of 1 John castigates his prophetic rivals for refusing to acknowledge Jesus' uniqueness and claiming for themselves the same status that he attributes to Jesus.[127] In this situation of prophetic rivalry, the Johannine author encourages his readers to examine the content of prophetic speech in order to determine the nature of its source. Only those spirits that confess Jesus Christ has come in the flesh are legitimate (1 John 4:1–3). We see here the beginnings of a concern for orthodoxy. In contrast, the Didachist (11.1–12) explicitly forbids such an evaluation, preferring like Matthew the option of assessing the prophet's conduct and way of life (Matt 7:15–23), thus emphasizing orthopraxy. Paul's criteria of evaluating ASC experiences in terms of their community-building effects falls closer to the criteria provided by the *Didache* and Matthew. With the exception of Luke-Acts, then, all of the texts that we have

---

[126] Patterson, *Gospel of Thomas and Jesus*, 207.

[127] Von Wahlde, *The Johannine Commandments*, 145; Grayston, *The Johannine Epistles*, 18–26; See also John Painter, "The Farewell Discourse and the History of Johannine Christianity," *NTS* 27 (1981): 525–43, and idem, "The 'Opponents' in 1 John," *NTS* 32 (1986): 48–71.

examined suggest some criteria for judging the authenticity of those who claim divine inspiration for their messages. Our final evidence for prophets and ASC experiences comes from the letters of Ignatius of Antioch, who in many ways represents a synthesis of Pauline and Johannine concerns.

Ignatius

Ignatius, bishop of Antioch and martyr for Christ, is generally recognized as a prophetic figure.[128] This identification is based primarily on Ign. *Phld.* 7.1–2, where the bishop describes how the Spirit made him cry out with the "voice of God." The Holy Spirit, and not Ignatius, proclaimed, "Do nothing without the bishop." Although some Philadelphian church members rejected this prophecy as staged, arising from advance information supplied to the Syrian bishop, it does, in fact, appear to conform to the expectations of prophetic speech as practiced in the ancient world.[129]

This letter is not the only evidence of Ignatius' prophetic activity. He promises to write more to the Ephesians about the divine plan if the Lord reveals anything to him (Ign. *Eph.* 20.1–2). His explication of the significance of the star that shone at Jesus' birth (Ign. *Eph.* 19.2–3) may be an example of the sort of thing he had in mind.[130] The Syrian bishop asserts that he knows "heavenly things" that the Trallian Jesus-followers are not mature enough to receive (Ign. *Trall.* 4.1–5.2). He assures the Roman church that they can obey his written instructions concerning his martyrdom because there is "living and speaking water" in him, that is, a prophetic spirit, calling him to come to the Father (Ign. *Rom.* 7.2).[131] I would like to argue that Ignatius' prophecies, revelations, and knowledge of heavenly things are indicators of ASCs. They mark him as a person particularly favored by God and, therefore, able to act as an intermediary between God/Christ and the churches.

Ignatius' prophetic role is closely connected to his situation as a martyr-elect. He asserts that "living and speaking water," that is, the Spirit, in him is calling him

---

[128] B. H. Streeter, *The Primitive Church Studied with Reference to the Origins of the Christian Ministry* (London: Macmillan and Co., 1930), 152; Christine Trevett, "Prophecy and Anti-Episcopal Activity: A Third Error Combated by Ignatius?" *Journal of Ecclesiastical History* 34 (1983): 5; Maier, *Social Setting of the Ministry,* 162.

[129] Aune, *Prophecy in Early Christianity,* 290–93; Trevett, "Prophecy and Anti-Episcopal Activity," 6; Maier, *Social Setting of the Ministry,* 162.

[130] Maier, *Social Setting of the Ministry,* 161; Schoedel, *Ignatius of Antioch,* 87.

[131] Maier, *Social Setting of the Ministry,* 162; Bruce J. Malina, "The Social World Implied in the Letters of the Christian Bishop-Martyr (named Ignatius of Antioch)," SBLSP (1978), 77.

to die a martyr's death in Rome (Ign. *Rom.* 7.2). Although this connection may at first appear somewhat peculiar, it makes sense when we examine what it means to be a martyr-elect. As Malina demonstrates, Ignatius was a liminal person, suspended between two socially defined states. The Roman judicial process had tried, convicted, and labeled him a deviant so that he was on the way to permanent removal from normal society. In the meantime, the Syrian bishop was bound and chained, signs of his liminal status as a person condemned but not yet executed. For Ignatius and many, if not most, of the Christ-followers he encountered in transit to Rome, his condemnation and imprisonment were not part of a process of social degradation but of status elevation.[132] His death will not signify his final destruction; rather it will mark his attainment of God (Ign. *Eph.* 12.2) and his entry into a post-mortem existence in the presence of the divine Father.[133] His execution will complete and perfect his discipleship (Ign. *Eph.* 3.1; 1.2); it will affirm and sanctify his career and confirm that he is a follower of the great apostles (Ign. *Eph.* 12.2).

Ignatius' liminal status places him not only outside the boundaries of normal society but also to a certain extent beyond the boundaries of his Jesus-group subculture. In the early church's interpretation of the situation, the martyr-designate is no longer wholly of this world; hence its norms and conventions are no longer binding and may even be scrutinized critically.[134] Ignatius evokes precisely this aspect of the liminal position to justify his otherwise presumptuous instructions to communities in which he has no personal role or status. Moreover, the prisoner for Christ awaiting execution is a person poised on the threshold of the heavenly and spiritual realm, and thus, is especially open to communications from that invisible world.[135] Not only does a prophetic call justify the Syrian bishop's martyrdom, his liminal status enhances his prophetic abilities. Prophet and martyr are mutually reinforcing roles played by the Syrian bishop.[136] Together they empower him to address, instruct, and criticize the members of churches to which he is an outsider.

Ignatius uses his status as a martyr and a prophet to advocate for greater obedience to and solidarity with church leaders. As we can see from the opening lines of

---

[132] Malina, "The Social World," 78–80.

[133] Corwin, *St. Ignatius and Christianity in Antioch*, 37.

[134] Rosemary Rader, *Breaking Boundaries: Male/Female Friendship in Early Christian Communities* (New York: Paulist, 1983), 44–61; Malina, "The Social World," 80.

[135] Malina, "The Social World," 78; Rader, *Breaking Boundaries*, 53, 571.

[136] G. W. H. Lampe, "Martyrdom and Inspiration," in *Suffering and Martyrdom in the New Testament: Studies presented to G. M. Styler by the Cambridge New Testament Seminar* (ed. William Horbury and Brian McNeil; Cambridge: Cambridge University Press, 1981), 119, 122–29.

his letter to the Jesus group in Philadelphia, he believes that these are divinely appointed leaders:

> Ignatius, also called Theophorus, to the church of God the Father and the Lord Jesus
> Christ which is in Philadelphia in Asia. . . . which I greet in the blood of Jesus Christ
> which is joy, eternal and constant, *especially if they are at one with the bishop and with the elders*
> *and deacons who are with him, who have been appointed in the purpose of Jesus Christ, whom according*
> *to his own will he has established in strength by his Holy Spirit.* (Ign. *Phld.* inscription; emphasis
> mine)

This quotation is the clearest statement in Ignatius' letters concerning the origins and basis of the tripartite form of leadership consisting of bishop, elders and
deacons. While Ignatius never tells us anything about the precise mechanism for
appointing elders and deacons, he does indicate how at least one bishop acquired
his office. Ignatius asserts that the unnamed bishop of Philadelphia "acquired his
ministry to the community not of himself, nor through human beings, not yet
with reference to empty conceit, but in the love of God the Father and of the Lord
Jesus Christ" (Ign. *Phld.* 1.1). He emphasizes the absence of human agency and the
partiality of the church's divine patrons. Ignatius' choice of words echoes Gal 1:1,
where Paul describes himself as an apostle, not from human beings nor through
humans, but through Jesus Christ and God the Father. Paul's apostolic calling was
based in a revelatory (ASC) experience. Is Ignatius suggesting that bishops were
also called through some sort of divinatory, prophetic, or visionary process?

The use of various forms of prophetic or revelatory mechanisms in the selection of church leaders is well attested in a number of early Jesus-group texts. Acts
records that Judas' replacement in the Jerusalem church was chosen by lot (Acts
1:21–26) and asserts that the elders of the Ephesian church were made bishops of
the church by the Holy Spirit (Acts 20:28). Peter is given the keys of authority because he receives a revelation concerning the true identity of Jesus (Matt
16:17–19). Thomas' preeminence results from an ecstatic experience in which the
hero is "intoxicated," that is, possessed by Jesus (*Gos. Thom.* 13). Among the
Johannine Christ-followers, Peter's pastoral guardianship of the church is bestowed in a resurrection appearance of Jesus (an ASC; John 21:15–19). The author of the Pastoral Epistles associates Timothy's leadership with prophecy and
the laying on of hands by the elders (1 Tim 4:14; 1:18).

Later writings also attest to the ideal of divine actions and judgment as determining episcopal election. Clement of Alexandria depicts John going about Asia
Minor appointing as bishops those who were drawn by lot from a pool of persons
indicated by the Spirit (*Quis div.* 42). Origen prefers that the choice of bishop be

made by a spiritual man to whom God's will has been revealed in answer to prayer (*Hom. Num.* 13.4). Eusebius recounts how a child's cry and a dove settling on the head of a church member were interpreted as omens and indicators of the divine will in electing bishops (*Hist. eccl.* 6.29).

Ignatius' letter to the Philadelphians begins with an unequivocal assertion that the Holy Spirit has appointed the bishop, presbyters, and deacons of this church. Their bishop, in particular, acquired his ministry through divine preferment and not through the efforts of humans (Ign. *Phld.* 1.1), pointing to a revelatory selection process. Ignatius personally testifies that this bishop's demeanor appropriately reflects that of his divine patron (Ign. *Phld.* 1.2). Commitment to God and to Christ, consequently, requires the acknowledgement of this bishop as the community's legitimate "shepherd" (Ign. *Phld.* 2.1).

The remainder of the letter is given over to a defense of Ignatius' position and actions while in Philadelphia, especially his own prophetic speech. Ignatius insists that the Spirit prompted him to cry out with the "voice of God," exhorting the Philadelphians to "give heed to the bishop and to the council of elders and to the deacons," and to "do nothing apart from the bishop" (Ign. *Phld.* 7.1–2). From this defense we can draw two conclusions. First, this Syrian bishop believes that Spirit-inspired speech is authoritative and thinks that his listeners should too.[137] Second, Ignatius explicitly seeks to reinforce the status and honor of church leaders, either because he perceives that reinforcement to be the Spirit's will or because he thinks that presenting it that way will persuade his listeners.

Ignatius' appeals to the Spirit as ultimately and definitively legitimating church leaders, especially bishops, are highly illustrative, pointing to the origins of this office in the Syrian environment from which Ignatius emerges. His appeals suggest that he comes from a Christ-confessing community or circle in which prophets speaking in the Spirit in the name of Jesus introduced this form of leadership.[138] From Ignatius' lack of appeal to commandments or tradition, we might infer that this role is a rather recent development. The Fourth Gospel provides an account of just such a situation. In John's final chapter, Peter acquires the role and status of shepherd over the community in a post-resurrection encounter with Jesus that is legitimated by a prophetic figure, the beloved disciple (John 21:15–19). Here Ignatius wishes to play a similar role.

---

[137] Trevett, "Prophecy and Anti-Episcopal Activity," 5–6.

[138] Cyril C. Richardson, "The Church in Ignatius of Antioch," *Journal of Religious History* 17 (1937): 436; A. J. Mason, "Conception of the Church in Early Times," in *Church, Ministry, and Organization in the Early Church Era* (ed. Everett Ferguson; Studies in Early Christianity; vol. 13; New York: Garland, 1993), 30.

Conclusions

Jesus and his earliest followers lived in a cultural milieu in which prophetic figures were needed to communicate with the spirit world. Jesus' contemporaries understood and believed that this communication took place in altered states of consciousness. It should not be a surprise, then, that the writings of post-Jesus groups are filled with references to various forms of ASCs. The following table sums up the results of my analysis.

Texts	Types of ASCs	Social Location of ASC practitioners	Functions of ASCs
Jesus	Visions, shamanic journey, prayer, possession	Jesus was peripheral to Israelite political religion.	ASCs affirm Jesus status as prophet, and are the source of his healing and teaching re: the kingdom of God.
Paul	Visions, shamanic journey, revelations, possession	Paul was a peripheral figure in the house churches, but ASC was a central component of their communal life.	ASCs affirm Paul's apostolic status and are the source of his peculiar eschatological teachings. In the house churches ASCs are a cause of rivalry.
Luke-Acts	Dreams, visions, revelations	ASC experiences are central.	ASC legitimates the lives and ministries of Jesus, Paul, and the other apostles. ASCs provide the impetus for innovation in missionary practice.
Didache	Speaking "in spirit"	Practitioners are potentially central to the group, but their behavior and practices must be tested against the teaching of the twelve apostles. Their functions can be carried out by bishops and deacons.	Approved practitioners serve as the community's high priests, living off the tithes of the community, performing liturgies, and improvising the eucharistic prayers.
Matthew	Dreams, visions, revelations	Prophets are marginal figures, coming from outside or being sent out. Their conduct must be tested vis-à-vis Jesus' Torah.	ASCs legitimate Jesus' life and ministry, the scribal status of Peter, and the community's teaching mission; but otherwise are viewed with suspicion.

Johannine Texts	Visions, spirit-possession	ASC experiences are central but highly problematic. Prophetic speech must be tested vis-à-vis christological confessions.	Prophetic speeches reveal the true identity of Jesus (i.e., new teaching about Jesus), and legitimate the status/ministry of the prophetic beloved disciple and the pastoral status Peter.
Thomas	Christ-intoxication (i.e., possession)	Practitioners are peripheral to churches. ASC experiences are central to their experience, but their content is "secret" and must be guarded for fear of hostility and violence.	ASC experience is the source of Thomas' superiority, and legitimates counter-cultural lifestyle in imitation of Jesus.
Ignatius	Revelations, spirit-possession	Ignatius is a peripheral figure to the churches he addresses, and as a liminal person en route to his execution.	ASCs provide the basis for new or deeper understandings of God's mysteries, and legitimate the emerging threefold ministry of bishop, elders, and deacons.

In all of the persons and texts that we have examined, prophetic activity (ASCs) functions in relation to and in tension with social structures and tradition. Jesus, a peripheral prophet, operated outside the structures of Israelite political religion and to a large degree in opposition to the household structures of his day (as discussed in chapter one). Although ASC experiences were the foundation of Paul's apostolic status, he occupied no unassailable position of leadership within the larger Jesus movement or even within the house churches that he himself established. Within these communities ASCs such as a glossolalia and prophecy were valued so highly that they inspired intramural rivalry for honor and status. In Luke-Acts every innovation in missionary practice, from the first acceptance of Gentiles to the appointment of the Ephesian elders as bishops, is unabashedly legitimated by ASC experience. The writer of the *Didache* sought to regularize the status of ASC-inspired prophets by making authentic prophets high priests within the community, serving alongside other teachers, bishops, and deacons. This move is validated neither by ASCs nor by the remembered words of Jesus given in ASCs, but by the teaching of the apostles. Matthew's community kept alive the memory of the itinerant prophetic ministries of Jesus and his disciples while growing increasingly suspicious of similar persons in their environment. Among these messianic Jesus followers, ASCs validated the emergence of both a scribal leadership, epitomized by Peter, and a scribal teaching ministry summed up in Matt 28:16–20. In the Johannine community prophetic activity resulted in the articulation of a christological tradition that was, then, used to test and limit the activity of prophets. ASCs eventually legitimated a pastoral leadership (as epitomized by Peter) committed to keeping Jesus' words and commandments. In reaction to these developments, Thomas' Christ-intoxicated itinerants sought to keep their ASC-inspired interpretation of Jesus' sayings a secret entrusted to only a few. For Ignatius, information received in ASC enhances and deepens his understanding of the mysteries surrounding the life of faith, and in particular, legitimates the emerging structure of episcopal leadership.

Jesus' ministry ended about 30 C.E.; Paul's, by 64 C.E. Paul's house churches stand in both continuity and discontinuity with the group initiated by Jesus. Where Jesus saw himself as a prophet speaking for the God of Israel and sometimes for Holy Wisdom, Paul regarded himself to be an apostle of Christ Jesus. Hence Paul's message focused more on the significance of the Christ for his non-Israelite audiences. Where their two visions coalesced is in the way that Paul held up Christ's self-emptying solidarity with alienated humanity as a paradigm for his own practice of apostleship and stewardship. Consequently both were critical of the patriarchal structures of their times. As an alternative Jesus built a movement of mothers, brothers, and sisters in which there were no human fathers or patriarchs to whom one owned obedience and submission; similarly Paul lifted up the values of sibling solidarity and general reciprocity as the basis for building up the *ekklesiai*.

Another thirty years separates Paul from the bulk of the texts that we have examined here, all of which were composed approximately between 85–110 C.E. That thirty-five year period shows a remarkable diversity in terms of ministry choices— scribal/teaching ministries, pastoral ministries, episcopal ministries—all derived from ASC-inspired insights. During the very same time period, itinerant prophetic ministries were kept alive in memory of the practice of Jesus and his instructions to his first followers, and settled prophetic/priestly ministries were instituted in keeping with "apostolic" teaching. This is not a one-directional movement from prophetic or charismatic leadership to church offices. Although frequently relegated to the peripheries of the church as an institution, the prophetic element has remained throughout subsequent Christian history. In Syria and the Christian East, the "holy man" continued to play an important role in community life alongside church officials for many centuries.[139] The challenge for contemporary Christian communities is to recognize authentic prophetic voices in our context.

---

[139] Peter Brown, *Society and the Holy in Late Antiquity* (London: Faber & Faber, 1982), 80–101, 153–65, provides a good look at the importance of the holy man in Syria from the fourth to sixth centuries. Although Brown argues that the holy man was a new phenomenon, I believe that these holy men were simply continuing a tradition long established.

4
KEEPERS OF THE WORD

WE BEGAN OUR STUDY by examining the ancient Mediterranean houses and households that provided both the physical spaces for the churches to gather in and the social structures for organizing their members. These groups functioned as fictive kinship groups in which the values of sibling solidarity and general reciprocity bound participants to one another in a common loyalty to one God and one Lord, Jesus Christ. It is in this context that Paul and his followers adopted the images of the faithful, prudent, and even shrewd steward, or household manager, as a model of authority and leadership from below. In the previous chapter we saw how prophets, those who communicated with the divine in altered states of consciousness, authorized and legitimated innovation and change. The utterances of prophets also produced tension and even conflict within church groups, resulting in the need for various tests of the authenticity of prophetic communications. These ranged from the message's potential to build up the community rather than the individual, to careful scrutiny of a prophet's lifestyle (praxis) and/or beliefs (orthodoxy). The fourth evangelist even declared that the Holy Spirit's function was that of reminding present-day Christ-followers of the words and teaching of Jesus (John 14:26). It is to this remembering function of leadership that we turn in this chapter, exploring how tradition, the collective memory of the past, provides continuity and supports change by integrating the new into the old.

Writing and Reading in a Predominantly Oral Culture

According to John 14:23, Jesus declared to the disciples at the Last Supper, "Those who love me will keep my word." As contemporary readers of the gospel, our common sense understanding of Jesus' instruction to his disciples is that they (and we) remember and observe his teachings. That the first disciples did so seems evident in the written text before our eyes. Jesus' followers dutifully wrote down the words of Jesus to ensure that they would not be forgotten. Our tasks as modern-day disciples of Christ are to read and interpret these teachings, apply them in our daily lives, and transmit our understandings to future generations through electronic and print media as I am doing in the production of this book. It seems like a fairly simple and straightforward process from our perspective, but what did it mean to keep the word of Jesus in a first-century Mediterranean context?

Once again, we are confronted by a dramatic difference between our social and cultural context and that of Jesus and his earliest followers. We are a highly literate people living in an industrialized, urban society in which mass communication is made possible by the widespread use of print and electronic media. The vast majority (96–99 percent) of the U.S. population and other similarly industrialized urban societies can read and write.[1] We take literacy for granted. In contrast, the first-century Mediterranean region consisted of pre-industrialized, agrarian societies in which only two to four percent of the population was literate.[2] Higher rates of literacy may have existed in urban centers, but "at no period from the invention of the Greek alphabet to the end of the Roman Empire did literacy exceed 10–15 percent of the entire population, women and slaves included."[3] In other words, the primary mode of communication for the vast majority of people in the world of Jesus and his earliest followers was oral-aural, that is, speaking and listening.[4] The same would have been the case in the eastern Mediterranean cities in which Paul operated and the early churches emerged.

Characteristics of Oral Cultures. As Walter Ong reminds us, communication in primarily oral cultures takes the form of sound rather than the visual images of print and electronic media. As sounds, words are evanescent and dynamic.[5] These characteristics have serious implications for the way that non-literate peoples both think and articulate their thoughts. Ong explains succinctly these processes in primarily oral cultures:

> You have to do your thinking in mnemonic patterns, shaped for ready oral recurrence. Your thought must come into being in heavily rhythmic, balanced patterns, in repetitions or antitheses, in alliterations and assonances, in epithetic and other for-

---

[1] Statistics for global, national, and regional literacy rates can be found at http://www.uis.unesco.org.

[2] Malina and Rohrbaugh, *Social-Science Commentary on the Synoptic Gospels,* 7; Esler, *Conflict and Identity in Romans: The Social Setting of Paul's Letter* (Minneapolis: Fortress, 2003), 177; Richard A. Horsley with Jonathan A. Draper, *Whoever Hears You Hears Me: Prophets, Performance, and Tradition in Q* (Harrisburg: Trinity International, 1999), 125–27.

[3] Kim Haines-Eitzen, *Guardians of Letters: Literacy, Power, and the Transmitters of Early Christian Literature* (Oxford: Oxford University Press, 2000), 7.

[4] Esler, *Conflict and Identity,* 177.

[5] Walter J. Ong, *Orality and Literacy: The Technologizing of the Word* (New York: Methuen, 1982), 32.

mulary expressions, in standard thematic settings . . . in proverbs which are constantly heard by everyone so that they come to mind readily.[6]

Thought and its transmission in oral cultures are, thus, bound up with memory systems, particularly social or collective memory, a subject to which we will return below.

Since oral thought and expression are mnemonically based, they are characterized by formulaic styling, simpler grammatical structures (e.g., the use of additive rather than subordinate clauses), the use of aggregative rather than analytic categories (e.g., not "the soldier," but "the brave soldier" or "the braggart soldier"), redundancy, and repetition.[7] Predominantly oral cultures tend toward traditionalism, for they place a high value on conserving what has been learned in the past.[8] At the same time "oral societies live very much in a present which keeps itself in equilibrium or homeostasis by sloughing off memories which no longer have present relevance."[9] Non-literate peoples conceptualize and verbalize knowledge in close reference to the world of human life and in situational rather than abstract constructions.[10] Learning and knowing require close, empathetic, communal identification rather than detached, impersonal, individualistic objectivity, and often take the form of agonistic verbal and intellectual interactions.[11]

Transmission of Information. Mass communication is almost entirely local. Heralds or public criers (*kerukes, praecones*) who walk about a town or city crying out their announcements make official government "news" known to the general public.[12] Such information reaches people living in outlying rural villages if and when persons travel to and from town for marketing or other purposes. Practical knowledge is learned through both informal and formal apprenticeship—from observation and practice accompanied by verbal explanation.[13] We ought, therefore, to imagine Jesus as growing up and acquiring his skills as a *tekton* (builder or carpenter) at his father's side rather than at a trade school. Similarly, Paul would have learned tentmaking as an apprentice to a family member or friend. Social, religious, ethical, and wisdom forms of knowledge were propagated by storytellers,

---

[6] Ibid., 34.
[7] Ibid., 37–41.
[8] Ibid., 41.
[9] Ibid., 46.
[10] Ibid., 42–43, 49–57.
[11] Ibid., 43–46.
[12] Joanna Dewey, "Textuality in an Oral Culture: A Survey of the Pauline Tradition," *Semeia* 65 (1994): 45–46.
[13] Ong, *Orality and Literacy*, 9, 43.

actors, musicians, and street entertainers, some of whom made their living from their oral performances. At festival times, for example, Greco-Roman temples employed storytellers to recount the amazing deeds of the deity inhabiting the sacred precincts. Many oral artists did not perform for a living but were known in their village, town, or region as "good tellers of tales." They entertained and taught in their work places, at neighborhood gatherings, or while traveling.[14] Oral artistry was acquired by listening; by repeating what one heard; by memorizing formulary materials such as proverbs, clichés, and other set phrases or expressions; and by mastering the art of combining and recombining these materials in the composition of a song, poem, or story.[15]

In Israelite communities, the teaching and learning of Scripture were carried out by public oral recitation from memory at Sabbath assemblies.[16] The costliness of scrolls made it unlikely that all or even many village assemblies could afford them; those scrolls that were available would hardly have been legible to any but trained scribes.[17] Like most Israelites, Jesus became familiar with the Scriptures through their oral performance. Jesus would have learned the content of Israelite religious and social practice from stories told and psalms sung at Sabbath gatherings, re-enacted during commemorative ceremonies such as Passover, and recited and chanted while walking to a job site in Sepphoris or Tiberias. Jesus' mastery of proverbs, metaphors, riddles, parables, and other forms of oral discourse would have been acquired in verbal contests in the yards and lanes of Nazareth, on the job site, and in other public settings. While thus immersed in a predominantly oral culture, Jesus would also have encountered writing, if nowhere else, as inscriptions on monuments in urban centers such as Sepphoris and Jerusalem and on coins, although he himself never seems to have any coins (any time a question related to currency arises Jesus has to ask someone for a coin or send Peter fishing for a fish with a coin in its mouth! see Matt 22:19; 17:27 and parallels). Like other rural peasants Jesus would have come into contact with literate culture through the village scribes who kept records of legal and business transactions and who functioned as teachers and adjudicators of disputes and conduct in general.[18] These scribes were often representatives of elite landowners and government officials. Although the Gospels frequently present Jesus engaging in verbal challenge

---

[14] Dewey, "Textuality in an Oral Culture," 45–46.

[15] Ong, *Orality and Literacy*, 9, 24–26.

[16] Horsley, *Whoever Hears You Hears Me*, 127; Dewey, "Textuality in Oral Culture," 46.

[17] Horsley, *Whoever Hears You Hears Me*, 135–37.

[18] William E. Arnal, *Jesus and the Village Scribes: Galilean Conflicts and the Setting of Q* (Minneapolis: Fortress, 2001), 195.

and riposte contests with scribes (*grammateis*) associated with the chief priests or Pharisees, there is no evidence that Jesus produced written texts or documents of any sort. The reference in John 8:6 to Jesus' writing or drawing (*kategraphen*) on the ground "proves nothing about his ability to write, even if it is a historically reliable tradition, since nothing is specified about what he drew."[19]

Rudimentary Writing Skills and Resources. In the social world of Jesus—and indeed until the invention of the printing press in the mid-fifteenth century—writing was limited largely to members of the elite and to "professionals" for whom writing was a trade or craft. In part this limitation was due to the nature of available technologies for writing. Papyrus and parchment were too expensive to be accessible to all but the wealthiest members of society. A single sheet of papyrus in second century C.E. Egypt sold for two obols, a sum representing about a third of a laborer's daily wage, while the production of fifty parchment manuscripts of the Bible in the fourth century C.E. required skins from at least 2,500 sheep or goats.[20] Wax tablets, wooden tablets, and *ostraca* (pottery fragments recycled for use as tax-receipts, lists, and children's school lessons) that were more readily available did not lend themselves to the production of extensive texts.

Another factor limiting a widespread reliance on writing was the amount of skill and labor needed to write legibly with wooden or goose quill styli on these rather crude surfaces. Even the literate elites found writing so laborious as to be ignoble, as is evident in the following comment by the anonymous first century B.C.E. author of the *Rhetorica ad Herennium:*

> The laborious is not necessarily the noble. There are many things that are laborious, which you would not necessarily boast of having done; unless, you actually thought it glorious to copy out stories and whole speeches in your own hand. (4.6)

It should come as no surprise, therefore, that much of the physical production of texts was carried out by slaves and freed persons employed in the households of elites and their retainers, in public administration, and in the few bookshops and libraries that existed. Inscriptional evidence indicates that women as well as men were engaged in such scribal activity.[21] There were varying degrees of literacy even among trained scribes. Cicero notes that, in taking down dictation, his freedman

---

[19] Thomas E. Boomershine, "Jesus of Nazareth and the Watershed of Ancient Orality and Literacy," *Semeia* 65 (1994): 22.

[20] Robert A. Derrenbacker Jr., "Writings, Books and Readers in the Ancient World," *American Theological Library Association Summary of Proceedings* 52, no. 1 (1998): 207–8.

[21] Haines-Eitzen, *Guardians of Letters,* 43–52.

Tiro "can follow whole sentences," in contrast to Spinthano, to whom he must dictate "syllable by syllable" (*Epistulae ad Atticum* 13.25). The early second-century Christ-follower Hermas asserts that when given a little book he "copied everything letter by letter, for I could not find the syllables" (*Herm. Vis.* 2.1.4). The lady who gave him the book later reveals to him actual "knowledge of the book" (*Herm. Vis.* 2.1.4). These references demonstrate the disassociation of the act of writing from composing and of writing from reading. Paul's reference in Gal 6:11 to the "large letters" that he makes when he writes in his own hand may be an indicator of his limited proficiency in the physical performance of writing.[22] Not surprisingly, he regularly used scribes in the production of his letters (Rom 16:22; 1 Cor 16:21; Phlm 19), as did his disciples and imitators (2 Thess 3:17; Col 4:18).

Preference for Oral Transmission. Not only did rudimentary technologies for writing limit its diffusion in the ancient world, but both elite and non-elite members of society were deeply ambivalent about its human and social effects. Perhaps the best examples come from Plato, who wrote at a time when increasing literacy was beginning to transform the consciousness of elite Greeks. In the *Phaedrus* (268–276) and the *Seventh Letter* (341–343), writing is disparaged as "a mechanical, inhuman way of processing knowledge, unresponsive to questions and destructive of memory."[23] At best, written words "remind the reader of what he already knows on any given subject" (*Phaedrus* 275) but can never serve as adequate substitutes for "live" oral teaching. When Plato himself writes, he produces "dialogues," that is, written texts that imitate and seek to preserve to some degree the active relationships intrinsic to oral discourse.[24]

This notion that books are secondary to oral teaching appears to be a common cultural assumption extending through to the first and second centuries C.E., as the following examples show.[25] After promising to send books to a friend, Seneca reminds him, "However, you will gain more from the living voice and from sharing someone's daily life than from any treatise" (*Epistulae Morales* 6.5). Quintilian argues that students in a rhetorical school will benefit more from their teacher's live performance of an oration than from reading speeches by others, because "the living voice, as the saying goes, provides more nourishment" (*Institutio Oratoria* 2.2.8). Using the same phrase, Pliny claimed that "the living voice, as the common saying

---

[22] Dewey, "Textuality in an Oral Culture," 49.

[23] Ong, *Orality and Literacy,* 24.

[24] Pieter J. J. Botha, "Living Voice and Lifeless Letters: Reserve towards Writing in the Greco-Roman World," *HvTSt* 49, no. 4 (1993): 750.

[25] Ibid., 752.

has it, is much more effective" to urge a friend to go and listen to an orator rather than to stay at home and read a book (*Epistulae Morales* 2.3). Even in the context of learning medicine, Galen insists, "There may well be truth in the idiom current among most craftsmen, that reading out of a book is not the same as, or even comparable to, learning from the living voice" (*De compositione medicamentorum secundum locum*, 6.1). Papias, bishop of Hierapolis in the early second century, explains his habit of questioning visitors who knew Jesus' disciples by asserting, "I did not imagine that things out of books would help me as much as the utterances of a living and abiding voice" (Eusebius, *Hist. eccl.* 3.39.4). From craftsmen to physicians to professors to imperial advisers to bishops of the early church, there was a strong and marked preference for oral teaching and performance that was expressed, appropriately enough, in the form of a proverb (an oral genre) about the superiority of the "living voice."[26]

What I wish to emphasize here is that Greco-Roman literacy "was highly oral. . . . A text was something to be vocalized, an aid to memory and a repository for the voice of an author."[27] Not only were texts composed orally as authors recited or dictated to their scribes, but the finished product was almost always read aloud to a group of hearers in some specific social context.[28] Many, if not most, early Mediterranean manuscripts, therefore, came into existence as "voiced texts" that were intended for oral performance.[29] Given the nature of ancient manuscripts, "written in *scripta continua* with no word breaks or punctuation," a person "needed to be quite familiar with a text to read it aloud, a familiarity that was perhaps more likely to have been gained by hearing it orally than by prior reading."[30] For the

---

[26] See James Fentress and Chris Wickham, *Social Memory* (Oxford: Blackwell, 1992), 9–10 for further discussion of the relationship between writing and oral memory.

[27] Botha, "Living Voice," 746.

[28] Ibid., 745.

[29] John M. Foley, "Indigenous Poems, Colonialist Texts," in *Orality, Literacy, and Colonialism in Antiquity* (Semeia Studies 47; ed. Jonathan A. Draper; Atlanta: Society of Biblical Studies, 2004), 9–35. Foley proposes a four-part spectrum of media categories for oral poetry: (1) oral performance in which composition, performance and reception are oral-aural, (2) voiced texts composed in writing but intended for oral performance and aural reception, (3) voices from the past captured in manuscripts that may be either direct transcriptions of oral performances or copies of voiced texts often edited and recopied many times, in which composition, performance and reception may have been some combination of oral-aural and written (4) written oral poems in which oral forms and structures are deliberately composed in writing for literate audiences. Foley's categories (especially voiced texts and voices from the past) may be useful for helping us understand the complex oral-scribal texts of the Jesus movement, even though they are not, strictly speaking, oral poetry.

[30] John S. Kloppenborg, *Excavating Q: The History and Setting of the Sayings Gospel* (Edinburgh: T&T Clark, 2000), 60; Horsley, *Whoever Hears You Hears Me*, 132–33; Dewey, "Textuality in an Oral Culture," 51.

same reasons, when Greco-Roman authors refer to and/or recite from ancient "texts," they are much more likely quoting from memory than copying from a manuscript.[31]

Rhetorical Training, Jesus, and New Testament Authors. The foundation of ancient Greek education and culture, as in all Western societies until the Age of Romanticism, was the study of rhetoric—the art of public speaking.[32] Like other predominantly oral forms of discourse, Greco-Roman rhetoric was "basically agonistic and formulaic."[33] The presumed point of rhetorical discourse was to prove or disprove a point against some opposition. The process of "inventing" a line of argumentation involved culling from the store of traditional sayings called commonplaces (*topoi*) those that were most applicable to the case at hand. Writing enabled the aspiring speaker to organize and treat these inherited materials analytically and produce a voiced rhetorical text intended for oral performance.[34] Writing, therefore, was used in the service of verbal art, particularly for the venue of the law courts (forensic rhetoric), the civic assembly (deliberative rhetoric), and civic and religious celebrations (epideictic rhetoric). The experience of rhetorical culture in these contexts was limited to the elite, who had the time and leisure to devote to extensive education and for whom eloquent oratory was a mark of status and honor.

Jesus did not engage in the rhetorical culture of Greco-Roman elites. While he would have had some contact with written materials, there is no evidence that he could write. Jesus may have occasionally heard Scriptures read aloud, perhaps in a larger village such as Capernaum, where a synagogue might have possessed a Torah scroll; but it is more likely that he became familiar with Israelite religious

---

[31] Paul J. Achtemeier, "Omne verbum sonat: The New Testament and the Oral Environment of Late Western Antiquity," *JBL* 109 (1990): 3–27. M. Carruthers, *The Book of Memory: A Study of Memory in Medieval Culture* (Cambridge: Cambridge University Press, 1990) argues that, even in the Middle Ages, written materials were disseminated through memorization and oral transmission.

[32] Ong, *Orality and Literacy*, 108–9, asserts that the commitment to the formal study and practice of rhetoric is an index of the amount of residual orality in a given culture. As Dewey ("Textuality in Oral Culture," 39) appropriately points out, to speak of the Greco-Roman world as possessing high residual orality is to define it from the perspective of the elite—the 2 to 4 percent who could read and write. I would like to add that orality was not "residual" for the vast majority of people in Greco-Roman antiquity, rather it was primary. Indeed any literacy that anyone possessed would have been secondary. Writing and reading cultures did not become culturally dominant until the expansion of literacy in the seventeenth and eighteenth centuries (see Jeffrey K. Olick and Joyce Robbins, "Social Memory Studies: From 'Collective Memory' to the Historical Sociology of Mnemonic Practices," in *Annual Review of Sociology* 24 [1998]: 114).

[33] Ong, *Orality and Literacy*, 110.

[34] Ibid., 110–11; see also Foley, "Indigenous Poems, Colonialist Texts," 17.

traditions through oral performance in the absence of manuscripts.[35] Luke's story of Jesus reading from a scroll in the synagogue at Nazareth (4:14–30) cannot be regarded as a demonstration of Jesus' literacy. The text that Jesus allegedly "reads" consists of bits of Isa 61:1–2 and 58:6 that in the form cited corresponds to no known ancient text of Isaiah. If this "reading" actually goes back to Jesus, it provides, at best, evidence of his ability to recite and paraphrase from memory Scriptures suitable for the occasion.[36] Such abilities do not require literacy in a primarily oral context. Within that milieu Jesus appears to have been a gifted oral storyteller and a master of verbal challenge and riposte, as is evident in the gospel accounts of his encounters with Judean teachers and Scripture experts.

In contrast to Jesus, Paul seems to have been literate. He could write, albeit not with professional scribal proficiency.[37] He certainly heard Scripture and other writings (such as drafts of his own letters) read aloud. We have no evidence that he himself read aloud to others.[38] He dictated the contents of his letters to scribes, composing them in his head and/or in oral collaboration with Sosthenes (I Cor 1:1), Timothy (2 Cor 1:1; Phil 1:1; see Col 1:1), or Timothy and Silvanus (I Thess 1:1; see 2 Thess 1:1).[39] Not only did some of Paul's congregants in Corinth find him lacking in rhetorical skills, but he himself admits that he was not a good speaker (I Cor 2:1; 2 Cor 10:10; 11:6). Yet, Paul's letters are dominated by

> . . . his own arguments defending or advocating certain conduct in highly provocative ways. He uses accusation and praise, oaths and blessings, instructions and explanations, quoting written even more than oral traditions and in general responding to his own difficult questions with yet more difficult answers.[40]

The evidence of the letters suggests that Paul possessed what Robbins calls "significant 'progymnastic' skills."[41] The *progymnasmata* were the first or preliminary

---

[35] Vernon K. Robbins, "Oral, Rhetorical, and Literary Cultures: A Response," *Semeia* 65 (1994): 79 makes the grossly exaggerated claim that hearing the Scriptures read was Jesus "sole source" of knowledge of them.

[36] Chilton, *Rabbi Jesus*, 99–102, treats the paraphrase as originating with Jesus and interprets the crowd's response as "Who is this illiterate *mamzer* who thinks he can manipulate Scripture?" Boomershine, "Jesus of Nazareth and the Watershed of Ancient Orality," 21–22 casts doubt on the historicity of the Lukan scene but still concludes that Jesus was literate.

[37] Pieter J. J. Botha, "Letter Writing and Oral Communication in Antiquity," *Scriptura* 42 (1992): 23, argues that Paul probably could not write Greek at all, asserting that Gal 6:11 is too similar to illiteracy formulas to ignore.

[38] Robbins, "Oral, Rhetorical, and Literary Cultures," 80.

[39] Werner H. Kelber, "The Case of the Gospels: Memory's Desire and the Limits of Historical Criticism," *Oral Tradition* 17, no. 1 (2002): 73; Botha, "Letter Writing," 22.

[40] Antoinette Clark Wire, "Performance, Politics and Power: A Reponse," *Semeia* 65 (1994): 133.

[41] Robbins, "Oral, Rhetorical, and Literary Cultures," 82.

exercises that students had to master in preparation for advanced training in rhetoric. We can surmise, therefore, that Paul had been introduced at least to the initial stages of a rhetorical education and the production of voiced rhetorical texts.
We have no evidence that he participated beyond this training in Greco-Roman
rhetorical culture. These skills enabled Paul to remain in contact with his geographically dispersed congregations through letters that were sent not as texts to
be read in the way that we read, but as frameworks for oral performances that
made Paul present and audible in his physical absence. Paul's emissaries recited,
interpreted, and extended the contents of these letters in order to make Paul's
voice heard among his congregants.[42] Ironically, neither the content of Paul's letters nor a reputation for writing letters shaped the early churches' memory of Paul
as captured in the Acts of the Apostles, the Apocryphal Acts of Paul, and the Pastoral Epistles. This may be because rhetoric, unlike narrative, is not easily remembered in a context that relies primarily on oral memory and the authority of the
living voice.[43]

The majority of New Testament texts appear to have been composed by authors possessing similar progymnastic skills. The Epistle to the Hebrews is the
only text in the canon that can be regarded as an example of advanced rhetorical
composition, while Luke-Acts represents a level of skill somewhat inferior to Hebrews but superior to the other New Testament texts.[44] These and other early
Jesus-group texts come to us as "voices from the past," captured in manuscripts
that may be either direct transcriptions of oral performances or copies of voiced
texts often edited and recopied many times. The composition, performance, and
reception of these materials may have been oral-aural, written, or some combination of both.[45]

Social Memory (a.k.a. Collective Memory or Cultural Memory)

As indicated above, thought and its articulation in primarily oral cultures were
closely linked with both individual and collective systems of memory. Even literacy in the Greco-Roman world was highly oral and, thus, dependent on memory.
Due to the difficulties of reading ancient manuscripts, most "quotations" of these
written texts were actually recitations that persons who had read them or perhaps

---

[42] Richard F. Ward, "Pauline Voice and Presence as Strategic Communication," *Semeia* 65 (1994):
102.

[43] Dewey, "Textuality in an Oral Culture," 55.

[44] Robbins, "Oral, Rhetorical, and Literary Cultures," 81.

[45] See Foley, "Indigenous Poems, Colonialist Texts," 20–26.

heard them read later recalled from memory. The reliance on traditional materials (commonplaces) as the basic building blocks of rhetorical performance points to continued reliance on the remembered wisdom of the social group. Recognition of these relationships has led to the proposal that the societies of antiquity (and the Middle Ages) might, in fact, be described as "memorial" cultures, in contrast to the documentary, textual cultures that emerged from the Enlightenment and in which we operate.[46] Analysis of memory systems in the ancient world demonstrates that

> the measure of remembering was not historical verification as such, but rhetorical persuasiveness. One was inclined to remember primarily what was deemed worthy of remembering, and what merited remembering depended on the bearing it had for present time and circumstances.[47]

Social memory studies confirm these observations arising from explorations of ancient texts.

Social memory studies originate in the work of French sociologist Maurice Halbwachs (1877–1945). In his pioneering study, *The Social Frameworks of Memory* (originally published in 1925), Halbwachs argues that "individual memory is . . . a part or an aspect of group memory."[48] All persons not only acquire but also "recall, recognize and localize their memories" within social groups.[49] Halbwachs used the term "collective memory" to refer to the interpenetration of autobiographical memory (memories acquired through personal experience) and historical memory (memories mediated by other individuals and groups or through written records). Halbwachs asserts that through the process of preserving and continually reproducing memories of different periods in our lives, we develop and perpetuate a sense of identity.[50] Significantly, however, our minds reproduce and reconstruct these memories of the past under the influence and pressures of the present social situation by touching them up, shortening them, or completing them as necessary.[51] Our memories "hang together" not because they are contiguous in time, according to Halbwachs, but because they are "part of a totality of thoughts common to a group . . . with whom we have a relation at this

---

[46] Kelber, "The Case of the Gospels," 56, following Carruthers, *The Book of Memory* 1990.

[47] Kelber, "The Case of the Gospels," 56, summarizing Janet Coleman, *Ancient and Medieval Memories: Studies in the Reconstruction of the Past* (New York: Cambridge University Press, 1992).

[48] Maurice Halbwachs, *On Collective Memory* (ed. and trans. Lewis A. Coser; Chicago: Chicago University Press, 1992), 53.

[49] Ibid., 38.

[50] Ibid., 47.

[51] Ibid., 49–51.

moment."[52] Those shared memories, consisting of a series of individual images of the past that reproduce the group's history, significantly define its nature, qualities, and attitudes.[53] As we pass from one group to another, "we change our memories along with our points of view, our principles and our judgments."[54] Similarly, as social circumstances change over time and a society modifies its representations of the past, so do individuals. Thus, the past in itself is not preserved in individual or group memories, but is adjusted and distorted in the interests of making that past cohere with the variable conditions of the present.[55]

Contemporary social scientists, building on the foundations laid by Halbwachs, have adopted the phrase "social memory" to designate "the varieties of forms through which we are shaped by the past, conscious and unconscious, public and private, material and communicative, consensual and challenged."[56] Social memory itself is defined as "a process, not a thing" that "works differently at different points in time."[57] It is deeply implicated in the formation and perpetuation of identities, is subject to contestation, and is characterized by both malleability and persistence.[58]

Like social memory, identity-making is an ongoing constructive process.[59] Our identities emerge from our ability "to relate fragmentary experiences across temporal boundaries," that is, to remember the past and to anticipate the future in the present.[60] Through the processes of socialization, we acquire the ability to articulate not only an autobiographical memory (the memory of events personally experienced) but also a "sociobiographical memory" that integrates us into the past, present, and future of the social groups to which we belong.[61] Personal and social identities are established, reinforced, and maintained through commemoration, that is, remembering together common *commemoranda* in the form of artifacts, practices, rituals, and productions of the verbal arts.[62] These *commemoranda* might

---

[52] Ibid., 52.

[53] Ibid., 59.

[54] Ibid., 81.

[55] Ibid., 172–73, 182–83.

[56] Olick and Robbins, "Social Memory Studies," 112.

[57] Ibid., 122.

[58] Ibid.

[59] Ibid.

[60] Esler, *Conflict and Identity*, 22; Alan Kirk, "Social & Cultural Memory," in *Memory, Tradition, and Text: Uses of the Past in Early Christianity* (Semeia Studies 52; ed. Alan Kirk and Tom Thatcher; Atlanta, Society of Biblical Literature, 2005), 4–5.

[61] Olick and Robbins, "Social Memory Studies," 123.

[62] Kirk, "Social and Cultural Memory," 7–8.

include public monuments (e.g., tombs), commemorative ceremonies and celebrations, collections of various objects, and myths and stories.[63]

Memory contestation takes place because "in any given social context individuals and groups disagree over what people and events in the past are significant in the present and on the nature of any claimed significance."[64] Who defines and interprets a group's shared memories is directly tied to claims about who has status and power within the group itself. If one can influence or control memories, one can decisively shape personal and social identities. Struggles over the possession and interpretation of social memory can result in the development of "counter-memories," that is, interpretations of the past that differ from and challenge the official or dominant version. "Popular memory" refers to the interpenetration of official and unofficial, public and private interpretations of the past.[65] Consequently, any given commemoration—oral, written, or material artifact—of a person or event is not so much a window into the past as "a description or performance designed for specific pragmatic and rhetorical purposes" tied to ongoing processes of memory contestation.[66]

The recognition that social memory is a product of contestation leads to an awareness that "the past is produced in the present and is thus malleable."[67] Inevitably we interpret the world—including the past—on the basis of our own personal experience and within our own cultural contexts. Social memory undergoes instrumental changes when we intentionally manipulate the past to serve particular interests in the present, treating the past as a resource to exploit in pursuing current social struggles. Cultural changes may cause elements and images within social memory to lose their relevance and/or fit with present understandings. Inertial changes in social memory result when the carriers of images from the past die, decay, are lost, or are forgotten. Certain aspects of the remembered past, however, appear to be quite persistent under certain conditions. Inertial persistence occurs when certain aspects of the past are reproduced out of sheer force of habit. Cultural persistence results from the continuing relevance or adaptability of elements from the past for current cultural projects and formations. Instrumental persistence occurs when persons or groups within a society deliberately seek to maintain a particular version of the past.[68]

---

[63] Olick and Robbins, "Social Memory Studies," 124.
[64] Esler, *Conflict and Identity*, 174.
[65] Olick and Robbins, "Social Memory Studies," 126–27.
[66] Esler, *Conflict and Identity*, 175.
[67] Olick and Robbins, "Social Memory Studies," 128.
[68] Ibid., 129–30.

Additionally, social memories "form genres that unfold over time by referring not only to their contexts and to the 'original' event, but their own histories and memories as texts."[69]

Trying to capture the dynamic nature of social memory as both malleable and persistent, sociologist Barry Schwartz describes it both as a model of society and for society. Social memory reflects and shapes social reality by providing language for articulating present predicaments and a map for getting through them "by relating where we are to where we have been."[70] It accomplishes this "relating" through the operations of framing and keying. Framing refers to the way that shared memories of a "primary event"—an earlier event that unifies, animates, and orients or reorients a group in some fundamental way—provides frameworks or perspectives for perceiving and comprehending current events.[71] Keying is the mechanism whereby the meaning of events in one frame is understood comparatively or analogically in relation to activities in another frame. Keying "matches publicly accessible (i.e., symbolic) models of the past (written narratives, pictorial images, statues, motion pictures, music, and songs) to the experiences of the present."[72] The result is that "as models *of* society, past events are *keyed to the present;* as models *for* society, past events are *keyed by the present.*[73]

In the cultural world of Jesus' followers, oral performance and social memory were inextricably intertwined. The commemoration of Jesus and his words occurred in the form of various oral performances—the reciting of his teachings, the telling of his deeds, the composing of poems and songs of praise at group gatherings. The regular repetition of these commemorative oral performances would inevitably result in transmission over time. If a group stopped reciting a particular discourse or telling a particular story, it vanished without a trace. The materials that persisted from one generation to another consisted of those elements of the Jesus traditions that were most memorable, most inspiring, and most useful in forming and maintaining a particular group's sense of identity. Consequently, we no longer have access to many oral traditions that emerged and flourished in the decades following Jesus' life and ministry.

---

[69] Ibid., 130.

[70] Barry Schwartz, "Memory as a Cultural System: Abraham Lincoln in World War II," *American Sociological Review* 61 (October 1996): 910.

[71] Ibid., 911.

[72] Ibid.

[73] Ibid.

It is fortunate for us that the earliest followers of Jesus lived in a world where writing could be and was put in the service of oral performance. Followers of Jesus at various times and places produced texts either as scripts for oral performances (voiced texts) or as transcriptions of oral performances (voices from the past). In this way some of the earliest commemorations of Jesus have been preserved until today. I intend to examine a sample of these texts in order to assess how words of and about Jesus were "kept," by whom, and for what purposes. Whose voices within those early groups were recorded? What values and attitudes were they promoting as constitutive of a Christ-confessing identity? What values and attitudes were they opposing? What role did the words of Jesus play in their community-identity building projects?

Keeping the Words of Jesus

The Lost Sayings Source "Q." The starting point for my examination will be a document that exists today only as a hypothesis originally formulated to account for the literary relationships among the Synoptic Gospels. The Two Document Hypothesis proposes that the writers of the Gospels of Matthew and Luke independently from one another had access to the Gospel of Mark and to a lost sayings source. The latter, known as Q, is posited as the source for the approximately 235 verses that Matthew and Luke share with one another but do not appear in Mark. In spite of its hypothetical status and some recent criticism, Q continues to "offer the most economic and plausible accounting of the form and content of the Synoptic Gospels."[74] Not only are the contours of Q discernible in the Gospels of Matthew and Luke, references to and recitations of its contents appear in a number of other documents that early Jesus groups produced. The diffusion of these sayings in texts as varied as the letters of Paul, the *Didache*, and the *Gospel of Thomas*, in addition to the Gospels of Matthew and Luke, make Q ideal for the type of analysis undertaken here.

While traditionally referred to as the "sayings" source, Q is perhaps better understood as a collection of speeches or discourses built around the theme of the kingdom of God. The following is a simplified outline of the reconstructed text.[75]

---

[74] Kloppenborg, *Excavating Q*, 11.
[75] Adapted from Horsley, *Whoever Hears You Hears Me*, 88.

Q/Luke	Matthew	Discourse
3:7–9, 16–17	3:7–12	John's speech on the crisis of impending judgment and deliverance
6:20–47	5:1–12, 39–48; 7:1–5, 15–27	Jesus' opening speech announcing the kingdom and presenting instruction for interaction in kingdom communities
7:18–35	11:2–19	Affirmation of the fulfillment of age-old longings now happening with Jesus and the kingdom
9:57–10:16	8:18–22; 9:37–8; 10:5–15	Instructions on the mission of spreading the kingdom movement
11:2–4, 9–11	6:9–13; 7:7–11	petitioning God boldly for the kingdom
11:14–26	12:22–30, 43–45	Reassurance of the kingdom's presence, with a warning about movement discipline
11:29–32, 39–52	12:38–43, 15:1–9; 7:1–9	Jesus' warning and condemnation of "this generation," that is, scribes and Pharisees who block people's entry into the kingdom
12:2–12	16:5–6; 10:26–33	An exhortation to confidence in confession when faced with opposition
12:22–31	6:25–34, 19–21	A discourse declaring that, despite their poverty, they need have no anxiety if they remain single-minded in pursuit of the kingdom
12:39–40, 42–46	24:42–51	Sanctions
12:49–59	10:34–36; 16:2–3; 5:25–26	The crisis constituted by Jesus' mission
13:18–21	13:31–33	Two encouraging parables about growth of the kingdom
13:28–29, 34–35; 14:16–24	7:13–14, 22–23; 8:11–12; 19:30	Condemnation of the ruling house in Jerusalem
14:26–27, 34–35; 15:4–7; 16:13, 17, 18; 17:1–6	10:37–38; 5:13; 18:12–14; 11:12–13; 5:18; 19:9	Group discipline
17:23–27	24:26–8, 37–9	Sanctioning discourse
22:28–30	20:24–28; 19:28	Closing declaration of the kingdom of God as the renewal of Israel

As a voiced text, village or town scribes would have produced Q to address "a network of villages sympathetic to Jesus' kingdom message or a subculture or counterculture within the larger towns and cities of Lower Galilee."[76] As a text that was composed and performed orally, Q was embedded in the historical and social circumstances of its framers and hearers, encoding their values, attitudes, and expectations.[77] Analysis of the contents of Q point to a "struggle on two fronts: in support of town and village culture against the encroachments of the cities and in support of local forms of Israelite religion in the face of pressures from the hierocratic worldview of Judea."[78]

Q/Luke 11:47–51 as Social Memory. Alan Kirk utilizes the insights of social memory studies to illustrate the dynamics of commemoration at work not only within the text, but in the emergence of Q as both oral tradition and written document. His entry point into the text is Q/Luke 11:47–51:

> Woe to you, for you build the tombs of the prophets, but your forefathers killed them. Thus you witness against yourselves that you are the sons of your forefathers. Therefore also Wisdom said, "I will send them prophets and sages, and some of them they will kill and persecute" so that a settling of accounts for the blood of all the prophets poured out from the founding of the world may be required of this generation, from the blood of Abel to the blood of Zechariah, murdered between the sacrificial altar and the House. Yes, I tell you, an accounting will be required from this generation![79]

Kirk asserts that this passage may be read on three intersecting planes. Delivered by Jesus in response to "aggressive challenges to [his] prophetic credentials," this speech projects a premonition of mortal danger.[80] From the perspective of Q, it refers both retrospectively to the death of Jesus and presently to the situation

---

[76] Kloppenborg, *Excavating Q*, 171, 200–201. Horsley, *Whoever Hears You Hears Me*, 304, argues that "as spokespersons for Jesus the Q performers were cast into prophetic roles, serving in a prophetic office." Kloppenborg, 193, notes the absence of "standard signs of prophetic speech." This factor, together with the form of the text itself as well as indications in the text that its performers were familiar with instructional and judicial processes, lends itself to the conclusion that Q was both composed and performed by village scribes. See also Arnal, *Jesus and the Village Scribes*, 168–72.

[77] Kloppenborg, *Excavating Q*, 193; Horsley, *Whoever Hears You Hears Me*, 147.

[78] Kloppenborg, *Excavating Q*, 261.

[79] From *The Critical Edition of Q* (ed. James M. Robinson, Paul Hoffmann, and John S. Kloppenborg; Minneapolis: Fortress, 2000), reproduced in Alan Kirk, "The Memory of Violence and the Death of Jesus in Q," in *Memory, Tradition, and Text: Uses of the Past in Early Christianity* (ed. Alan Kirk and Tom Thatcher; Semeia Studies 52; Atlanta: Society of Biblical Literature, 2005), 195–96.

[80] Kirk, "Memory of Violence," 196.

of the Q people as threatened by, if not subject to, violent persecution.[81] This
"conflation of the present, or recent past, with the epic past to form a unified
picture is one of the characteristic operations of social memory."[82] Jesus' death is
thus "keyed" to a particular Israelite (possibly deuteronomistic) cultural script
about the violent fate of the prophets and the killing of innocent men like
Abel and Zechariah.[83] The integration of Jesus' terrible death into an existing
Israelite sacred narrative as its climactic episode not only gives it meaning, but also
transforms it into "memory" (i.e., it is commemorated).[84] This commemorative
keying, argues Kirk, is evidence of an effort to "eradicate and transform the hor-
rific public stigma attaching to the executed person and by extension to the identity of the affiliated group" in a context where the memory of Jesus is being
contested.[85]

Kirk demonstrates that the appearance of such a commemorative passage in Q,
an overtly instructional text, coheres with the finding that "group constitutive
norms are immanent in memories of foundational persons and events."[86] Greek funeral orations and funerary epigrams provide evidence that the "inculcation of em-
blematic norms" is a feature of such commemorations.[87] The same dynamics of
social memory evident in Q 11:47–51 would have been operative in the generation
of Q as a coherent body of oral tradition soon after Jesus' death. His ethical teachings, aligned with the group's new understanding of his violent demise in light of Israel's store of cultural memories, enable this particular Jesus group to "reconstitute
itself as a moral community centered on commemoration of Jesus."[88] Kirk suggests
that Q's emergence as a written memory artifact may have coincided with the
"breakdown of 'communicative memory,' that is, of face-to-face, oral forms of
transmission that begins to occur approximately at the forty-year threshold," al-

---

[81] Ibid.

[82] Ibid., 197.

[83] Kloppenborg, *Excavating Q*, sees a deuteronomistic view of history as determinative of Q's overall structure (210); he attributes this however to redactional activity in the second stage of Q's formation (128). Kirk ("The Memory of Violence," 196–97) seems to see it as present already at the
initial emergence of Q as oral tradition. The entire notion of a deuteronomistic view is challenged
by Horsley (*Whoever Hears You Hears Me*, 110–11) who connects this theme to Jeremiah (7:21–35;
25:4; 29:17–19; 35; 44), the penitential prayers of Neh. 9 and Baruch 1–3, and to late second
temple legends, i.e., to popular "little" tradition rather than to "great tradition."

[84] Kirk, "The Memory of Violence," 197–98.

[85] Ibid., 199–200.

[86] Ibid., 200.

[87] Ibid., 201.

[88] Ibid., 206.

though he allows for the possibility of earlier scribal formation.[89] Even as Q's speeches continued to be performed in oral environments, it became available as a document for the authors of Matthew and Luke to use.

Kirk, breaking new ground, highlights the dynamics of social memory in the emergence of Q. He shows how the operations of social memory can generate both oral and written forms of commemoration. By highlighting the inherent connections between commemoration and moral exhortation, Kirk clarifies why Jesus' teaching was so important for the Q people. His use of commemorative keying enables us to see more clearly how the Q people appropriated and reinterpreted images and scripts drawn from Israelite cultural memory to make sense of their own experience and to ensure the persistence and demonstrate the malleability of these images and scripts.

Q/Luke 11:47–51 in Jesus' Context. We can see the same process at work with the words of Jesus. Q11:47–51 is, after all, presented to us as a speech of Jesus. It is part of a longer exchange (11:39–52) involving an honor-shame contest—a trading of insults—between Jesus and representatives of the Jerusalem elite, Pharisees and/or Torah experts (lawyers).[90] In this context, as Jesus utters a series of "woes," he accuses his interlocutors of violating basic covenantal principles or laws and warns them of punishment to come.[91] Their obsession with ritual purity (11:39, 44), tithing (11:42), social status (11:43), and building tombs for prophets whom their forefathers killed (11:47) cannot hide their failure to practice the covenantal principles of justice and mercy on which the very same prophets staked their lives (see Q11:42, 46). Reflected in Jesus' woe against these scribal elites is, in part, a contest over the memory of Israel's prophets, who were increasingly memorialized in the construction of commemorative tombs and shrines and in legends of persecution and martyrdom, some of which were written down.[92] Jesus' words both raise and answer the question: do monuments built at great cost most appropriately commemorate the prophets, or does practicing the justice and love of God that the prophets preached?

Jesus' words that were spoken in an agonistic context evoke a contested memory within first-century Israelite society. As remembered and recited in Q 11:47–51, Jesus' stance on that contested memory comes to epitomize the

---

[89] Kirk, "The Memory of Violence," 205–6. Q is generally dated vaguely to the era before the First Jewish Revolt (66–70 C.E.); Arnal, *Jesus and the Village Scribes,* 167–68, makes a case for dating the scribal redaction referred to as Q2 in the 40s with Q1 appearing even earlier.

[90] Malina and Rohrbaugh, *Social-Science Commentary on the Synoptic Gospels,* 275–76.

[91] Horsley, *Whoever Hears You Hears Me,* 285; Kirk, "The Memory of Violence," 196.

[92] See discussion in Horsley, *Whoever Hears You Hears Me,* 285–91.

normative position of the Q people vis-à-vis the scribal elites within their own environment. They see themselves as Wisdom's persecuted sages who commemorate the latest member of that band of murdered prophets, not by building monuments, but by speaking and living out the way of Jesus.

Q/Luke 11:47–51 in Paul's Context. Paul's first letter to the assembly in Thessalonica, which he co-authored with Timothy and Silvanus (ca. 51 C.E.), likewise involves the same social memory dynamics, especially in the passage that evokes the tradition memorialized in Q 11:47–51:

> For you, brothers and sisters, became imitators of the churches of God in Christ Jesus that are in Judea, for you suffered the same things from your own compatriots as they did from the Jews, who killed both the Lord Jesus and the prophets, and drove us out; they displease God and oppose everyone by hindering us from speaking to the Gentiles so that they may be saved. Thus they have constantly been filling up the measure of their sins; but God's wrath has overtaken them at last. (2:14–16)

As in Q, the tradition about the violent fate of the prophets serves as a frame for keying not only Jesus' death and the persecution of the Judean *ekklesiai,* but also the circumstances of the non-Israelite Christ-followers in Thessalonica. What is implicit in Q, Paul and his co-authors express explicitly: Jesus' death is the latest or perhaps the last stanza in the ongoing epic saga of the rejection and killing of Israel's prophets, a story that now includes the followers of Jesus. A piece of contested Israelite tradition has been appropriated as a significant aspect of the collective memory of the Jesus movement. It is identified neither as a saying of Jesus nor as a derivative of any particular text, but appears as part of the oral tradition of Jesus' followers.[93] Paul and his co-workers evoke it in a non-Israelite environment to affirm the social identity of the Thessalonian Christ-followers as "imitators" of the persecuted Judean Christ-assemblies. The intended hearers of the letter share experiences of mistreatment and harassment with these geographically and ethnically distant siblings in faith and with the authors as well (see 1:6; 2:2; 3:3–4). By keying these experiences to the sacred narrative of Jesus and the prophets, their suffering is not only rationalized but valorized as intrinsic to membership in a Jesus group. The point, of course, is to encourage group maintenance and solidarity in a hostile milieu.

Summary. Q presents the Israelite cultural memory of the elite's rejection of the prophets as a speech of Jesus, only retrospectively and implicitly interpreting it

---

[93] See discussion in Arnal, *Jesus and the Village Scribes,* 166–67, especially n. 16.

as a reference to Jesus' death. Paul and his co-authors use a Jesus-group interpretation that explicitly links Jesus' death to the fate of the prophets to affirm the social identity of their intended hearers. These differences in presentation and function point to the fluidity of oral traditions and the malleability of social memories. This particular social memory appears again only in Acts 7:52 and seems to have played a role in the interpretation of the parable of the wicked tenants or dispossessed peasants (Mark 12:1–12; Matt 21:33–46).[94] In each case we see that the same oral tradition has been presented with modifications in different social situations and has consistently featured polemical engagement with influential or powerful opponents.[95] The memory of the rejected Israelite prophets did not persist, however, to become a dominant aspect in the early church's social memory. Paul neither refers to this tradition in any of his other letters nor refers to it in explicating his understanding of the significance and meaning of Jesus' death. For that understanding he prefers other emerging collective commemorations of Jesus.

The Words of Jesus in Paul's Letters. Communicating a few years later with the *ekklesia* in Corinth (ca. 54 C.E.), Paul (together with Sosthenes) reminds his hearers of the gospel that was transmitted to them. His statement clearly demonstrates that he is evoking a recent collective memory of his congregants, but in doing so he is also referring to an emerging tradition of the wider Jesus movement. Paul declares, "I handed on to you as of first importance what I in turn had received, that Christ died for our sins . . . that he was buried, and that he was raised from the dead" (15:3–4). A list of resurrection appearances follows, beginning with Cephas and the twelve; then five hundred brothers and sisters, James, and all the apostles, and concluding with Paul himself (15:5–11). Paul recalls these persons not to commemorate them for posterity as witnesses to Christ's resurrection but to incorporate himself into their illustrious company. Paul's use of this emerging tradition clearly indicates his understanding of it as a piece of tradition/collective memory that is adaptable to suit the particular circumstances he is addressing. The passage functions to set Paul up as an authoritative interpreter of the meaning of Christ's resurrection in a context where some members of the Corinthian community are calling into question the whole notion of resurrection from the dead (15:12ff.). This polemical use does not militate against the importance of Jesus' death, burial, and resurrection for Paul, as we can see in his treatment of the Eucharist in the same letter (11:17–34).

---

[94] See discussion in Malina and Rohrbaugh, *Social Science Commentary on the Synoptic Gospels,* 199–200.
[95] Kloppenborg, *Excavating Q,* 210.

Paul indicates that he cannot commend his hearers for their practice of the Lord's Supper (11:17). Indeed, their conduct at these ceremonial gatherings, where "one goes hungry and another becomes drunk" and those who have nothing are humiliated, demonstrates that they are not eating the Lord's Supper at all (11:20–22). By proceeding without "discerning the body" of the Lord in their eating and drinking, they bring judgment and condemnation upon themselves (11:29–30). In other words, the Corinthians' meal does not function as such a ceremony ought; it no longer creates, affirms, and maintains their social identity as members of the one body of Christ (see 10:17). Their practices replicate current Greco-Roman values and not those of Christ's body, a fictive kinship group in which sibling relations of mutual reciprocity replace hierarchical relations based on social status, ethnic affiliation, and gender.

In an effort to set his hearers straight, Paul reminds them:

> For I received from the Lord what I also handed on to you, that the Lord Jesus on the night when he was handed over took a loaf of bread, and when he had given thanks, he broke it and said, "This is my body that is for you. Do this in remembrance of me." In the same way he took the cup also, after supper, saying, "This cup is the new covenant in my blood. Do this, as often as you drink it, in remembrance of me." For as often as you eat this bread and drink the cup, you proclaim the Lord's death until he comes. (11:23–26)

Paul once again reminds his hearers of materials that he transmitted to them. The temporal indicator that the instructions for the meal were given "on the night when he was betrayed" (11:23) locate them within an already existing narrative of Jesus' passion. The central acts of eating and drinking are to be done "in remembrance of me," a phrase that is repeated twice (11:24, 25), thus explicitly and definitively signaling the commemorative nature of the meal. By attributing the instructions to eat and drink in his memory to the Lord Jesus, Paul and/or the early tradition makes Jesus himself the founder and initiator of this memorial activity.

The description of the cup as "the new covenant in my blood" (11:25) relates the action of drinking to the making and renewing of Israel's historic covenant (Exod 24, Jer 31). In this scenario Jesus' death is the blood offering that ratifies the covenant.[96] Again, Paul transmits a tradition that has appropriated Israelite social memories related to the notion of covenant and covenant ratification rituals

---

[96] See discussion in Ellen Bradshaw Aitken, "*ta dromena kai ta legomena:* The Eucharistic Memory of Jesus' Words in First Corinthians," in *Harvard Theological Review* 90 (1997): 359–70.

(contributing to their persistence), but this tradition has re-interpreted these memories in ways that would have been abhorrent to many within Israelite communities (see John 6:60). Paul concludes his recitation of the transmitted tradition by adding his own interpretation, "For as often as you eat this bread and drink the cup, you proclaim the Lord's death until he comes" (11:26). The meal, thus, commemorates the past death of Jesus and anticipates his forthcoming return in glory. The meal also provides a ritual participation in the blood and body of Christ that transforms the many who share the same cup and bread into "one body" (10:16–17)—a ritual declaration and enactment of the notion that "we are what we eat."[97] As a central and ongoing ceremony of the *ekklesia,* the meal serves to affirm their social identity as a group who commemorates Jesus' death in anticipation of his return. Paul insists that for the meal to function effectively in producing and affirming the group as those who remember Jesus, it must be conducted in ways that reflect the values of the kingdom for which he died.

On a slightly different tangent, I find it interesting that even though Paul never met or knew the historical Jesus, he claims to have received "from the Lord" the words allegedly spoken at the Last Supper. The common explanation insists that Paul received the words "not from Jesus directly, but by way of the church's liturgical tradition."[98] Church tradition may be Paul's source, but as we have seen (in chapter three), Paul introduces new teaching, received in altered states of consciousness, into the nascent Resurrected Jesus tradition by labeling it a "word of the Lord," that is, a prophetic oracle. In each of the instances examined in chapter three, Paul's focus is "eschatological." In this instance, Paul's eschatological statement of the Eucharist as commemorating Jesus' death in anticipation of his return at least derives from such experiences, if not the actual words of institution.

Since these communities exist to commemorate the death of their "founder," we might expect to see a fair amount of moral exhortation in Paul's letter. We are not disappointed. What is surprising is that Paul so very rarely draws on Jesus' teachings; for only twice does he refer explicitly to sayings of Jesus. In I Corinthians, within the context of a debate about the appropriateness of marriage and sexual intimacy for followers of Christ, he declares to them:

---

[97] Jerome H. Neyrey, *Paul in Other Words: A Cultural Reading of His Letters* (Louisville, Ky.: Westminster John Knox, 1990), 168.

[98] Victor Paul Furnish, Notes to "The First Letter of Paul to the Corinthians," in *The Harper Collins Study Bible* (ed. Wayne A. Meeks; San Francisco: HarperSanFrancisco, 1993), 2155 n. 11.23.

To the married I give this command—not I but the Lord—that the wife should not separate from her husband (but if she does separate, let her remain unmarried or else be reconciled to her husband), and that the husband should not divorce his wife. (7:10–11)

Both Q and Mark attribute a similar sort of teaching to Jesus. To enable a quick comparison, they are as follows:

Q/Luke 16:18	Matthew 19:9	Matthew 5:32	Mark 10:11–12
. . . anyone who divorces his wife,	. . . whoever divorces his wife,	anyone who divorces his wife,	whoever divorces his wife
	except for unchastity,	except on the ground of unchastity,	
[and marries another] commits adultery, and	and marries another commits adultery.		and marries another commits adultery against her;
		causes her to commit adultery,	
whoever marries a woman divorced from her husband commits adultery.		and whoever marries a divorced woman commits adultery;	
			and if she divorces her husband and marries another, she commits adultery.

As we can see immediately, Paul is not actually quoting any extant version of this saying. In Q and the Gospels, the saying addresses the situation of husbands and does not appear to prohibit divorce per se; instead, it rules out the possibility of remarriage since the second marriage would be an adulterous one. Paul makes no reference to adultery at all; he simply asserts that husbands are not to divorce their wives. Paul does, however, envision a wife separating from or divorcing her husband. Mark's allowance for this possibility suggests that he, like Paul, is adapting Jesus' teaching for a Greek or Roman community in which both men and women are able to sue for divorce.[99] Jesus' teaching that remarriage following divorce is adulterous may inform Paul's insistence that a wife who separates from her husband must remain unwed or be reconciled to her husband, but Paul never actually says so. No doubt a detailed explanation and rationale for this ruling

---

[99] Greek and Roman law allowed husband or wife to initiate a divorce, in contrast to the teaching of Deut 24:1–4.

would have been communicated verbally first to and later by those who delivered the letter to Corinth. Paul refers to Jesus' command to validate his judgment that husbands and wives ought not to divorce. While regarding Jesus' teaching as authoritative in this matter, Paul is unconcerned with verbatim recitation or application of that teaching. In a manner consistent with his predominantly oral culture, Paul freely paraphrases and adapts the saying to meet the needs of his particular circumstances.

Paul also cites an explicit command of Jesus within the context of defending his personal practice of refusing material support from the Corinthian assembly. Paul's argument begins with the rhetorical question, "Do we not have the right to our food and drink?" (I Cor 9:3). The answer, of course, is that apostles do have a right to financial and other forms of material support. Paul contends that this right derives not from human authority but from both Torah and a command of the Lord: "For it is written in the law of Moses, 'You shall not muzzle an ox while it is treading out the grain'" (9:9; Deut 25:4). Just as those who serve in the Temple get their food from the temple, so "the Lord commanded that those who proclaim the gospel should get their living by the gospel" (9:13–14). Thus, having established the right of apostles to demand and receive material support from those to whom they preach, Paul explains why he has not and will not take advantage of this right (see chapter two).

Our interest here is in the command attributed to the Lord that those who proclaim the gospel should make their living by the gospel (9:14). Although this command is not a verbatim recitation of any statement found on Jesus' lips in any of the Gospels, it seems to summarize the intent of Jesus' instructions to the seventy, "Remain in the same house, eating and drinking whatever they provide, *for the laborer deserves to be paid*" (Q/Luke 10:7). A similar saying is recorded in Matthew, but in the context of instructions to the twelve apostles about the conduct of their mission: "Take no gold, or silver, or copper in your belts, no bag for your journey, or two tunics, or sandals, or a staff; *for laborers deserve their food*" (Matt 10:9–10). Once again, it is obvious that Paul, writing in the middle of the first century without access to written sources for his "commands of the Lord," paraphrases freely the gist of sayings retained in the collective memory of the Jesus movement. The situation is quite different at the end of the first century, as is illustrated by the use of this same saying in the pseudo-Pauline text I Timothy. There the author asserts that ruling elders who preach and teach are worthy of double compensation, "for the scripture says, 'You shall not muzzle an ox while it is treading out the grain,' and '*The laborer deserves to be paid*'" (5:18). The pseudo-Pauline author not only quotes Q/Luke 10:7 verbatim, but locates the saying in *he graphe*, literally "the writing," but frequently translated as "the scripture." A saying that once in-structed itinerant apostles to depend on their hosts for sustenance, a right that Paul refused to make use of, now justifies the financial support of locally resident elders. Once again, the hallmarks of an oral cultural are evident even in the literary use of the saying.

This quick study of Paul's references to words, commands, or sayings of the Lord demonstrates that he did not rely heavily or very frequently on such potentially authoritative sources to make his points. Only twice—in prohibiting divorce (1 Cor 7:10–11) and in defending the apostolic right to material support (1 Cor 9:14)—does Paul utilize loosely paraphrased commands of Jesus to sup-port his position. In the case of the latter, Paul obviously does not consider Jesus' command to make a living from proclaiming the gospel to be binding on him per-sonally. Indeed, he refuses material support from the Corinthian congregation, preferring to rely on his own labors and the gifts from the assembly in Philippi (2 Cor 11:9; Phil 4:15). For Paul, the word or command of the Lord includes in-sights gleaned from personal ASC experiences as well as sayings that we can trace back to both the historical Jesus and significantly nascent commemorative tradi-tions about Jesus. When Paul evokes the collective memory of a particular church group or the broader store of Jesus movement social memory, he does so not to preserve them for future generations but to bolster his own position within the context of hammering out values and guidelines for his fledgling assemblies.

The Words of Jesus in the Didache. One of the earliest and most fascinating treat-ments of the sayings/words and memory of Jesus occurs in the *Didache*, a training manual for non-Israelite recruits who are being initiated into an already existing network of Israelite household-based Jesus assemblies.[100] The *Didache* comes to us as "voices from the past," that is, as a written text documenting a particular social-ization program of a specific network of Israelite Jesus people.[101] It was com-posed, performed, and received both as oral performance and as a written text preserving the discourses of persons, allegedly the apostles, speaking on behalf of

---

[100] Milavec, *The Didache*, vii; Draper, "Ritual Process," 123; Jonathan A. Draper, "The Role of Rit-ual in the Alternation of Social Universe: Jewish-Christian Initiation of Gentiles in the Didache," *List* 32 (1997): 49; Milavec, "The Social Setting of 'Turning the Other Cheek' and 'Loving One's Enemies' in Light of the Didache," *BTB* 25 (1995): 137.

[101] "Voices from the past" and "voiced texts" are terms proposed by Foley, "Indigenous Poems, Colonialist Texts," 13–26, for classifying oral poetry. They are taken up by Martin S. Jaffee, "Rab-binic Oral Tradition in Late Byzantine Galilee: Christian Empire and Rabbinic Ideological Resis-tance," in *Orality, Literacy, and Colonialism in Antiquity* (Semeia Studies 47; ed. Jonathan A. Draper; Atlanta: Society of Biblical Literature, 2004), 172–79, in relation to rabbinic texts. I think they can work well for understanding early Jesus-group texts as well.

the Lord. The *Didache* is a written artifact of social memory that preserves orally composed elements such as the sayings of Jesus, proverbial Israelite wisdom, and various prayers. The incorporation of these disparate elements of the composer's (or composers') heritage in the text transforms them into *commemoranda* in the form of teachings and rituals that, when remembered and reenacted together, decisively establish, reinforce, and maintain social identity. For the teachers and ritual leaders who "read" the *Didache*, it functioned as a "voiced text" providing a script for oral performances in which recruits were initiated and integrated into their new social identity as Jesus people.[102] Our examination of this text will focus on the *sectio evangelica* and the rituals of baptism and the Eucharist.

The *Didache* begins with catechetical instructions addressed to prospective non-Israelite recruits. These instructions are introduced with the statement, "There are two ways, one of life and one of death" (1.1) and include a long series of commands and prohibitions characterizing the way of life (1.2–4.14), a brief description of the way of death (5.1–2), and a concluding instruction about the desirability of Torah observance (6.1–3). Although evidence confirms that this "two ways" device was widespread in the early Mediterranean world, the form of the device that appears here derives from Israelite models, or perhaps more specifically from Israelite followers of Jesus.[103] Of particular interest to us is the *sectio evangelica* in 1.2–2.1, which has frequently been regarded as either "a subsequent interpolation in the text of the 'basic document'" or "a piece of redaction that was of special significance for the Didachist and his writing."[104] Given what we know about the oral nature of text production in the ancient world, the composer of the *Didache* was less likely to have worked directly from written texts than to have woven together orally transmitted and aurally received versions of these traditions.

The *sectio evangelica* consists of characteristic teachings of Jesus memorialized in Q and its Synoptic Gospel descendants. The following table enables us to compare the *Didache*'s version of Jesus' words with their parallels in Q, Matthew, Luke, and occasionally other early Jesus-group texts.

---

[102] See also Milavec, *The Didache*, xxxii–xxxiii, 715–25; Ian H. Henderson, "The Didache and Orality in Synoptic Comparison," *JBL* 111 (1992): 283–306.

[103] See discussion in Hubb van de Sandt and David Flusser, *The Didache: Its Jewish Sources and Its Place in Early Judaism and Christianity* (Minneapolis: Fortress, 2002), 55–80, 140–80; Kurt Niederwimmer, *The Didache: A Commentary*, (Minneapolis: Fortress, 1998), 30–41. Milavec, *The Didache*, 111, argues that since (1) no Jewish source has come down to us that uses the Two Ways teaching as it is found in the *Didache*, and (2) all variations of the Two Ways teaching appear only in early Jesus movement texts, it is likely that this particular model of the Two Ways teaching was "crafted expressly by disciples of Jesus for use in a gentile environment."

[104] Niederwimmer, *The Didache*, 68.

Didache	Q/Luke	Matthew	Other
1.2 On the one hand, the way of life is this: "First, you will love the God who made you; second your neighbor as yourself. On the other hand: as many [things] as you might wish not to happen to you, likewise, do not do to another.	10:27 You shall love the Lord your God . . . and your neighbor as yourself	22:37–39 You shall love the Lord your God . . .You shall love your neighbor as yourself.	Mark 12:30–31 you shall love the Lord your God . . .You shall love your neighbor as yourself.
	6:31 Do to others as you would have them do to you.	7:12 In everything do to others as you would have them do to you; for this is the law and the prophets.	*Thomas* 6.3 and don't do what you hate
1.3 And [for an assimilation] of these words, the teaching is this: Speak well of the ones speaking badly of you, and pray for your enemies, and fast for the ones persecuting you; for what merit [is there] if you love the ones loving you? Do not even the gentiles do the same thing? You, on the other hand, love the ones hating you, and you will not have an enemy.	6:27–28 . . . Love your enemies, do good to those who hate you, bless those who curse you, pray for those who abuse you.	5:43–44 You have heard that it was said. . . . But I say to you, Love your enemies and pray for those who persecute you.	Rom 12:14 Bless those who persecute you; bless and do not curse them.
	6.32 If you love those who love you, what credit is that to you? For even sinners love those who love them.	5:46–47 For if you love those who love you, what reward do you have? Do not even the tax collectors do the same? . . . Do not even the Gentiles do the same?	
1.4 Abstain from fleshly and bodily desire. [How so?] If anyone should strike you on the right cheek, turn to him/ her also the other, and you will be perfect; if anyone should press you into service for one mile, go with him/her two; if anyone should take away your cloak, give to him/her your tunic; if anyone should take from you [what is] yours, do not ask for	6:29–30 If anyone strikes you on the cheek, offer the other also; and from anyone who takes away your coat do not withhold even your shirt. . . . and if anyone takes away your goods, do not ask for them again.	5:38–42 You have heard. . . . But I say to you, Do not resist an evildoer. But if anyone strikes you on the right cheek, turn the other also; And if anyone wants to sue you and take your coat, give your cloak as well; and if anyone forces you to go one mile, go also the second mile.	

it back; for you are not even able [to do so].

1.5 To everyone asking you [for anything], give [it] and do not ask for it back; for, to all, the Father wishes to give [these things] from his own free gifts. Blessed is the one giving according to the rule; for s/he is blameless. Woe to the one taking; for, on the one hand, if anyone having need takes, s/he will be blameless; on the other hand, the one not having need will stand trial . . . why s/he took and for what [use]; and being in prison, s/he will be examined thoroughly certaining [the things] s/he has done, and s/he will not come out from there until s/he gives back the last quadrans.	6:30 Give to everyone who begs from you. . . .

12:57–59 And why do you not judge for yourselves what is right? Thus, when you go with your accuser before a magistrate, on the way make an effort to settle the case, or you may be dragged before the judge, and the judge hand you over to the officer, and the officer throw you in prison. I tell you, you will never get out until you have paid the very last penny. | 5:42 Give to everyone who begs from you, and do not refuse anyone who wants to borrow from you.

5:25–26 Come to terms quickly with your accuser while you are on the way to court with him, or your accuser may hand you over to the judge, and the judge to the guard, and you will be thrown into prison. Truly I tell you, you will never get out until you have paid the last penny. | *Thomas* 95 [Jesus said], "If you have money, don't lend it at interest. Rather give [it] to someone from whom you won't get it back." |

It is striking that in the *Didache's* *sectio evangelica* the words of Jesus are not introduced as such. In contrast, Q includes these particular sayings as part of Jesus' inaugural announcement of the kingdom and its agenda; Luke incorporates the same teachings into Jesus' address from the level place (6:17ff.); and Matthew contextualizes them in Jesus' Sermon on the Mount (5:1–7:29). In the *Didache* Jesus' instructions—to bless, pray, and fast for one's enemies and persecutors; to turn the other cheek, to go the second mile, to give one's tunic along with one's cloak, and to give to everyone who asks—appear simply as applications of the double command to "love the God who made you, [and] your neighbor as yourself." While the content of these teachings recalls the sayings recorded in Q and its descendants, their form and structure is sufficiently different that we can conclude that the composer(s) of the *Didache* was (were) reciting oral tradition and not quoting from written documents.[105]

The same situation applies to the double commandment itself. It is not introduced as Scripture or commandment or law (Torah), again in contrast to the Synoptic Gospels where it is explicitly identified as such. In Mark and Matthew a Torah expert—a scribe (Mark) or a lawyer who is a Pharisee (Matt)—asks Jesus which of the commandments is the greatest. Jesus responds by reciting the double commandment (Mark 12:28–34//Matt 22:34–40). In Luke the Torah expert (a lawyer) himself recites the double commandment in response to Jesus' questions, "What is written in the law? What do you read there?" (10:25–27). In each of these instances the double commandment is explicitly identified as a commandment and/or related to "the law" (Torah), which in Luke is explicitly identified as a written text. In the *Didache*, however, the double commandment defines "the way to life" (1.1) and is described simply as "words" from which the "teachings" that follow are derived (1.3a). Furthermore, the double commandment is recited in an abbreviated proverbial form that is oral and that recurs only in Barnabas 19.2.[106]

The composer(s) of the *Didache* appear to be working with oral expressions of emerging Jesus traditions and Israelite popular memory rather than anything approaching the status of official texts. These two sources—oral Jesus traditions and popular memory—are treated as complementary and are integrated into a single script defining the way to life, that is, Israelite Jesus-group norms and values over against the way of death, that is, non-Israelite values and norms.[107] The *Didache*'s use of the sayings of Jesus illustrates both the fluidity of these oral traditions and their intrinsic embeddedness in Israelite traditions. The sayings also function as a part of covenant renewal discourse for Israelite village communities in Galilee, thereby displaying their fluidity and embeddedness.[108] Matthew presents the same Jesus traditions in a context where the interpretation of shared traditions is being contested. Matthew's Jesus speaks polemically in antitheses— "you have heard that it is said . . . but I say . . ."—in order to flesh out what truly honorable behavior exceeding that of Matthew's rivals, the scribes and Pharisees, might look like (see Matt 5:20).[109] Luke's version appears to be addressed to urban elites in the eastern Mediterranean who may experience social ostracism by

---

[105] Milavec, *The Didache*, 714–20; Draper, "Ritual Process," 153; Niederwimmer, *The Didache*, 80.
[106] Niederwimmer, *The Didache*, 64.
[107] Draper, "The Role of Ritual," 54.
[108] Horsley, *Whoever Hears You Hears Me*, 216–27.
[109] See discussion in Malina and Rohrbaugh, *Social Science Commentary on the Synoptic Gospels*, 42–47.

joining Jesus groups[110] and seems to be the least connected with specifically Israel-ite concerns. Each text represents instrumental changes in social memory as their writers intentionally manipulate the remembered words of Jesus in order to serve specific needs within local networks of Jesus people. At the same time, that these diverse groups continue to find the words of Jesus relevant and adaptable to their needs ensures their cultural persistence.

This brief examination of the opening section of the *Didache*, therefore, enables us to see social memory as it is being made, that is, as it emerges from the com-poser's (or composers') integration of elements from the nascent Jesus tradition with particular aspects of Israelite cultural memories. The same dynamics are op-erative in the remainder of the Two Ways discourse. While the Two Ways dis-course includes commandments from the second half of the Decalogue (2.2), it excludes others, such as "honor thy mother and father," possibly since these would create impossible situations for non-Israelite converts. How could one honor a polytheistic parent and his/her gods as filial piety demanded and at the same time love the God of Israel? Recitations from the Decalogue are intertwined with six additional prohibitions forbidding pederasty, illicit sex, the practices of magic, making potions, abortion, and infanticide (2.2). Judeans stereotypically associated these activities with the polytheistic cultures surrounding them, activities that many non-Israelites would have condoned.[111] The end result is a new social memory built by linking past (Israelite cultural memories), recent past (Jesus tradition de-rived from the apostles), and present (counter-cultural experience in a non-Israelite environment and/or sub-cultural experience within the larger Israelite commu-nity). As an articulation of that social memory, the Two Ways discourse functions as a model of the values and norms ideally epitomized by the *Didache*'s Judean Jesus society and as a model for shaping the social identity of non-Israelites wishing to join this group.

Drawing on insights gleaned from theories of ritual processes, Jonathan Draper demonstrates how the Jesus tradition in the *Didache* functions in the remaking of the initiate's social identity through enacting a "ritual and social death to the old universe."[112] In the honor-shame cultures of the ancient Mediterranean world, following the instructions in 1.3–4 that prohibit any response to insult or physi-cal injury would result in a loss of honor that, in turn, could lead to "social ostra-cism, first by one's family, who would have to avenge the loss of honor, and

---

[110] Ibid., 250.
[111] Milavec, *The Didache*, 121–40.
[112] Draper, "The Role of Ritual," 55.

secondly by society in general." The ability to endure both social humiliation and ostracism indicates to the novice that he or she is "perfect" (1.4), that is, acting in obedience with the way of life of the *Didache* people.[113] The second set of sayings that encourage letting go of money and property (1.5–6) would only widen the breach with one's kin, "since property was held by and redeemed by the kinship group."[114] However, giving to everyone who asks establishes "God as the new Father for the novice."[115] As a result of following these teachings the initiate "would die socially to their kinship and social group" while simultaneously entering into reciprocal fictive kinship relations with both the God of Israel and the members the *Didache* group.[116]

The process of re-socialization into the social memories of the *Didache* people can be seen beginning in chapter 3. Addressing the novice as "my child," the ritual elder explains that anger, lust, divination, falsehood, and grumbling are to be avoided because they lead respectively to murder, adultery, idolatry, theft, and blasphemy (3.1–6). In place of these qualities, the initiate must learn to be gentle, long-suffering, merciful, harmless, calm, and good (3.7–8). The ritual elder standing *in loco parentis* for God, the new fictive Father, supported the novice in this task:[117]

> My child, the one speaking to you the word of God, you will remember night and day, and you will honor him/her as [the] Lord, for where [the] dominion [of the Lord] is spoken of, there [the] Lord is. And you will seek every day the presence of the saints in order that you rest in their words. (4.1–2)

Daily meetings are envisioned not only with the ritual elder but with others in the *Didache* community for the purpose of supporting the novice in the process of re-socialization. The novice is encouraged to bring his or her children and slaves into the new society (4.9–10). While the slaves of group members are instructed to be subject to their "masters as replicas of God" (4.11), no similar direction is given children in relation to their parents or to wives with respect to their husbands. This instruction probably reflects the reality that non-Israelite men and women sometimes joined the *Didache* people over the objections of their polytheistic parents and/or husbands.[118] After a brief description of the way of death (5.1–2), the Two Ways discourse concludes with the exhortation to "bear the whole yoke

---

[113] Ibid., 56.

[114] Ibid., 57.

[115] Ibid.

[116] Ibid., 58. For more on this see also Milavec, *The Didache*, 758–68, on "the social setting for 'turning the other cheek.'"

[117] Draper, "The Role of Ritual," 59.

[118] See discussion of 1 Cor 7:12–16 and *The Acts of Thecla* in chapter 1.

of the Lord" and to observe Israelite food laws (6.2–3) as much as possible. Full observance of Torah is desirable—it leads to perfection (6.2)—but is "not a prerequisite for joining the community."[119] The only absolute requirement is the avoidance of things that have been sacrificed to idols (6.3), a stipulation which "functions to produce and maintain clear lines of demarcation between the old and the new social universe."[120]

As a written artifact of the social memory of the *Didache* people, the Two Ways discourse commemorates a ritual process of initiation in which the novice becomes separated from previous kin and social groups and in a state of liminality "undergoes a simulated primary socialization . . . with new fictive parents and new fictive peers."[121] The final stage of this process, Draper argues, is described in *Did.* 7.1–10.7 as a sequence of ritual actions consisting of "fasting, ritual lustration in the Name of God, a special prayer to be uttered by the initiands and a sacred meal."[122]

Once the novice has learned the behaviors appropriate for membership in the *Didache*'s society, he or she is to be baptized "in the name of the Father and of the Son and of the Holy Spirit, with living water" (7.1) or other ritually pure water (7.2–3). This ritual follows a communal fast, a ritual signaling a "break between the food of the old life and the life-giving food of the new community."[123] Baptism will incorporate the initiate into "a permanent and separate community in opposition to the rules and order" not only of non-Israelite society but also of rival Israelite groups.[124] Already prohibited from eating food sacrificed to idols (6.3) and hence from participation in many aspects of non-Israelite social life, the newly baptized convert is now instructed to fast regularly on Wednesday and Friday, not on Monday and Thursday like the hypocrites (8.1). In this way *Didache* people publicly declared their social identity as distinct from that of other pious Israelites in the community, who may or may not be Pharisees.[125]

Similarly, the newly baptized are directed to pray, not as the hypocrites do, but as the Lord instructed in the gospel:

---

[119] Draper, "The Role of Ritual," 63.

[120] Ibid., 64.

[121] Draper, "Ritual Process," 124.

[122] Ibid., 131.

[123] Ibid., 135.

[124] Ibid., 136.

[125] Draper, "Ritual Process," 136, asserts that the "hypocrites" are Pharisees; Niederwimmer, *The Didache*, 131–32, prefers to see them simply as "the pious within Israel"; Milavec, *The Didache*, 304–5, argues that the "hypocrites" are Judeans and/or Judean Christ-followers promoting temple piety.

Our Father who is in heaven,
may your name be acclaimed as holy,
may your kingdom come,
may your will come to pass on earth as it does in heaven.
Give us today our daily bread
and cancel for us our debt
as we cancel [debts] for those who are indebted to us,
and do not bring us into temptation
but preserve us from evil [or, from the evil one]
For power and glory are yours forever.[126]

The novice first uttered this prayer at his/her baptism. Here the newly baptized received instruction to pray this way "three times within the day" (8.3). Since the prayer had to be said aloud at the right time wherever the person happened to be, this ritual practice served as a continuing public affirmation of the person's membership in the *Didache* group, setting him/her apart from other Judeans as well as non-Israelites.[127] Thus group members commemorated Jesus' words on a thrice daily basis, not for their own sake, that is, out of any interest in historical preservation, but as a public declaration of allegiance to their new fictive kin group headed by the heavenly Father.

The initiation process culminates in the celebration of a sacred meal. Participation in this meal is restricted to those who have undergone baptism (9.5), a ritual ceremonially finalizing their transition from "outsider to insider, from pagan to saint, from stranger to brother or sister."[128] The text (9.1) identifies this meal as "a thanksgiving" (*eucharistias*) and gives the following directions for how ritual leaders should "give thanks" (*eucharistesate*):

> First, concerning the cup: "We give you thanks, our Father, for the holy vine of your servant David which you revealed to us through your servant Jesus. To you [is] the glory forever." And concerning the broken [loaf]: "We give you thanks, our Father, for the life and knowledge which you revealed to us through your servant Jesus. To you [is] the glory forever. Just as this broken [loaf] was scattered over the hills [as grain], and having been gathering together, became one; in like fashion, may your church be gathered together from the ends of the earth into your kingdom. Because yours is the glory and the power through Jesus Christ forever." (9.2–4)

The *Didache* people connect the elements of their sacred meal, not with the body and blood of Jesus as in the Pauline (I Cor 11:23–26) and Synoptic traditions

---

[126] *Did.* 8.2 see parallels in Matt 6:9–13 and Q/Luke 11:2–4.
[127] Draper, "Ritual Process," 138.
[128] Milavec, *The Didache*, 254.

(Mark 14:22–25//Matt 26:26–30//Luke 22:14–23), not with the flesh and blood of Jesus as in the Johannine (6:54–59) and Ignatian texts (Ign. *Rom.* 7.3; Ign. *Smyrn.* 12.2), but with the "vine of David your servant" and with "life and knowledge."[129] Jesus' role is explicitly identified as that of a servant through whom God revealed "life and knowledge." Only in the final doxology is Jesus referred to as the Christ, a notion that is not taken up anywhere else in the text.[130] A petition for the gathering of the Father's church into God's kingdom follows the thanksgivings.

Parallel structure and content characterize the thanksgiving prayers recited at the end of the meal:

> We give you thanks, holy Father, for your holy name, which you tabernacle in our hearts, and for the knowledge and faith and immortality which you revealed to us through your servant Jesus. To you [is] the glory forever. You, almighty Master, created all things for the sake of your name, both food and drink you have given to people for enjoyment in order that they might give thanks; to us, on the other hand, you have graciously bestowed Spirit-sent food and drink for life forever through your servant [Jesus]. Before all [these] things, we give you thanks because you are powerful [on our behalf]. To you [is] the glory forever. Remember, Lord, your church, to save [her] from every evil and to perfect [her] in your love and to gather [her] together from the four winds [as] the sanctified into your kingdom, because yours is the power and the glory forever. Come, grace [of the kingdom]! And pass away, [O] this world! Hosanna to the God of David! If anyone is holy, come! If anyone is not, convert! Come Lord! Amen! (*Did.* 10.1)

Here thanks is given for (1) the Father's holy name, which tabernacles in the believers' hearts; (2) the knowledge, faith, and immortality revealed through the servant Jesus; (3) the material food that nourishes all people; and (4) the Spirit-sent nourishment of the community for life eternal through God's servant, Jesus. Again the prayers conclude with a petition for the protection of the church from evil, its perfection, and its inclusion in God's kingdom.

What the *Didache* people commemorate in the meal is quite different from the focus on the death of Jesus in the Pauline tradition. This community celebrates God's actions as made known through the revelatory work of Jesus. The prayers before the meal connect the cup of wine with "the vine of David" (9.2), that is, the renewal of the house and lineage of David and, by extension, the restoration of Israel,

---

[129] Ibid., 663–66.
[130] Draper, "Ritual Process," 148.

the kingdom over which he ruled as God's servant.[131] By drinking the cup, the newly baptized are joined to Israel and its eschatological hopes,[132] perhaps even imagining themselves as becoming "members of the new royal household . . . a kind of alternative *familia caesaris*."[133] The meal functions to affirm the status of the newly (and formerly) baptized, not only as full members of the community, but also as "saints"—holy ones—in whose hearts the holy name of the holy Father tabernacles (10.2). God's presence, thus, is located in the assembly of the saints gathered in thanksgiving at the sacred meal. As such, the meal constitutes the community's "sacrifice," whose purity depends on each person's confession of failures (14.1) and reconciliation of interpersonal conflicts within the community (14.2). By describing this meal as "sacrifice," the composer(s) of the *Didache* enhance(s) its focus as a celebration of life with God and with one another.[134]

The "broken loaf" is bread, which was the staple of ancient Mediterranean diets and, thus, both a literal and metaphorical symbol of life. In Israelite traditions it is also a "common cultural symbol of knowledge/wisdom,"[135] frequently associated with the giving of Torah.[136] The sharing of the broken loaf with the newly baptized affirms their transition from unknowing to knowing, from the way of death to the way of life revealed through God's servant Jesus. In the prayers after dinner this knowledge is connected with "faith and immortality" (10:2). Faith means trust in the divine Father, commitment to the way of life, and trust in the forthcoming renewal of the kingdom revealed by Jesus. Immortality is simply freedom from death-dealing lifestyles and modes of thought now and forever. The sharing of the broken loaf in the sacred meal of the *Didache* community also enacts a proleptic participation in the coming kingdom.[137] Just as grain once scattered on the hills was gathered into the one loaf that now feeds the assembly, so the church consisting originally of Israel alone but now including the newly baptized non-Israelite will also be gathered into the Father's kingdom. In this way the community commemorates God's past

---

[131] Milavec, *The Didache*, 361–64.

[132] Draper, "Ritual Process," 150.

[133] Milavec, *The Didache*, 535, following Bruce J. Malina, "Mediterranean Sacrifice: Dimensions of Domestic and Political Religion," *BTB* 26:1 (Spring 1996): 36; Draper, "Ritual Process," 147.

[134] Milavec, *The Didache*, 152.

[135] Ibid., 373.

[136] Ibid., 374.

[137] Draper, "Ritual Process," 148, asserts that it is as king of the renewed kingdom that Jesus reveals the vine of David; Milavec, *The Didache*, 666, limits Jesus' role to that of revealer who will be among the 'holy ones' (*Did.* 16.7) coming with the Lord on the last day.

kingdom-building work, initiated through David while anticipating its forth-coming culmination as revealed through Jesus.

Jesus, like David, is identified as *tou paidos sou* ("your servant," "your child," or "your son") in relation to the divine Father. Here we see again the operations of social memory at work through framing and keying. Long-standing Israelite cul-tural memories about David provide the frame for keying the *Didache*'s presenta-tion of Jesus. Just as David, the servant/son of God, established a kingdom for God's people, so Jesus, the servant/son of God, reveals the forthcoming restora-tion of that same kingdom together with knowledge of and faith in the way of life now and forever. Jesus is further acclaimed as the Christ through whom God's power and glory are revealed (9.4). If Davidic traditions indeed key the *Didache* people's understanding of Jesus, then we might surmise that Jesus is or will be the king of the renewed kingdom, even though the text mentions nothing explicit about his role in the establishment or operations of that kingdom.[138] Undoubt-edly, more would have been said about that role within the context of the group's gatherings, but unfortunately nothing was recorded.

Jesus is commemorated in the prayers and rituals of the *Didache* people as the servant/son and anointed of the God of David. This community honors Jesus by doing what Jesus did: teaching the way of life and gathering for celebratory, life-affirming meals that anticipate the coming of God's kingdom.[139] Jesus' words and practices are remembered, repeated, and re-enacted because they define the group's social identity as the church waiting to be gathered into the kingdom. Jesus' words had been integrated into popular Israelite traditions and set the agenda for the group's way of life and mission in the interim—the initiation of non-Israelites into this kingdom movement.

The Words of Jesus in the Gospel of Thomas. Another early Jesus movement text, equally intriguing as the *Didache*, is the *Gospel of Thomas*. Like our hypothetical lost sayings source Q, the *Gospel of Thomas* is a collection of sayings. Its very existence strength-ens the case for the existence of the former. Indeed, the editors of *The Critical Edi-tion of Q* list fifty-six parallels between these two documents.[140] A small sample of these common sayings/discourses will suffice to demonstrate the continuing flu-idity of the Jesus tradition, not only in its early stages, as evidenced in Paul's letters

---

[138] Milavec, *The Didache*, 391–92.

[139] Kloppenborg et al., *Q Thomas Reader*, 78, 85.

[140] Kloppenborg et al., *Q Thomas Reader*, 88–93. Patterson, *Gospel of Thomas and Jesus*, 113–20; Davies, *The Gospel of Thomas and Christian Wisdom*, 3, 16–21. See also Valantasis, *Gospel of Thomas*, 13–20.

and the *Didache,* but still later at the end of the first or the beginning of the second century C.E., when the *Gospel of Thomas* was compiled in Syria.[141]

Whereas the sayings in Q (at least as reconstructed) are arranged in topical discourses, the majority of sayings in the *Gospel of Thomas* are not.[142] They appear to be organized without any thought to themes, topics, theological direction, or logical structure.[143] Yet the collection is not aimless. Valantasis argues that the *Gospel of Thomas* is best understood as an ascetical text that seeks to create "a new person as a minority person within a larger religious culture."[144] This process involves a reconstruction of the reader/hearer's subjectivity (personal identity), a redefinition of social relationships (social identity), and the construction of an alternative way of living.[145] The goal of the *Gospel of Thomas* is, therefore, similar to that of the *Didache,* which gives directions for the transformation of social identity through teaching and ritual performance. The *Gospel of Thomas,* however, seeks to re-create its reader/hearer's personal identity through a communal interpretative process, that Valantasis describes as a mode of discourse and a method of theology that "revolves about effecting a change in thought and understanding in the readers and hearers."[146] The hearer begins as a seeker trying to uncover the interpretation of the Gospel's secret sayings and emerges as an enlightened and empowered solitary or single person who is both young and old (Saying 4) and is neither male nor female but transformed (Saying 22). As a solitary, one lives alone and adopts a detached stance toward the world crystallized in the command to "be passersby" (Saying 42) or even homeless itinerants (Saying 86).[147] Amazing powers over the physical world (Saying 106), an intimate relationship with Jesus (Sayings 75, 108), and immortality (Sayings 1, 11, 18, 19, 111) follow.

Valantasis' ascetic reading of the *Gospel of Thomas* will be particularly helpful in assessing how this text works as social memory and, in particular, how it introduces instrumental changes into the tradition of Jesus' sayings in order to construct its own peculiar model for and of society. We will begin with a comparison of the Beatitudes:

---

[141] Horsley, *Whoever Hears You Hears Me,* 84–85.

[142] Valantasis, *Gospel of Thomas,* 6.

[143] Ibid., 22.

[144] Ibid., 10, 24.

[145] Ibid., 7, and especially 54, in contrast to Horsley, *Whoever Hears You Hears Me,* 147, who asserts that the Thomas people engaged in solitary reading and meditation.

[146] Valantasis, *Gospel of Thomas,* 11; Patterson, *Gospel of Thomas and Jesus,* 128–31.

[147] Malina and Rohrbaugh, *Social-Science Commentary on the Synoptic Gospels,* 41.

Q/Luke	*Gospel of Thomas*	Matthew
6:20—Blessed are you who are poor, for yours is the kingdom of God.	54—Jesus said, "Blessed are the poor, for to you belongs Heaven's domain."	5:3—Blessed are the poor in spirit, for theirs is the kingdom of heaven.
6:21—Blessed are you who are hungry now, for you will be filled. . . .	69.2—Blessed are those who go hungry, so the stomach of the one in want may be filled.	5:6—Blessed are those who hunger and thirst for righteousness, for they will be filled.
	69.1—Jesus said, "Blessed are those who have been persecuted in their hearts: they are the ones who have truly come to know the Father.	5:10—Blessed are those who are persecuted for righteousness' sake, for theirs is the kingdom of heaven.
6:22—Blessed are you when people hate you, and when they exclude you, revile you, and defame you on account of the Son of Man.	68—Jesus said, "Blessed are you when you are hated and persecuted; and no place will be found, wherever you have been persecuted.	5:11—Blessed are you when people revile you and persecute you and utter all kinds of evil against you falsely on my account.

The first noteworthy feature is the point that was made above. The macarisms in the *Gospel of Thomas* are not clustered together to form an extended discourse as they are in Q/Luke or Matthew. In all of these instances, however, the Beatitudes do ascribe honor to those to whom honor is not normally granted in the ancient world.[148] Just as Q/Luke's first beatitude addresses its hearers directly as "the poor," so does the *Gospel of Thomas*. In Matthew, however, the poor in spirit are referred to in the third person. To be poor in the ancient world meant that one lacked not primarily economic resources but the ability to maintain one's inherited status and honor because of misfortune or the injustice of others.[149] The *Gospel of Thomas'* version of the saying about hunger speaks of physical hunger, just as Q/Luke's does; in contrast, Matthew's version refers to a hunger for righteousness or justice. Yet, the condition of hunger itself is not what is blessed or honorable, according to *Thomas'* Jesus, but going hungry so that the stomach of another needy person may be filled. In a situation of limited resources, the sharing of food is particularly praiseworthy (see Luke 3:11).

The features most characteristic of the *Gospel of Thomas* occur in the sayings about persecution. Q/Luke 6:22 asserts that it is blessed or honorable to be

---

[148] Ibid., 400.
[149] Valantasis, *Gospel of Thomas*, 148.

persecuted on account of the Son of Man, who in Matthew is explicitly identified as Jesus (5:11). This connection to the Son of Man may be assumed but is not stated explicitly in the *Gospel of Thomas*, where persecution is universalized: "the seekers will be persecuted and hated in every place."[150] Persecution is thus valorized and becomes a defining characteristic of being a seeker and a solitary in a social context where these are not normative or highly valued lifestyles. In the *Gospel of Thomas* another macarism that turns the focus of persecution inward immediately follows this beatitude: those who have been persecuted in their hearts are the ones who have truly come to know the Father (*Gos. Thom.* 69.1). True knowledge of God that is intimate and relational emerges from internal conflict and/or mastery of contrary elements within one's own heart, rather than from reflection or mentalization.[151]

Just as Matthew added five additional beatitudes to Q's four, so we find additional macarisms scattered throughout the *Gospel of Thomas*. I will highlight four of them here, beginning with the one most characteristic of this work:

> Jesus said, "Blessed are those who are alone and chosen, for you will find the Father's domain. For you have come from it, and you will return there again" (*Gos. Thom.* 49).

Valantasis marks this saying as particularly illustrative of the way in which the *Gospel of Thomas* constructs personal identity. The two generalized categories ("those who are alone" and "chosen") become descriptors of the hearer and seeker through the designation in the second phrase as "you."[152] In this way they learn that not only are they solitaries but, as such, they are chosen and will find the kingdom. Why? The Father's domain is their origin and their destiny. As Valantasis asserts, "this sets the stage for their understanding of every other aspect of their lives."[153] *Gospel of Thomas* 19, where Jesus declares, "Blessed is the one who came into being before coming into being," gives a temporal dimension to the origins of those whom he calls to be his disciples since he promises that if they "pay attention to my sayings, these stones will serve you" (19.2). Related to this beatitude is *Gos. Thom.* 58, "Blessed is the person who has toiled and found life." Here "toil" refers to the work of recovering the interpretation of Jesus' sayings that results in renewed life in the present and guarantees that one will not "taste death" (*Gos. Thom.* 2).

The saying in *Gos. Thom.* 7 is somewhat different from the previous ones, but illustrates an important element of the Thomas people's worldview and practices:

---

[150] Ibid.

[151] Ibid., 126.

[152] Ibid., 127.

[153] Ibid., 65.

Jesus said, "Blessed is the lion that the human will eat, so that the lion becomes human. And foul is the human that the lion will eat, and the lion still will become human."

This beatitude assumes a hierarchically organized universe in which the human represents a higher life form or state of being than the lion. Whether the lion is eaten by the human or eats the human, the lion benefits by rising up to the level of the human. The process works in reverse for the human who is polluted or made foul by eating or being eaten by the lion; in other words, the human moves down in the chain of being. One interpretation of this saying "applauds the transformation of base into higher forms of life" and might be applied to welcome the unenlightened into the circle of seekers. Another reading of it might illustrate the principle that "you are what you eat," and function to problematize the eating of meat either by the Thomas people or by the Egyptian monks who later copied and preserved the text.[154]

Particularly interesting is the *Gospel of Thomas'* treatment of Q/Luke 11:9–10 (//Matt 7:7–8), in which Jesus promises, "Ask, and it will be given you; search, and you will find. . . . everyone who searches finds." In both the Gospels of Matthew and Luke, this saying is related to prayer and functions to assure the hearer that God hears and will respond appropriately.[155] The closest literary parallel to this saying can be found in *Gos. Thom.* 94: "One who seeks will find, and for [one who knocks] it will be opened." In these sayings the gratification of one's desires is immediate, occurring "with the speed of the opening of a door after someone knocks on it."[156] Searching and finding, however, emerge as recurring themes in the *Gospel of Thomas*. Indeed, they lie at the very heart of the task to which its hearers are called: to discover the interpretation of Jesus' secret sayings (*Gos. Thom.* 1). *Gospel of Thomas* 2 immediately sets out the nature of this project for the hearer:

> Those who seek should not stop seeking until they find. When they find, they will be disturbed. When they are disturbed, they will marvel, and will rule over all.

Discovering the interpretation of Jesus' sayings turns out not to be as quick or easy as having a door open as soon as one knocks on it. Seeking will not result in immediate finding; rather the seekers must persist until they find that for which they are searching. The finding will not end the process, however, since what is found will be disturbing, will cause them to marvel, and only at the end will empower them. Valantasis identifies this saying as describing the "performative

---

[154] Malina and Rohrbaugh, *Social-Science Commentary on the Synoptic Gospels*, 53, 272–73.
[155] Valantasis, *Gospel of Thomas*, 174.
[156] Ibid., 56.

process" through which Thomas' ascetic program for creating a new personal identity in the hearer is accomplished.[157]

Two sayings highlight the various frustrations associated with this process:

> Jesus said, "Often you have desired to hear these sayings that I am speaking to you, and you have no one else from whom to hear them. There will be days when you will seek me and you will not find me." (Gos. Thom. 38)

> Jesus said, "Seek and you will find. In the past, however, I did not tell you the things about which you asked me then. Now I am willing to tell them, but you are not seeking them." (Gos. Thom. 92)

In the first saying, Jesus indicates that only he can satisfy the seekers' desire to hear his words. Also, perhaps the narrator of this voiced text who speaks as and through the voice of Jesus can satisfy this hunger. In other words, no other performance (or text) of Jesus' sayings can have the effect that this particular one does.[158] If one searches outside of its boundaries, one will not find Jesus.[159] The second saying highlights a different problem. In the past Jesus did not answer all the questions that were put to him, and now that he is willing to do so, his followers no longer ask them. Valantasis notes that this saying is the only one in the entire *Gospel of Thomas* that "develops the barest outlines of an historical narrative"; he suggests that it may provide an historical rationale for the existence of the Thomas people and their peculiar understanding of Jesus.[160]

This brief examination of a few sayings from the *Gospel of Thomas* demonstrates the same social memory processes that we have seen at work in other early Jesus-group texts. The compiler of the sayings had an agenda that had little or nothing to do with the historical preservation of the words of Jesus. In recording these particular sayings, "Thomas" was providing a script for a set of oral performances that involved not only the recitation of the sayings but also their interpretation by a select group of hearers. In accepting the invitation to participate in this enterprise, the hearers become seekers whose goals are enlightenment and empowerment here and beyond, summarized in the promise that they will not "taste death." Through a process of communal interpretation, the seeker acquires a new personal (and social) identity. The sayings themselves provide the model of and for this transformation.

---

[157] Ibid., 114–15.
[158] A similar theme occurs in John 7:31; 8:21; 13:33.
[159] Valantasis, *Gospel of Thomas*, 173.
[160] Patterson, *Gospel of Thomas and Jesus*, 126–48.

On the basis of those sayings, the Thomas people may be described as a scattered and loosely structured movement of socially radical itinerants who are instructed to walk about the countryside, healing the sick and eating whatever is served to them (*Gos. Thom.* 14). They are instructed to set aside family ties, property, conventional economic activities, and even traditional religious disciplines such as fasting, prayer, almsgiving, dietary, and purity observances.[161] As we have seen in chapter three, the ideal seeker is epitomized in the character of Thomas, an "intoxicated" (i.e., Jesus-possessed) mediator of divine secrets, a prophetic or shamanic figure who is ultimately indistinguishable from Jesus himself (*Gos. Thom.* 108). As such, Thomas "records" and transmits the gospel's secret wisdom. The sectarian nature of the Thomas people is reflected in *Gos. Thom.* 13, where other understandings of Jesus are rejected and Thomas' special revelation is presented as eliciting hostility from other Jesus people.

The Jesus whom the *Gospel of Thomas* memorializes is unlike both the prophet of Q, who renews ancient covenantal relations in Galilean villages, and the healer and sage of the Synoptics. He is certainly not similar to the Davidic son of God to whom the *Didache* people look for the revelation of the way of life and the restoration of David's kingdom. In contrast, Thomas' text commemorates the work of the "living Jesus" and portrays him as a living presence who speaks directly to the reader/hearer.[162] Although Jesus' identity is rarely a subject of discussion in the sayings (in contrast to the discourses of John's gospel, for example), when it is discussed, he is described as a panentheistic divine figure, perhaps best exemplified in *Gos. Thom.* 77:

> Jesus said, "I am the light that is over all things. I am all: from me all came forth, and to me all attained. Split a piece of wood; I am there. Lift up a stone and you will find me there.

For this Jesus, "no person, no place, no event" is or can be outside of his purview.[163] As a corollary, there is no person to whom this living Jesus is not completely and directly accessible. This image of Jesus emerges early in the second century, in a context where the memory of Jesus is being contested within and between various Jesus groups and by their leaders (see *Gos. Thom.* 13). This contest over the memory of Jesus concerns not only the question "Who is Jesus?" but also "Who are the true keepers of Jesus' words and memory?" The *Gospel of Thomas*

---

[161] Valantasis, *Gospel of Thomas*, 8–9.

[162] Ibid., 155–56.

[163] Malina and Rohrbaugh, *Social-Science Commentary on the Gospel of John*, 221–22.

provides one answer; the Gospel of John provides another that is closely related but differently nuanced.

The Words of Jesus in the Gospel of John. The editors of *The Critical Edition of Q* identify about a dozen parallels between the Gospel of John and Q. Aside from John's version of the healing of the centurion's son in John 4:46–54 (or servant in Luke 7:1–10//Matt 8:5–13), these parallels almost always take the form of phrases or decontextualized word strings that the Johannine evangelist incorporates into his own peculiar narrative. The majority of these can be found in the farewell discourses, that is, in Jesus' final words as recorded in chapters 13–17. As is typical in ancient Mediterranean kin-based societies, Jesus' final words consist of predictions about forthcoming events of significance to his disciples, advice for how to keep the group together, and assurances of continuing interpersonal relations.[164]

Just a few examples will suffice to restate the point that the gospel writer had an agenda that had little or nothing to do with the historical preservation of the words of Jesus. The proverb, "servants are not greater than their master," occurs in Matthew's mission discourse (10:24–25), where it serves as a rationale for the anticipated labeling of the apostles as demon possessed. A similar saying may be found in Luke 6:40, located in the Sermon on the Plain. The same proverb occurs twice in John. In John 13:16, it functions as a mandate for mutual "footwashing," that is, forgiveness of sins within the Jesus group; in John 15:20, it valorizes the anticipated persecution of the disciples and points to "the antisocietal character of the John group."[165] The saying "Ask and you will receive" (John 16:24b) is related to prayer in the Synoptic Gospels, where it functions as an assurance of God's openness and willingness to provide. In the *Gospel of Thomas*, as we have seen, the same saying both assures and problematizes the seeker's confidence in receiving answers. The Johannine author makes it clear that the request must be in the name of Jesus: "if you ask anything of the Father in my name, he will give it you" (16:23). What the disciples receive is assurance that Jesus will continue to act as a broker between them and the heavenly Father, even after his death.[166]

The Q sayings that were incorporated into the Gospels of Matthew, Luke, and Thomas, however, play a very limited role in the Gospel of John. As noted in the previous chapter, the characteristic speech form of the Fourth Gospel is the prophetic oracle of self-commendation, in which the Johannine Jesus declares himself to be the bread of life (6:35, 41, 48, 51); the light of the world (8:12; 9:5); the

---

[164] Ibid., 223.

[165] Ibid., 242.

[166] Ringe, *Wisdom's Friends*, 61.

gate of the sheep (10:7, 9); the way, truth, and life (14:6–7); and the true vine (15:1). Through these terms Jesus claims to be (or at least speak for) divine Wisdom herself.[167] The oracles function in two ways: (1) to commemorate a particular understanding of Jesus, and (2) to legitimize the leadership of a particular group within the Johannine community who advocates this understanding. One example should suffice to make my point.

In the bread of life discourse (John 6:31–59), Jesus claims to be "the living bread that came down from heaven," and asserts that "the bread that I will give for the life of the world is my flesh" (v. 51). Only the one who eats the flesh of Jesus and drinks his blood will experience true life, eternal life, resurrection on the last day, and the mutual abiding in and of Jesus (vv. 53–56). By urging that his followers eat his flesh and blood, the Johannine Jesus apparently advocates "what has been prohibited as food to humans from the time of Noah, and . . . what is truly cannibalistic."[168] This eating is not intended to be understood literally, but as insider coded language (anti-language) in which "ingesting Jesus' flesh and blood is synonymous with welcoming, accepting, receiving, believing in" him "in spite of his being 'lifted up' and 'glorified' on the cross."[169]

Jesus does not speak these words during the Last Supper, but after the feeding of the five thousand when he engages in challenge-riposte interaction with a crowd in Capernaum's synagogue (vv. 24, 59). Thus, the discourse does not present Jesus as the initiator of a meal commemorating his life or death, as do Paul and the Synoptics, but as the true broker of God's life-giving bread who asserts his claim over that of Moses. It also functions to separate insiders, that is, Johannine Jesus people, from outsiders, that is, those who look to Moses and his Torah (or by implication any other source) for the bread of life. Although nothing in John's gospel explicitly connects this discourse with any ritual of commemoration like the Eucharist, Ignatius of Antioch does refer to the Eucharist as the "flesh and blood" of Christ (Ign. *Rom.* 7.3; Ign. *Smyrn.* 12.2), and the "bread of God" (Ign. *Eph.* 5.2; Ign. *Rom.* 7.3) that bestows immortality (Ign. *Eph.* 20.2), suggesting another alternative to the Pauline/Synoptic and the Didachist's commemorations.

The bread of life discourse (as well as the other distinctive Johannine discourses) preserves not the words of the historical Jesus but words about Jesus that derive from prophetic articulations of his importance to the Johannine group. These words are the ones the hearers of John's gospel are instructed to keep if they

---

[167] Malina and Rohrbaugh, *Social-Science Commentary on the Gospel of John*, 136.
[168] Ibid.
[169] Ibid., 133.

love Jesus (14:23). These words have been codified as the Johannine Jesus people's social memory, that is, the model of and for their society. Even in this one example, we see evidence for the group's sectarian or anti-societal stance that is not limited to other Israelites, but includes other Jesus people whom it sees as rivals. The Johannine Jesus and his words emerge from the conflict and crisis resulting from the death of its first generation of leaders, and epitomized by the beloved disciple. Prophetic rivalry (1 John; John 13:31–14:26), schism (1 John 2:19), and the breakdown of fellowship (3 John; 2 John) followed. Hence, the writer of 1 John argues that Spirit possession alone is not the sign of a true prophet, but must be accompanied by the dual confession that Jesus is the Christ and that he has come in the flesh (1 John 4:1–6). For this community the Gospel of John provides a definitive integration of prophetic activity in a narrative about the Jesus who came in the flesh. The evangelist seeks to resolve the problem of prophetic rivalry by producing a text that legitimates prophetic performances (perhaps his own?) while simultaneously limiting Spirit-inspired activity to the recollection of the meaning of what Jesus said and did (14:12–26; 16:12–14). The last chapter of the gospel presents a final resolution when the Risen Lord, present in the community as the Paraclete, chooses Peter to take on the role of the shepherd responsible for maintaining the community's integrity and fidelity to its remembered (memorialized) words of and about Jesus.

Conclusion

Social memory processes are evident in the way that the words of Jesus were preserved and transmitted by various early Jesus-group writers. Q/Luke 11:47–51 presents the Israelite cultural memory of the elite rejection of the prophets as a speech of Jesus, retrospectively and implicitly interpreting it as a reference to his death that incorporates him into the sacred narrative of the prophets. The same saying functions in 1 Thess 2:13–16 to affirm the social identity of the persecuted and harassed Thessalonian Christ-followers as belonging to the same tradition. A quick study of Paul demonstrates that he did not rely heavily or frequently on the sayings of Jesus to make his points. Only twice—in prohibiting divorce (1 Cor 7:10–11) and in defending the apostolic right to material support (1 Cor 9:14)—does Paul use loosely paraphrased commands of Jesus to support his position. Significantly, for Paul the word or command of the Lord is not limited to sayings that we can trace back to the historical Jesus but includes also nascent commemorative traditions about Jesus, as well as insights gleaned from personal ASC experiences.

In the *Didache's sectio evangelica* the words of Jesus are not introduced as such but are presented simply as applications of the double command to "love the God who made you, [and] your neighbor as yourself." As we can see, this is recited in an abbreviated proverbial—i.e., characteristically oral—form. In this text Jesus traditions and Israelite popular memory are integrated to form a single script defining the way of life. The end result is a new social memory, built by linking past, recent past, and present, that functions as a model of the values and norms ideally epitomized by the *Didache's* Israelite Jesus society and for shaping the social identity of non-Israelites wishing to join this group. Jesus' words and practices are remembered, repeated, and re-enacted because they define the group's social identity as the church waiting to be gathered into the kingdom. Jesus' words integrated into popular Israelite traditions set the agenda for the group's way of life and mission in the interim—the initiation of non-Israelites into this kingdom movement.

A brief examination of Q sayings that appear in the *Gospel of Thomas* demonstrate the same social memory processes at work. The compiler of the sayings has an agenda that had little or nothing to do with the historical preservation of the words of Jesus. Rather the *Gospel of Thomas* provides a script for a set of oral performances that involved both recitation and interpretation by a select group of hearers whose goal was enlightenment and empowerment here and beyond. Through the interpretive process the seeker acquired a new personal (and social) identity with the sayings themselves providing the model of and for this transformation. A similar set of conclusions pertains to the use of Q sayings in the Gospel of John. In fact they play a very small role in the Fourth Gospel, being limited to the farewell discourses in chapters 13–17. The characteristic speech form in John is the prophetic oracle of self-commendation, in which the Johannine Jesus declares himself to be the bread of life, and so forth. These oracles preserve not the words of the historical Jesus but the words about Jesus that derive from prophetic articulations of his importance to the Johannine group. It is these words that the hearers of John's gospel are instructed to keep if they love Jesus (14:23). It is these words that are codified in the midst of social conflict as the Johannine Jesus people's social memory (i.e., model of and for their society).

This study demonstrates that, for these early Christ-followers, keeping the words of Jesus did not and could not mean anything like a literalistic preservation and transmission of what the historical Jesus really said. In every case what was preserved and transmitted was a social memory in which past and present were integrated to tell a new story for a new audience in a new time and place.

5

CONCLUSIONS AND IMPLICATIONS

Roads go ever ever on under cloud and under star, yet feet that wandering
have gone turn at last to home afar.
(J. R. R. Tolkien)

IF BOOKS MAY BE compared to roads, then we have reached that point in this
journey where it is necessary to look back over the roads we have traveled in order
to ascertain where we have been and where we might go from here. I began with
the intention of examining in their Greco-Roman context the roles of stewards,
prophets, and keepers of the word in the early church. My expectation was that
stewards would represent the influence of existing social structures, prophets the
impact of religious experience, and keepers of the word the importance of tradition. What I have discovered is that stewards could be shrewdly subversive of
dominant power structures, prophets were innovators whose vision and imagina-
tion had to be controlled, and keepers of the word were creative interpreters of the
past. These roles were and are most effective when combined; the leaders who
have made the greatest impact are those persons who were simultaneously stewards, prophets, and keepers of the word. Jesus and Paul are perhaps the best
examples.

Jesus

Jesus lived in a group-oriented society where the house and household were the
basis of social organization at all levels. First-century Mediterranean households
consisted of co-residential, multigenerational groups related by kinship, marriage,
or other social arrangements, such as slavery. These households were patriarchal,
patrilineal, and patrilocal units of production and consumption. In other words,
these ancient families not only lived together but also worked and worshipped together in the same house, which served both as a private residence and as a place of
business and religious life, commerce, and worship.

In this society, access to scarce resources was dependent on having and maintaining the right social networks. Patronage relationships enabled persons not related by blood, law, or other traditional means to interact as fictive kin. In these interactions the party that controlled the needed goods or services played the role of surrogate father or patron, while those in need were clients playing the role of dependents. These relationships were often brokered or mediated by persons who enjoyed physical or emotional proximity to the potential patron. By acting as brokers, persons who otherwise lacked status and authority (such as women, slaves, and freed persons), could and did exercise considerable influence and power. Jesus' habit of addressing God as "father" is indicative of the ancient cultural pattern of imagining human-divine relationships as analogous to human patron-client relations. In fact, the Gospels, and especially the Gospel of John, most frequently present Jesus functioning as a broker of his heavenly Father's resources.

Jesus conducted his ministry in such houses, in the midst of such households and fictive kinship relationships. They provided the physical and social milieu in which he was born, raised, and lived out his vocation. We have seen in chapter one that Jesus critiqued and redefined these traditional patriarchal arrangements. Those who left their fathers' (or husbands') houses to join Jesus' movement found themselves in a surrogate family, a fictive kinship circle in which no human person held the power and privileges of a father or patriarch. As followers of Jesus they were all equally dependents, whether mothers, brothers, or sisters, in relation to one heavenly Father. Just as no one was to assume the role of father, no human person was to act as a patron. Just as there was only one father—the one in heaven—so there was to be only one patron—the heavenly one. Jesus sought to replace patron-broker-client relations that grew out of the vertical stratification of patriarchy with a dependent and sibling solidarity that emphasized general reciprocity and mutual support. In this way Jesus used one aspect (dependent and sibling solidarity) of what we might call "traditional family values" to subvert another element of those very same family values (patriarchal domination).

The status of the household as the primary and paradigmatic social organization in the ancient Mediterranean world meant that the city and even the empire were considered direct analogues. Where public offices existed, they were often based on household models, as in the case of the *oikonomos* ("steward") who administered the affairs of elite households, cities, social clubs, religious associations (including temples), and so forth. Within the context of limited goods and honor consciousness of the ancient Mediterranean world, the management of financial and other resources was most frequently in the hands of slaves or freedpersons that their elite masters regarded as lacking the appropriate sensibilities for honorable activities. Yet slaves and freed-persons coveted such positions as one of the very rare avenues available for upward mobility. As slaves and freed-persons, *oikonomoi* were the clients of their masters, whose patronage and favor ensured their positions. They occupied an in-between status involving a sort of derivative authority from their roles as agents and representatives of their masters. As such, they frequently functioned as brokers for other clients seeking favors from their masters.

Although Jesus never explicitly calls himself a steward, his modus operandi is not unlike that of the shrewd steward in the parable preserved in Luke 16:1–8.[1] In a world where persons like the rich man regard the equitable sharing of material resources as "unjust," the steward acts shrewdly by illicitly decreasing the amounts owed by his master's tenants. This move provides economic relief to the debtors, enables the rich man to acquire or retain a reputation for gracious generosity, and results in the master commending the steward. Everyone comes out ahead. The steward's methods are subversive, increasing his master's social capital (i.e., his good name and reputation among the tenants), at the expense of the master's greed for economic gain. In a similar way Jesus subverts traditional patriarchal household relations in order to build up a new surrogate family of equals for whom power is a resource to be used for others, not over others.

Jesus and his earliest followers lived in a cultural milieu in which prophetic figures were needed to communicate with the spirit world. Jesus' contemporaries understood and believed that this communication took place in altered states of consciousness. Sometimes these experiences took the form of possession, in which a god or spirit entered into and took control of the intermediary's personality, often signaled by loud or abnormal tones and rhythms of speech accompanied by excitement, ecstasy, or trance. Oracles that were understood as the direct speech of the possessing divinity or spirit would result. Meditative/mystic states and experiences such as soul flight could produce visions, auditions, or journeys through alternate reality.

As demonstrated in chapter three, Jesus was widely regarded as a prophet whose career seems to have manifested the characteristics of the "shamanic complex." ASC experiences—visions, vision quest, prayer, and possession—affirmed Jesus' calling and were the source of his healing and teaching. We described Jesus as a peripheral prophet operating outside the official structures of first-century Judean political religion, proclaiming the forthcoming reign of God. Jesus' heal-

---

[1] C. Brown, "The Unjust Steward," 121–45, in the process of making a different argument asserts that the "unjust steward" in the parable is Jesus.

ings and teachings demonstrated practically and theoretically how God's rule would function. In this anticipated theocracy, God would act as a father or patron to all of Israel, replicating Jesus' visionary experience of a God who interacted with him as a father/patron to a beloved son/favored client. All Israelites, elite and non-elite alike, would be siblings, equally dependents of the divine Father and Patron. Jesus' redefinition of patriarchal and patronal domination within the human community thus emerged from his prophetic vision. Such a social critique was consistent with his role as a prophet in Israel; he was following in the footsteps of Amos, Micah, Isaiah and others.

In the predominantly oral cultures of the ancient Mediterranean, thought and its articulation were closely linked with systems of memory, both individual and collective. Even literacy in the Greco-Roman world was highly oral and, thus, dependent on memory. Due to the difficulty of reading ancient manuscripts written in *scripta continua* (i.e., writing without word breaks or punctuation), most "quotations" of written texts were actually recitations of material recalled from prior reading or hearing of those texts. The reliance on commonplaces as the basic building blocks of rhetorical performance points to reliance on the remembered wisdom of the social group. In this cultural world, oral performance and social memory were inextricably intertwined. Social memory refers to the ways that human groups use the past in order to create and perpetuate social identities. Social memory provides models of and for society that are the subject of contestation, change, and persistence.

Although Jesus does not appear to have participated in the rhetorical culture of the Greco-Roman elites, he was a gifted oral storyteller and a master of verbal challenge and riposte. These skills are aptly displayed in Q/Luke 11:39–52 (see chapter four) where we encounter Jesus acting as a keeper of the word, recalling and interpreting the traditions of Israel. He reproaches the Pharisees for their devotion to purity, tithing, status, and building tombs for the prophets, while neglecting justice and love of God. Here Jesus speaks as a defender of the memory of the Israelite prophets and their message, criticizing the Pharisees for their failure to adequately preserve and transmit the prophetic traditions. Jesus' claim is that authentic commemoration of the prophets is demonstrated not by erecting elaborate shrines in their memory but in keeping their words alive by doing justice and loving God.

Jesus uses the prophetic call for justice to subvert the importance of public displays of piety (ritual cleansing, tithing, etc.) in much the same way that he uses the traditional family value of sibling solidarity to undermine patriarchal domination within the human community. Jesus as a keeper of the word functions both as a defender of an ancient and established tradition and as a shrewd steward of that same tradition by using it to critique and correct tendencies toward self-empowerment to the detriment of others in the community. Love of God, justice, and sibling solidarity work together as values and practices for the building up of community rather than individual reputations or egos. Community building rather than self-aggrandizement is what authentic prophets seek to accomplish. What we see in Jesus then is that the roles and functions of steward, prophet, and keeper of the word are inter-related and mutually reinforcing. Religious experience (ASCs) grounds Jesus' mission and empowers him to recall and lift up tradition (social memory) to speak subversively (like the shrewd steward) in order to build, maintain, and restore community.

Paul

Paul's ministry demonstrates the same sort of nexus between the roles of steward, prophet, and keeper of the word. Although Paul's mission field was the cities of the eastern Mediterranean, he too operated in houses (I Cor 1:11, 16:19; Rom 16:3–5, 13, 23; Phlm 2; see Col 4:15) that were the locus of work, worship, and family life. The nucleus of the Pauline *ekklesia* was often a household, such as that of Stephanas (I Cor 1:16) or Lydia (Acts 16:15). Individual persons could and did join these groups on their own, apart from other family members. The tensions created by this practice (e.g., "mixed" marriages) are hinted at in Paul's first letter to Corinth, highlighted in the *Acts of Thecla*, and confirmed by anthropological studies of conversion in contemporary Mediterranean cultures that share kinship orientations similar to those of Greco-Roman societies. Working out of ancient Mediterranean houses and households, Paul had to reckon with and carefully negotiate patron-broker-client relationships. The development of patronage relationships with persons such as Phoebe was necessary to facilitate his mission work but was fraught with tension, as evident in the delicacy with which he approached Philemon and even more so in his conflicts with elite members of the Corinthian congregation (see chapter one).

Paul's use of kinship language was intended to build and consolidate the social identity of church members as a surrogate family united in sibling solidarity with one another, regardless of their origins in different social classes or ethnic groups. We have seen in chapter one that, like Jesus, Paul lifted up the Mediterranean values of general reciprocity and mutual support that characterized sibling relations as a means of subverting patriarchal and hierarchical tendencies within the *ekklesiai*.

As we saw in chapter two, Paul's decision to describe himself as "a slave" of Christ (Rom 1:1; Phil 1:1; Gal 1:10) and a steward of God's mysteries (1 Cor 4:1) serves similar purposes. As Christ's slave and steward, Paul participates in the status and honor of his master. He represents Christ, acts on Christ's behalf, and speaks in Christ's name. Thus he can command a very high status and honor within the Christ-confessing community. Yet precisely as Christ's slave and God's steward, he is enslaved to all (1 Cor 9:19). Socially locating himself alongside manual laborers and slaves, Paul thus leads from below, in stark contrast to the dominant Greco-Roman ideology of benevolent patriarchalism assumed by the more well-to-do members of the Corinthian congregation. In the *ekklesia* the faithful steward imitates the crucified Christ in his solidarity with alienated humanity, rather than the benevolent patriarch of the dominant Greco-Roman ideology. For Paul, as for Jesus, the steward is a subversive figure standing in the margins between those who have status and power and those who do not. Faithful stewardship requires using that intermediary status and authority for the benefit of the weak.

Although Paul never called himself a prophet, our analysis in chapter three indicates that he possessed all the characteristics of one, and indeed was commemorated by the author of Acts as a prophetic figure. It is clear from his own letters that ASC experiences significantly determined the direction of Paul's life, transforming him from a persecutor to a promoter of the Jesus movement (Gal 1:15–16, 12). Altered states of consciousness were the source of Paul's eschatological teaching presented to his congregations as a word of the Lord (1 Thess 4:2–6, 15–17) and as divine mysteries revealed (1 Cor 15:51–52; Rom 11:25–26). For Paul, ASC experiences functioned as a source of innovative, and sometimes counter-cultural, teaching. It was in an ASC that he learned that God's "power is perfected in weakness" (2 Cor 12:9), a notion that is foundational to his understanding of the work of Christ (Phil 2:5–11) and to his own self-presentation as Christ's slave and steward.

Altered states of consciousness such as speaking in tongues and prophecy were prominently displayed in the Pauline *ekklesia*, as "the first fruits of the Spirit" given in anticipation of the forthcoming reign of God. When they became the basis for honor contests in the Corinthian church, Paul insisted that such experiences had to be evaluated in terms of their ability to build up the church rather than the individual. In other words, ASCs were not legitimate sources of personal status and power. Paul's preference for prophecy, for example, derived from its usefulness in building community by providing encouragement, consolation, instruction, and, when necessary, reproof (1 Cor 14:3–4, 19, 24). Thus Paul indicates that one criterion for determining the authenticity of ASC-based teaching and innovation is their commitment to and utility in building up the church as the body of Christ (cf. I Cor 12). As indicated in chapter one, the body metaphor once again connects us to the value of sibling solidarity. The church is thus a community characterized by mutual and reciprocal support. As the body of Christ it is called to embody and enact the crucified Christ's solidarity with alienated humanity, emptying itself in order to lift up the poor and the oppressed. As we have seen, for Paul, this is what faithful stewardship is all about.

In contrast to Jesus, Paul seems to have been introduced to the initial stages of a rhetorical education and the production of voiced rhetorical texts which enabled him to remain in contact with his geographically dispersed congregations. Paul's letters provide evidence for examining how he functioned as a keeper of the word (i.e., recalling and interpreting Israelite scriptural traditions, an examination of which was beyond the scope of this project) as well as the emerging social memories of Jesus groups. Hence, in chapter four we saw him using the tradition memorialized in Q/Luke 11:47–51 to affirm the social identity of his non-Israelite congregation in Thessalonica as "imitators" of the persecuted Judean churches, which in turn stand together with Jesus in a long line of persecuted Israelite prophets. In this way Paul enables the Thessalonian church not only to rationalize their suffering as part of an ongoing sacred narrative but also to see it as intrinsic to their identity as Christ-followers living in a hostile world.

Our study of Paul demonstrates that he did not rely heavily or frequently on sayings of Jesus to make his points. Only twice—in prohibiting divorce (I Cor 7:10–11) and in defending the apostolic right to material support (I Cor 9:14)— does Paul utilize loosely paraphrased commands of Jesus to support his position. Since Paul does not consider Jesus' command to make a living from gospel proclamation to be binding on him, it raises the question of how authoritative were the sayings of Jesus for Paul and/or for the early church? Paul regarded as of first importance the good news *about* Christ Jesus; that he died for our sins, was buried, and was raised from the dead (I Cor 15:3–4). Yet in writing to the Corinthian church he reminds them of this in order to introduce a list of witnesses to the resurrection of which he is the last (I Cor 15:5–11). The passage functions to set Paul up as an authoritative interpreter of the meaning of Christ's resurrection in a context where some members of the Corinthian community are calling into question the whole notion of a resurrection from the dead (15:12ff.). In explicating that meaning Paul engages in prophetic speech, revealing to his readers a mystery about the anticipated return of Christ (I Cor 15:51–52), discussed in chapter three. The emerging collective memory of historical witnesses to the resurrection event authorizes Paul to introduce a new eschatological understanding of that event, which he implies derives from ASC experience. Keeper of the word and prophet are in this instance mutually reinforcing roles.

The dynamic interaction of stewardship, prophecy, and tradition are even more clearly evident in Paul's treatment of the Lord's Supper. In I Cor 11:23–26 Paul recites what we know as the words of institution, which Paul says he received from the Lord (possibly as revelation?) and faithfully transmitted to his congregants. As we saw in chapter four, these words come from an existing narrative of Jesus' passion in which Israelite social memories of covenant making rituals have been appropriated and reinterpreted in new and scandalous ways. Paul concludes his recitation of the transmitted tradition by adding his own interpretation, "For as often as you eat this bread and drink the cup, you proclaim the Lord's death until he comes" (11:26). The meal, thus, commemorates the past death of Jesus and anticipates his forthcoming return in glory. The meal also provides a ritual participation in the blood and body of Christ that transforms the many who share the same cup and bread into "one body" (10:16–17). Paul insists that, for the meal to function effectively in creating, affirming, and maintaining the community's identity as the body of Christ in the world, the meal must be conducted in ways that embody the values of the crucified Christ. The Lord's Supper is not the Lord's Supper when some members of the community are hungry and/or humiliated (I Cor 11:20–22). Paul's words of institution, consisting of some combination of collective memory and prophetic vision, are used to subvert the hierarchical meal practices that the Corinthian Christ-followers brought with them into the church.

Religious experience (ASC) is the foundation of Paul's mission and his understanding of what it means to be an apostle of Christ. While Paul may not spend much time reciting words of Jesus, he keeps the word alive by striving to do what Jesus did. Like Jesus, Paul uses the traditional family value of sibling solidarity to build a community in which there is only one heavenly Father/Patron and one Lord, Jesus Christ, who is God's agent or broker (see I Cor 8:6). Paul, even more than Jesus, uses the language of stewardship to define what it means to function as a leader in community. Paul as a faithful steward eschews the dominant leadership paradigm of benevolent patriarchalism in order to re-present the crucified Christ's solidarity with the weak and lowly. This definition of stewardship is grounded not only in the example of Christ Jesus, but also in Paul's own ASC experience from whence he derives his understanding that divine power is perfected or made whole in weakness. Paul creatively interweaves emerging traditions about Jesus with his own prophetic insights to introduce new eschatological teachings and to undermine the hierarchical tendencies of his congregants. For Paul, as for Jesus, the roles and functions of steward, prophet, and keeper of the word are inter-related and mutually reinforcing.

Stewards in the Early Church and Today

In chapter two we saw that Paul was not alone in using slave terminology to identify himself in relation to Christ. Similar language is used by the authors of the epistles of James (1:1), 2 Peter (1:1), Jude (1), and Colossians (1:7; 4:7). In the book of Revelation both author (1:1) and recipients (1:1; 2:20, 19:5; 22:6) are identified as slaves of Christ or God. The word *oikonomos* does not, however, appear in these texts. It is used by the writer of 1 Peter in urging all Christ-follow-ers to be good stewards of God's manifold grace (4:10–11). This use of slave rhetoric reflects the reality that, among non-elite persons, service to persons of high status was a source of prestige. It also may have functioned to emphasize soli-darity between leaders and congregational members in the same way that fictive kinship terminology established the boundaries and nature of relationships with the *ekklesia*.

In the pseudo-Pauline texts the language of stewards and stewardship takes a different turn. The author of Colossians roots Paul's ministry in a divine commis-sion or perhaps in God's plan (1:24–25). This divinely commissioned Paul then proceeds to re-inscribe the dominant ideology of benevolent patriarchalism in the household code of 3:18–4:1. Likewise in Ephesians, Paul's ministry is described as consisting in the management of God's grace (3:2) and is the result of divine favor (3:7). This divinely favored Paul manages God's goods not only by bringing the gospel to the Gentiles (3:3–6), but by endorsing a household code firmly rooted in the ideology of benevolent patriarchalism (5:21–6:9). A similar valori-zation of dominant Greco-Roman values is to be found in the letter to Titus, where the bishop's role as God's steward requires him to possess all the character-istics of a Greco-Roman gentleman (1:7–9; see 1 Tim 3:1–3).

These Pauline trajectories lack Paul's emphasis on stewardship as an imitation of Christ's self-emptying solidarity with the weak. They also lack indicators of ASC. As artifacts of social memory these texts commemorate Paul as an authori-tative voice from the past, but his message is keyed to and by the authors' present desire and need to re-inscribe dominant Greco-Roman patriarchal household based values in the churches. This memory of Paul was not uncontested. The *Acts of Thecla* memorializes a Paul who endorses the renunciation of household and family commitments by valorizing the absolute value of ascetic chastity. Ignatius, who commemorates Paul as letter-writer and martyr (Ign. *Eph.* 12.1), represents a sort of middle way, affirming both marriage and celibacy (Ign. *Pol.* 5.1–2). He uses stewardship language to defend a bishop's lack of rhetorical skill (Ign. *Eph.* 6.1); thus grounding a bishop's authority in his role as God's representative in the congregation rather than in the possession of skills or attributes prized in the dominant culture (see Ign. *Mag.* 3.1). Ignatius is interested in securing the authority of bishops regardless of their qualifications while the pseudo-Pauline writers are committed to ensuring that traditional Greco-Roman householders are appointed to leadership roles in the church. Both use the language of stewardship to accomplish these different goals.

The question for us in the twenty-first century is how to measure faithful stewardship. Does it consist in unquestioning obedience to human masters, as demonstrated in the model of the two "successful" slaves in the parables of the talents and pounds? Does it consist in the uncritical endorsement of dominant cultural values, such as we find in the Pastoral Epistles and in so many contemporary models of stewardship that focus on financial growth? Or does faithful stewardship necessitate a subversive critique of culturally dominant models of leadership and success, such as we see in the parable of the shrewd steward? Does faithful stewardship call us to imitate Christ's solidarity with the weak, the poor, and the alienated, a model articulated and defended by Paul? Or perhaps some sort of middle road, as represented by Ignatius? How our ancestors in the faith answered these questions and how we answer them depend in large measure on social location, the presence or absence of authentic religious experience (ASCs), and how we define what we think it means to be keepers of the word.

Prophets in the Early Church and Today

Jesus and his earliest followers lived in a cultural milieu in which prophetic figures were needed to communicate with the spirit world. Jesus' contemporaries understood and believed that this communication took place in altered states of consciousness. Jesus' experience of God and Paul's experience of the resurrected Christ were foundational for their ministries and the counter-cultural directions that they took. We have noted that the pseudo-Pauline texts that re-inscribe the dominant Greco-Roman ideology of benevolent patriarchalism seem to lack interest in ASC experience. Is there a correlation then between religious experience (ASCs) and one's stance toward dominant culture?

Let us begin with our most socially radical texts. The *Gospel of Thomas* is rooted in ASC experience. The ideal disciple as portrayed by Thomas is an "intoxicated" (i.e., Jesus-possessed) mediator of divine secrets, a prophetic or shamanic figure who is ultimately indistinguishable from Jesus himself (*Gos. Thom.* 108). At first glance we might think of him as a figure quite similar to Jesus or Paul. The sayings he records and transmits, however, legitimate a loosely structured community of ascetics who live solitary lives marked by detachment from family ties, property, conventional economic activities, and even traditional religious disciplines. The goal is personal enlightenment and empowerment leading to immortality. There is none of the kinship or fictive kinship language that we associate with Jesus and Paul, no indicators that this text intends to create, affirm, or maintain a community. It is the individual who is to be transformed rather than the community, society, or the world.

The *Acts of Thecla* promotes a similar program of detachment from the world, especially from household and family life. Thecla's call to discipleship comes from overhearing Paul preach next door. She does experience an ASC, a vision of Christ in the form of Paul, while she is waiting to be executed in the arena at Iconium. Her personal power and authority increase as Thecla survives a series of potentially fatal ordeals. In each instance she is dramatically saved by divine intervention signaling that not only is she personally favored by God, her decision to leave her family is also divinely approved. At the end of the narrative, Paul affirms her call and sends her out dressed as a man to teach the word of God. Thecla is not a prophetic figure, although she is clearly a counter-cultural one. Her goal is personal liberation from the constraints of patriarchal society rather than the creation of a new and differently ordered society.

The *Gospel of Thomas* and the *Acts of Thecla* thus share a radical counter-cultural orientation and an interest in the transformation or liberation of individual persons. In both cases ASC experience and/or signs of divine favor serve to elevate the individual to a new status and/or role. This is precisely the sort of move that Paul opposes in I Corinthians 12–14. For Paul, authentic ASCs are characterized by the way that they build up the church as the body of Christ. The same sort of community orientation is found in Luke-Acts, where ASCs almost always serve to authorize the expansion of the church. Luke commemorates a Jesus who is particularly accessible to the poor, the marginalized, and women, and who consistently critiques the rich. His gospel is the one that preserved Jesus' parable of the shrewd steward. In other words, Luke regards ASCs positively as an instrument for building community, and maintains a critical stance toward dominant culture without demanding withdrawal from or rejection of the social world. This position seems closer to that of Jesus and Paul than the stances adopted by the *Gospel of Thomas* or the *Acts of Thecla*.

The other texts that we examined in chapter three demonstrate ambiguity and ambivalence about ASCs. The writer(s) of the *Didache* insist that only those prophets whose Spirit-inspired speech is not self-serving and whose conduct matches the truth they teach are authentic. These may assume positions of permanent leadership in the community. Yet by requiring such testing the *Didache* effectively subordinates the practitioners of ASCs to the judgments of local householders. The status of prophets is further eroded by indicating that their liturgical functions can be carried out by bishops and deacons chosen from among those same householders. Matthew shares the *Didache*'s concern for distinguishing genuine prophets from false ones and for subordinating them to the judgment of local community leaders. Unlike the *Didache*, Matthew makes no provisions for permanent prophetic leadership, although ASCs authorize Peter's scribal status and the community's teaching mission. In the Johannine literature, the Christological confession that Jesus Christ has come in the flesh is the standard by which authentic prophets are discerned; yet ASCs legitimate the pastoral ministry of Peter. None of these texts valorizes the dominant Greco-Roman ideology of benevolent patriarchy in quite the same way that the pseudo-Pauline texts do. In fact, each contains counter-cultural elements. The *Didache*'s teaching on the two ways, for example, omits the commandment to honor one's parents. Matthew's Jesus instructs his followers to call no man father, rabbi, or master (Matt 23:9–12). The Johannine Jesus insists that his followers are not his slaves or servants, but his friends (John 15:12–15). In all of these texts ASC functions dynamically in tension with social structures and tradition.

Religious experience, epitomized here as altered states of consciousness, is fraught with ambiguity. Their content is ambiguous, given meaning by the subject within the context of his or her worldview, and hence unverifiable by others. This is what makes it so difficult for many contemporary Western Christians to accept such experiences as anything but aberrant or pathological states. To do so, however, is to ignore or repress a vital source of spiritual insight. Spontaneous ASCs often provide powerful foundations for a sense of call or mission, as we see exemplified by the experiences of Jesus and Paul. For both of these persons, further ASCs provided not only what we might call spiritual resources for sustaining that call, but also functioned as a source of counter-cultural wisdom and innovation. It is equally important to note that their ASC experiences were filtered and interpreted through the prophetic traditions of Israel; Paul's were further shaped by the example of Jesus. Paul insisted that ASCs genuinely inspired by the Holy Spirit result in building up the church as the body of Christ, in which the weak are indispensable and the socially inferior are treated with respect and honor (1 Cor 12:22–24). Other early Christian writers suggested other criteria for discerning authentic Spirit-inspired speech and teaching (e.g., personal praxis, theological content). For religious experience to function effectively today, all these criteria ought to be evaluated for their ability to transcend the historical, social, and/or cultural boundaries separating contemporary Christians not only from the early church but also from each other.

Keepers of the Word in the Early Church and Today

As we demonstrated in chapter four, keeping the word in the ancient world did not, indeed could not, mean anything like a literalistic preservation and transmission of what some historical person really said. In every case, what has been preserved and transmitted in our texts is a social memory in which past and present are integrated to tell a new story for a new audience in a new time and place. Jesus, as a keeper of the word, lifted up particular aspects of Israelite scriptural and cultural traditions (e.g., the prophetic call for justice, the value of sibling solidarity) in order to critique dominant trends (e.g., public demonstrations of ritual piety and patriarchal hierarchies) in the society of his times. Although our study did not delve into Paul's use of Israelite scriptural traditions, Paul too was adept at highlighting one element in order to subvert another (e.g., the Abrahamic traditions over against the Mosaic covenant in Gal 3–4). Our examination of early Christian texts focused primarily on the notion of keeping the words of Jesus.

We saw that Paul emphasizes emerging traditions about Jesus' death and resurrection and eschatologically oriented revelations, far more than the words of Jesus in shaping the identity and consciousness of his *ekklesiai*. A dramatic contrast may be found in the *Gospel of Thomas*, which records words of Jesus to the exclusion of any and all narratives about his deeds, as the basis for self-transformation leading to immortality. The living Jesus, rather than Paul's crucified and resurrected Christ, is commemorated in the *Gospel of Thomas* as the source of life and salvation. In the *Didache*, Jesus' words and Israelite popular memory are integrated to form a single script for shaping the social identity of non-Israelites being integrated into this group. Jesus is commemorated as the Davidic servant/son of God who will soon restore his ancestor's kingdom. The Gospel of John commemorates a Jesus whose words consist of prophetic oracles of self-commendation, identifying himself as Wisdom. It is these words of the Word made flesh that Johannine readers are instructed to keep if they love Jesus (14:23), rather than the Q sayings we encounter occasionally in Paul, and so much more prominently in the *Didache* and the Synoptic Gospels.

Thus words about Jesus, words of Jesus, and words attributed to Jesus all held some sort of authoritative status in the various Jesus groups that produced our early Christian texts. These words functioned interactively with the various discourses that were occurring in these Jesus groups to create new social memories, new integrations of past and present that are memorialized in the texts that we have studied. We have seen that the early Christians, like other ancients, regarded these texts as scripts for oral performance, to be reconstructed anew at each retelling to meet the ever-changing needs of their audiences.

What does it mean to be a keeper of the word today? While we may at times dramatize texts, that is not our primary way of handling them. We read texts silently to ourselves and aloud in public contexts. We focus carefully on the words on the page, especially when the text in question is regarded as Scripture, as an authoritative guide for the Christian life in the world today. We are constrained by the words on the page in ways that the ancients were not. Yet it is possible to read the words on the page and arrive at quite different assessments of their meaning and value; it is possible to read the words on the page and miss the story in the text entirely. The challenge for us is to determine what constitutes a faithful interpretation of a text. If our early Christian texts are artifacts of the social memories of those communities that produced and preserved them, how do we use their content to frame and key our understanding of our present circumstances? In what ways should or could these texts provide models of and for the kinds of communities in which we want our children and grandchildren to live?

We have now come full circle. It is beyond the scope of this project to provide a blueprint for what it means to be a faithful steward, a true prophet, and/or a genuine keeper of the word. It is my hope that by examining the role of stewards, prophets, and keepers of the word in the early church we might be provoked to think more deeply about these three dimensions of leadership in our own time and in the many different places that we serve.

BIBLIOGRAPHY

Aarde, Andries G. van. "Fatherlessness in First-Century Mediterranean Culture: The Historical Jesus Seen from the Perspective of Cross-Cultural Anthropology and Cultural Psychology." *Hervormde teologiese studies* 55, no. 1 (1999): 97–119.

Aasgaard, Reidar. "Brotherhood in Plutarch and Paul: Its Role and Character." Pages 166–80 in *Constructing Early Christian Families: Family as Social Reality and Metaphor*. Edited by Halvor Moxnes. New York: Routledge, 1997.

Achtemeier, Paul J. "Omne verbum sonat: The New Testament and the Oral Environment of Late Western Antiquity." *Journal of Biblical Literature* 109 (1990): 3–27.

Aitken, Ellen Bradshaw. "*ta dromena kai ta legomena:* The Eucharistic Memory of Jesus' Words in First Corinthians." *Harvard Theological Review* 90 (October 1997): 359–70.

Arnal, William E. *Jesus and the Village Scribes: Galilean Conflicts and the Setting of Q.* Minneapolis: Fortress, 2001.

Ashton, John. *The Religion of Paul the Apostle.* New Haven: Yale University Press, 2000.

Aune, David E. *The Cultic Setting of Realized Eschatology in Early Christianity.* Supplements to Novum Testamentum 28. Leiden: Brill, 1972.

———. *Prophecy in Early Christianity and the Ancient Mediterranean World.* Grand Rapids: Eerdmans, 1983.

Barclay, John M. G. "The Family as the Bearer of Religion in Judaism and Early Christianity." Pages 66–80 in *Constructing Early Christian Families: Family as Social Reality and Metaphor*. Edited by Halvor Moxnes. New York: Routledge, 1997.

Bartchy, S. Scott. "Power, Submission, and Sexual Identity among the Early Christians." Pages 50–80 in *Essays on New Testament Christianity: A Festschrift in Honor of Dean E. Walker*. Cincinnati: Standard, 1978.

———. "Undermining Ancient Patriarchy: The Apostle Paul's Vision of a Society of Siblings." *Biblical Theology Bulletin* 29 (1999): 68–78.

Beare, Francis Wright. *The Gospel according to Matthew: Translation, Introduction, and Commentary.* San Francisco: Harper & Row, 1982.

Beavis, Mary Ann. "Ancient Slavery as an Interpretive Context for the New Testament Servant Parables with Special Reference to the Unjust Steward (Luke 16:1–8)." *Journal of Biblical Literature* 111 (1992): 37–54.

Boissevain, Jeremy. *Friends of Friends: Networks, Manipulators and Coalitions.* Oxford: Basil Blackwell, 1974.

Boomershine, Thomas E. "Jesus of Nazareth and the Watershed of Ancient Orality and Literacy." *Semeia* 65 (1994): 7–36.

Borg. Marcus J. "Jesus Before and After Easter: Jewish Mystic and Christian Messiah." Pages 53–76 in *The Meaning of Jesus: Two Visions.* Edited by Marcus J. Borg and N. T. Wright. San Francisco: HarperSanFrancisco, 1999.

Botha, Pieter J. J. "Letter Writing and Oral Communication in Antiquity." *Scriptura* 42 (1992): 17–34.

———. "Living Voice and Lifeless Letters: Reserve towards Writing in the Greco-Roman World." *Hervormde teologiese studies* 49, no. 4 (1993): 742–59.

Boulay, Juliet du. "Women: Images of Their Nature and Destiny in Rural Greece." Pages 139–68 in *Gender and Power in Rural Greece.* Edited by Jill Dubisch. Princeton: Princeton University Press, 1986.

Brown, Colin. "The Unjust Steward: A New Twist?" Pages 121–45 in *Worship, Theology and Ministry in the Early Church: Essays in Honor of Ralph P. Martin.* Edited by Michael J. Wilkins and Terence Paige. Journal for the Study of the New Testament: Supplement Series 87. Sheffield Academic Press, 1992.

Brown, Peter. *Society and the Holy in Late Antiquity.* London: Faber & Faber, 1982.

Brown, Raymond E. *The Epistles of John: Translated with Introduction, Notes, and Commentary.* Anchor Bible, vols. 29–29A. Garden City, N.Y.: Doubleday, 1982.

Burford, Alison. *Craftsmen in Greek and Roman Society.* London: Thames and Hudson Ltd, 1972.

Burtchaell, James T. *From Synagogue to Church: Public Services and Offices in the Early Christian Communities.* New York: Cambridge University Press, 1992.

Carey, M. J. and T. J. Haarhoff. *Life and Thought in the Greek and Roman World.* London: Methuen & Co., 1971.

Carney, T. F. *The Economics of Antiquity: Controls, Gifts, and Trade.* Lawrence, Kans.: Coronado, 1987.

Carruthers, M. *The Book of Memory: A Study of Memory in Medieval Culture.* New York: Cambridge University Press, 1990.

Chilton, Bruce, *Rabbi Jesus: An Intimate Biography.* New York: Doubleday, 2000.

Chow, John K. *Patronage and Power: A Study of Social Networks in Corinth.* Sheffield: Sheffield Academic Press, 1992.

Coleman, Janet. *Ancient and Medieval Memories: Studies in the Reconstruction of the Past.* New York: Cambridge University Press, 1992.

Corwin, Virginia. *St. Ignatius and Christianity in Antioch.* New Haven: Yale University Press, 1960.

Cory, Catherine. "Wisdom's Rescue: A New Reading of the Tabernacles Discourse (John 7:1–8:59)." *Journal of Biblical Literature* 116 (1997): 95–116.

Craffert, Peter. "Jesus and the Shamanic Complex: First Steps in Utilizing a Social Type Model." *Neotestamentica* 33, no. 2: 1999: 321–42.

Crossan, John Dominic. *The Historical Jesus: The Life of a Jewish Mediterranean Peasant.* San Francisco: Harper, 1991.

Crossan, John Dominic and Jonathan L. Reed. *Excavating Jesus: Beneath the Stones, Behind the Texts.* San Francisco: HarperSanFrancisco, 2001.

Davies, Stevan L. "The Christology and Protology of the *Gospel of Thomas*." *Journal of Biblical Literature* 111 (1992): 663–82.

———. *The Gospel of Thomas and Christian Wisdom.* New York: Seabury, 1983.

———. *Jesus the Healer: Possession, Trance, and the Origins of Christianity.* New York: Continuum, 1995.

Derrenbacker, Robert A., Jr. "Writings, Books and Readers in the Ancient World." *American Theological Library Association Summary of Proceedings* 52, no. 1 1998: 205–29.

deSilva, David A. "Patronage and Reciprocity: The Context of Grace in the New Testament." *Ashland Theological Journal* 31 (1999): 32–84.

Dewey, Joanna. "Textuality in an Oral Culture: A Survey of the Pauline Tradition." *Semeia* 65 (1994): 37–66.

Downey, Glanville. *Ancient Antioch.* Princeton: Princeton University Press, 1961.

Draper, Jonathan A. "Christian Self-Definition Against the 'Hypocrites' in *Didache* 8." SBLSP (1992): 362–78.

———. "Ritual Process and Ritual Symbol in Didache 7–10." *Vigiliae Christianae* 54 (2000): 121–58.

———. "The Role of Ritual in the Alternation of Social Universe: Jewish-Christian Initiation of Gentiles in the Didache," *Listening* 32 (1997): 48–67.

———. "Social Ambiguity and the Production of Texts: Prophets, Teachers, Bishops and Deacons in the Development of the Jesus Tradition in the Community of the *Didache*." Pages 284–312 in *The* Didache *in Context: Essays on Its Text, History and Transmission* edited by Clayton N. Jefford. Supplements to Novum Testamentum 77. Leiden: Brill, 1995.

————. "Torah and Troublesome Apostles in the *Didache* Community." *Novum Testamentum* 33 (1991): 347–72.

Drummond, Andrew. "Early Roman *Clientes*." Pages 89–115 in *Patronage in Ancient Society*. Edited by Andrew Wallace-Hadrill. London: Routledge, 1990.

Ehrman, Bart D. *Lost Scriptures: Books that Did Not Make It into the New Testament*. New York: Oxford University Press, 2003.

Eisenstadt, S. N. and L. Roniger, *Patrons, Clients, and Friends: Interpersonal Relations and the Structure of Trust in Society*. Cambridge: Cambridge University Press, 1984.

Elliott, John H. *A Home for the Homeless: A Sociological Exegesis of 1 Peter, Its Situation and Strategy*. Philadelphia: Fortress, 1981.

Esler, Philip F. *Conflict and Identity in Romans: The Social Setting of Paul's Letter*. Minneapolis: Fortress, 2003.

————. "Family Imagery and Christian Identity in Gal. 5:13 to 6:10." Pages 121–49 in *Constructing Early Christian Families: Family as Social Reality and Metaphor*. Edited by Halvor Moxnes. New York: Routledge. 1997

Fentress, James and Chris Wickham. *Social Memory*. Oxford: Blackwell, 1992.

Fledderman, Harry. "The Householder and the Servant Left in Charge." SBLSP 25 (1986): 17–26.

Foley, John M. "Indigenous Poems, Colonialist Texts." Pages 9–35 in *Orality, Literacy, and Colonialism in Antiquity*. Semeia Studies 47. Edited by Jonathan A. Draper. Atlanta: Society of Biblical Studies, 2004.

Ford, Richard Q. *The Parables of Jesus: Recovering the Art of Listening*. Minneapolis: Fortress, 1997.

Fredriksen, Paula. *Jesus of Nazareth, King of the Jews: A Jewish Life and the Emergence of Christianity*. New York: Alfred A. Knopf, 1999.

Furnish, Victor Paul. Notes to "The First Letter of Paul to the Corinthians." Page 2155 in *The Harper Collins Study Bible*. Edited by Wayne A. Meeks. San Francisco: HarperSanFrancisco, 1993.

Garland, Robert. "Priests and Power in Classical Athens." Pages 75–91 in *Pagan Priests: Religion and Power in the Ancient World*. Edited by Mary Beard and John North. Ithaca, N.Y.: Cornell University Press, 1990.

Garnsey, Peter and Richard P. Saller. *The Roman Empire: Economy, Society, and Culture*. Berkeley: University of California Press, 1987.

Garnsey, Peter and Greg Woolf. "Patronage of the Rural Poor in the Roman World." Pages 153–70 in *Patronage in Ancient Society*. Edited by Andrew Wallace-Hadrill. London: Routledge, 1990.

Goodman, Felicitas D. *Where the Spirits Ride the Wind: Trance Journeys and Other Ecstatic Experiences*. Bloomington & Indianapolis: Indiana University Press, 1990.

Gordon, Richard. "Religion in the Roman Empire: The Civic Compromise and Its Limits." Pages 235–55 in *Pagan Priests: Religion and Power in the Ancient World.* Edited by Mary Beard and John North. Ithaca, N.Y.: Cornell University Press, 1990.

―――. "The Veil of Power: Emperors, Sacrificers and Benefactors." Pages 201–31 in *Pagan Priests: Religion and Power in the Ancient World.* Edited by Mary Beard and John North. Ithaca, N.Y.: Cornell University Press, 1990.

Grayston, Kenneth. *The Johannine Epistles.* Grand Rapids: Eerdmans, 1984.

Haines-Eitzen, Kim. *Guardians of Letters: Literacy, Power, and the Transmitters of Early Christian Literature.* New York: Oxford University Press, 2000.

Halbwachs, Maurice. *On Collective Memory.* Edited and translated by Lewis A. Coser. Chicago: Chicago University Press, 1992.

Hanson, K. C. and Douglas E. Oakman. *Palestine in the Time of Jesus: Social Structures and Social Conflicts.* Minneapolis: Fortress, 1998.

Harill, J. A. "Slavery." Pages 1124–27 in *Dictionary of New Testament Background: A Compendium of Contemporary Biblical Scholarship.* Edited by Craig A. Evans and Stanley E. Porter. Downers Grove, Ill.: InterVarsity, 2000.

Harland, Philip A. *Associations, Synagogues, and Congregations: Claiming a Place in Ancient Mediterranean Society.* Minneapolis: Fortress, 2003.

Harrison, P. N. *Polycarp's Two Epistles to the Philippians.* Cambridge: Cambridge University Press, 1936.

Henderson, Ian H. "The Didache and Orality in Synoptic Comparison," *Journal of Biblical Literature* 111 (1992): 283–306.

Hopwood, Keith. "Bandits, Elites and Rural Order." Pages 171–87 in *Patronage in Ancient Society.* Edited by Andrew Wallace-Hadrill. London: Routledge, 1990.

Horsley, Richard A., with Jonathan A. Draper. *Whoever Hears You Hears Me: Prophets, Performance, and Tradition in Q.* Harrisburg: Trinity, 1999.

Horsley, Richard A. and Neil Asher Silberman. *The Message and the Kingdom: How Jesus and Paul Ignited a Revolution and Transformed the Ancient World.* Minneapolis: Fortress, 2002.

Hultgren, Arland J. *The Parables of Jesus: A Commentary.* Grand Rapids: Eerdmans, 2002.

Jacobs-Malina, D. *Beyond Patriarchy: The Images of Family in Jesus.* New York: Paulist, 1993.

Jaffee, Martin S. "Rabbinic Oral Tradition in Late Byzantine Galilee: Christian Empire and Rabbinic Ideological Resistance." Pages 171–91 in *Orality, Literacy, and Colonialism in Antiquity.* Semeia Studies 47. Edited by Jonathan A. Draper. Atlanta: Society of Biblical Literature, 2004.

Jefford, Clayton N. "Did Ignatius of Antioch Know the *Didache*?" Pages 330–51 in *The* Didache *in Context: Essays on Its Text, History, and Transmission*. Edited by Clayton N. Jefford. Supplements to Novum Testamentum 77. Leiden: Brill, 1995.

———. *The Sayings of Jesus in the Teaching of the Twelve Apostles*. Vigiliae Christianae Supplement 11. Leiden: Brill, 1989.

Johnson, E. Elizabeth. "Ephesians." Pages 338–42 in *The Women's Bible Commentary*. Edited by Carol A. Newsom and Sharon H. Ringe. Louisville: Westminster John Knox, 1992.

Johnson, Luke Timothy. *Religious Experience in Earliest Christianity: A Missing Dimension in New Testament Studies*. Minneapolis: Fortress, 1998.

Johnson, Terry and Christopher Dandeker. "Patronage: Relation and System." Pages 219–40 in *Patronage in Ancient Society*. Edited by Andrew Wallace-Hadrill. London: Routledge, 1990.

Kelber, Werner H. "The Case of the Gospels: Memory's Desire and the Limits of Historical Criticism." *Oral Tradition* 17, no. 1 (2002): 55–86.

Kirk Alan. "The Memory of Violence and the Death of Jesus in Q." Pages 191–206 in *Memory, Tradition, and Text: Uses of the Past in Early Christianity*. Semeia Studies 52. Edited by Alan Kirk and Tom Thatcher. Atlanta, Society of Biblical Literature, 2005.

———. "Social & Cultural Memory." Pages 1–24 in *Memory, Tradition and Text: Uses of the Past in Early Christianity*. Semeia Studies 52. Edited by Alan Kirk and Tom Thatcher. Atlanta, Society of Biblical Literature, 2005.

Kloppenborg, John S. *Excavating Q: The History and Setting of the Sayings Gospel*. Edinburgh: T&T Clark, 2000.

Kloppenborg Verbin, John S. "Patronage Avoidance in James." *Hervormde teolgiese studies* 55:4 (1999): 755–94.

Kloppenborg, John S. et al. *The Q Thomas Reader*. Sonoma, Calif.: Polebridge, 1990.

Kraemer, Ross S. *Her Share of the Blessings: Women's Religions among Pagans, Jews, and Christians in the Greco-Roman World*. New York: Oxford University Press, 1992.

———. "Mark 10:29–30: Sisters and Mothers Left for Jesus' Sake." Pages 93–105 in *Women in Scripture: A Dictionary of Named and Unnamed Women in the Hebrew Bible, The Apocryphal/Deutorcanonical Books, and the New Testament*. Edited by Carol Meyers. Grand Rapids: Eerdmans, 2000.

Lampe, G. W. H. "Martyrdom and Inspiration." Pages 118–35 in *Suffering and Martyrdom in the New Testament: Studies presented to G. M. Styler by the Cambridge New Testament Seminar*. Edited by William Horbury and Brian McNeil. Cambridge: Cambridge University Press, 1981.

Landry, David and Ben May. "Honor Restored: New Light on the Parable of the Prudent Steward (Luke 16:1–8a)." *Journal of Biblical Literature* 119:2 (2000): 287–309.

Lassen, Eva Marie. "The Roman Family: Ideal and Metaphor." Pages 103–20 in *Constructing Early Christian Families: Family as Social Reality and Metaphor.* Edited by Halvor Moxnes. New York: Routledge, 1997.

Lieu, Judith M. *The Theology of the Johannine Epistles.* Cambridge: Cambridge University Press, 1991.

Lightstone, Jack. "Christian Anti-Judaism in Its Judaic Mirror: The Judaic Context of Early Christianity Revisited." Pages 103–32 in *Anti-Judaism in Early Christianity.* Volume 2: Separation and Polemic; Studies in Christianity and Judaism 2. Edited by Stephen G. Wilson. Waterloo, Ont.: Wilfrid Laurier University Press, 1986.

Lygre, John G. "Of What Charges? (Luke 16:1–2)," *Biblical Theology Bulletin* 32, no. 1 (Spring 2002): 21–28.

MacDonald, Margaret Y. *Colossians and Ephesians.* Sacra Pagina Series, Volume 17. Collegeville, Minn.: Liturgical, 2000.

———. *Early Christian Women and Pagan Opinion: The Power of the Hysterical Woman.* Cambridge: Cambridge University Press, 1996.

Maier, Harry O. *The Social Setting of the Ministry as Reflected in the Writings of Hermas, Clement and Ignatius.* Dissertations SR 1. Waterloo, Ont.: Wilfrid Laurier University Press, 1991.

Malina, Bruce J. "Daily Life in the New Testament Period." Pages 355–70 in *Life and Culture in the Ancient Near East.* Edited by Richard E. Averbeck, Mark W. Chavalas and David B. Weisberg. Bethesda, Md.: CDL, 2003.

———. "The Maverick Christian Group—The Evidence of Sociolinguistics." *Biblical Theology Bulletin* 24, no. 4 (1994): 167–82.

———. "Mediterranean Sacrifice: Dimensions of Domestic and Political Religion." *Biblical Theology Bulletin* 26:1 (Spring 1996): 26–44.

———. "Mother and Son." *Biblical Theology Bulletin* 20 (1990): 57–61.

———. *The New Testament World: Insights from Cultural Anthropology.* Third Edition, Revised and Expanded. Louisville, Ky.: Westminster John Knox, 2001.

———. "Patron and Client: The Analogy behind Synoptic Theology." *Foundations & Facets Forum* 4, no. 1 (1988): 2–32.

———. *The Social Gospel of Jesus: The Kingdom of God in Mediterranean Perspective.* Minneapolis: Fortress, 2001.

———. "The Social World Implied in the Letters of the Christian Bishop-Martyr (named Ignatius of Antioch)." SBLSP (1978): 71–119.

Malina, Bruce J. and Richard L. Rohrbaugh. *Social-Science Commentary on the Gospel of John*. Minneapolis: Fortress, 1998.

————. *Social-Science Commentary on the Synoptic Gospels*. Minneapolis: Fortress, 2003.

Martin, Dale B. *Slavery as Salvation: The Metaphor of Slavery in Pauline Christianity*. New Haven: Yale University Press, 1990.

Mason, A. J. "Conception of the Church in Early Times." Pages 1–57 in *Church, Ministry, and Organization in the Early Church Era*. Edited by Everett Ferguson. Studies in Early Christianity 13. New York: Garland Publishing, 1993.

Matthews, V. C. and D. C. Benjamin. *Social World of Ancient Israel 1250–587 B.C.E.* Peabody, Mass.: Hendrickson, 1993.

Meeks, Wayne A. *The First Urban Christians: The Social World of the Apostle Paul*. New Haven: Yale University Press, 1983.

————. "The Man from Heaven in Johannine Sectarianism." *Journal of Biblical Literature* 91 (1972): 44–72.

Milavec, Aaron. *The Didache: Faith, Hope, and Life of the Earliest Christian Communities, 50–70 C.E.* New York: Newman, 2003.

————. "Distinguishing True and False Prophets: The Protective Wisdom of the *Didache*." *Journal for Early Christian Studies* 2, no. 2 (1994): 117–35.

————. "The Social Setting of 'Turning the Other Cheek' and 'Loving One's Enemies' in Light of the Didache," *Biblical Theology Bulletin* 25 (1995): 131–43.

Minear, Paul S. *To Heal and to Reveal: The Prophetic Vocation according to Luke*. New York: Crossroad, 1976.

Moxnes, Halvor. "What Is Family? Problems in Constructing Early Christian Families." Pages 13–41 in *Constructing Early Christian Families: Family as Social Reality and Metaphor*. Edited by Halvor Moxnes. New York: Routledge, 1997.

Neyrey, Jerome H. *Paul, in Other Words: A Cultural Reading of His Letters*. Louisville, Ky.: Westminster John Knox, 1990.

————. *An Ideology of Revolt: John's Christology in Social-Science Perspective*. Minneapolis: Fortress, 1988.

Niederwimmer, Kurt. *The Didache: A Commentary*. Minneapolis: Fortress, 1998.

North, John. "Diviners and Divination at Rome." Pages 51–71 in *Pagan Priests: Religion and Power in the Ancient World*. Edited by Mary Beard and John North. Ithaca, N.Y.: Cornell University Press, 1990.

Olick, Jeffrey K. and Joyce Robbins, "Social Memory Studies: From 'Collective Memory' to the Historical Sociology of Mnemonic Practices." *Annual Review of Sociology* 24 (1998): 105–40.

Ong, Walter J. *Orality and Literacy: The Technologizing of the Word.* New York: Methuen, 1982.

Osiek, Carolyn. "Slavery in the Second Testament World." *Biblical Theology Bulletin* 22 (1992): 174–79.

Osiek, Carolyn and David L. Balch. *Families in the New Testament World: Households and House Churches.* Louisville: Westminster John Knox, 1997.

Overholt, Thomas W. *Channels of Prophecy: The Social Dynamics of Prophetic Activity.* Minneapolis, Fortress, 1988.

Overman, J. Andrew. *Matthew's Gospel and Formative Judaism: The Social World of the Matthean Community.* Minneapolis: Fortress, 1990.

Pagels, Elaine H. *Beyond Belief: the Secret Gospel of Thomas.* New York: Random House, 2003.

Paine, Robert. "A Theory of Patronage and Brokerage." Pages 8–21 in *Patrons and Brokers in the East Arctic.* Edited by Robert Paine. Institute of Social and Economic Research, Memorial University of Newfoundland, 1971.

Painter, John. "The Farewell Discourse and the History of Johannine Christianity." *New Testament Studies* 27 (1981): 252–43.

———. "The 'Opponents' in I John." *New Testament Studies* 32 (1986): 48–71.

Patterson, Stephen J. *The God of Jesus: The Historical Jesus and the Search for Meaning.* Harrisburg, Pa.: Trinity, 1998.

———. *The Gospel of Thomas and Jesus.* Sonoma, Calif.: Polebridge, 1993.

Perdue, Leo G. "The Israelite and Early Jewish Family: Summary and Conclusions." Pages 163–222 in *Families in Ancient Israel.* Edited by Leo G. Perdue, et al. Louisville: Westminster John Knox, 1997.

Pilch, John J. "Altered States of Consciousness: A 'Kitbashed' Model." *Biblical Theology Bulletin* 26 (1996): 133–38.

———. "Altered States of Consciousness Events in the Synoptics." Pages 103–15 in *The Social Setting of Jesus and the Gospels.* Edited by Wolfgang Stegemann, Bruce J. Malina, and Gerd Theissen. Minneapolis: Fortress, 2002.

———. "Appearances of the Risen Jesus in Cultural Context: Experiences of Alternate Reality." *Biblical Theology Bulletin* 28 (1998): 52–60.

———. "Paul's Ecstatic Trance Experience Near Damascus in Acts of the Apostles." *Hervormde teologiese studies* 58 (2002): 690–707.

———. "Visions in Revelation and Alternate Consciousness: A Perspective from Cultural Anthropology." *Listening: Journal of Religion and Culture* 28 (1993): 231–44.

Pilch, John J. and Bruce J. Malina. *Handbook of Biblical Social Values.* Peabody, Mass.: Hendrickson, 1998.

Portefaix, Lillian. *Sisters Rejoice: Paul's Letters to the Philippians and Luke-Acts as Received by First-Century Philippian Women.* Stockholm: Almquist and Wiksell, 1988.

Powell, Mark Allen. *Fortress Introduction to the Gospels.* Minneapolis: Fortress, 1998.

Quast, Kevin. *Peter and the Beloved Disciple: Figures for a Community in Crisis.* Journal for the Study of the New Testament Supplement Series 32. Sheffield: Sheffield Academic Press, 1989.

Rader, Rosemary. *Breaking Boundaries: Male/Female Friendship in Early Christian Communities.* New York: Paulist, 1983.

Reinhartz, Adele. "The Johannine Community and Its Jewish Neighbors: A Reappraisal." Pages 111–38 in *What is John? Volume II, Literary and Social Readings of the Fourth Gospel.* Edited by Fernando F. Segovia. Society of Biblical Literature Symposium Series. Atlanta: Scholars Press, 1998.

Rensberger, David. "Sectarianism and Theological Interpretation in John." Pages 139–56 in *What is John? Volume II, Literary and Social Readings of the Fourth Gospel.* Edited by Fernando F. Segovia. SBL Symposium Series. Atlanta: Scholars Press, 1998.

Reumann, John. "*Oikonomia* = 'Covenant': Terms for *Heilsgeschichte* in Early Christian Usage." *Novum Testamentum* 3 (1959): 282–92.

———. "*OIKONOMIA:* Terms in Paul in Comparison with Lucan *Heilsgeschichte.*" *New Testament Studies* 12 (Jan 1967): 147–67.

———. "'Stewards of God': Pre-Christian Religious Application of *Oikonomos* in Greek." *Journal of Biblical Literature* 77, no. 4 (1958): 339–49.

———. *Stewardship and the Economy of God.* Grand Rapids: Eerdmans, 1992.

Richardson, Cyril C. "The Church in Ignatius of Antioch." *Journal of Religious History* 17 (1937): 428–43.

Ringe, Sharon H. *Wisdom's Friends: Community and Christology in the Fourth Gospel.* Louisville, Ky.: Westminster John Knox, 1999.

Robbins, Vernon K. "Oral, Rhetorical, and Literary Cultures: A Response." *Semeia* 65 (1994): 75–94.

Robinson, James M., Paul Hoffmann, and John S. Kloppenborg, eds. *The Critical Edition of Q.* Minneapolis: Fortress 2000.

Rousseau, John J. and Rami Arav. *Jesus and His World: An Archaeological and Cultural Dictionary.* Minneapolis: Fortress, 1995.

Ruis-Camps, J. *The Four Authentic Letters of Ignatius the Martyr.* Rome: Pontificium Institutum Orientalis Studiorum, 1980.

Saldarini, Anthony J. "The Gospel of Matthew and Jewish-Christian Conflict." Pages 38–61 in *Social History of the Matthean Community.* Edited by David Balch. Minneapolis: Fortress, 1990.

Saller, Richard P. "Patronage and Friendship in Early Imperial Rome: Drawing the Distinctions." Pages 49–62 in *Patronage in Ancient Society.* Edited by Andrew Wallace-Hadrill. London: Routledge, 1990.

――――. *Personal Patronage Under the Early Empire.* Cambridge: Cambridge University Press, 1982.

Sandnes, Karl Olav. "Equality Within Patriarchal Structures: Some New Testament Perspectives on the Christian Fellowship as a Brother- or Sisterhood and a Family." Pages 150–65 in *Constructing Early Christian Families: Family as Social Reality and Metaphor.* Edited by Halvor Moxnes. New York: Routledge, 1997.

Sandt, Hubb van de and David Flusser. *The Didache: Its Jewish Sources and Its Place in Early Judaism and Christianity.* Minneapolis: Fortress, 2002.

Schoedel, William R. *Ignatius of Antioch: A Commentary on the Letters of Ignatius of Antioch.* Hermeneia. Philadelphia: Fortress, 1985.

Schwartz, Barry. "Memory as a Cultural System: Abraham Lincoln in World War II." *American Sociological Review* 61 (October 1996): 908–27.

Smith, Robert H. "Matthew's Message for Insiders: Charisma and Commandments in a First-Century Community." *Interpretation* 46, no. 3 (1992): 229–39.

Spilsbury, Paul. "God and Israel in Josephus: A Patron-Client Relationship." Pages 172–91 in *Understanding Josephus: Seven Perspectives.* Journal for the Study of the Pseudepigrapha Supplement Series 32. Sheffield: Sheffield Academic Press, 1998.

Stambaugh, John E. and David L. Balch. *The New Testament and its Social Environment.* Philadelphia: Westminster, 1986.

Stegemann, Ekkehard W. and Wolfgang Stegemann. *The Jesus Movement: A Social History of Its First Century.* Minneapolis: Fortress, 1999.

Streeter, B. H. *The Primitive Church Studied with Reference to the Origins of the Christian Ministry.* London: Macmillan and Co., 1930.

Sullivan, Francis A. *From Apostles to Bishops: The Development of the Episcopacy in the Early Church.* Mahweh, N.J.: Newman, 2001.

Syrjanen, Seppo. *In Search of Meaning and Identity: Conversion to Christianity in Pakistani Muslim Culture.* Vammala: The Finnish Society for Missiology and Ecumenics, 1984.

Theissen, Gerd. *The Social Setting of Pauline Christianity: Essays on Corinth.* Philadelphia: Fortress, 1982.

Trevett, Christine. "Ignatius 'to the Romans' and I Clement LIV–LVI." *Vigilae Christianae* 43 (1989): 35–52.

――――. "Prophecy and Anti-Episcopal Activity: A Third Error Combated by Ignatius?" *Journal of Ecclesiastical History* 34 (1983): 1–18.

Tugwell, Simon. *The Apostolic Fathers.* London: Geoffrey Chapman, 1989.

Ukpong, Justin S. "The Parable of the Shrewd Manager (Luke 16:1–13): An Essay in Inculturation Biblical Hermeneutic." *Semeia* (1996): 189–210.

Valantasis, Richard. *The Gospel of Thomas.* New York: Routledge, 1997.

Vermes, Geza. *Jesus in His Jewish Context.* Minneapolis: Fortress, 2003.

Vyhmeister, Nancy Jean. "The Rich Man in James 2: Does Ancient Patronage Illumine the Text?" *Andrews University Seminary Studies* 33:2 (1995): 265–83.

Wahlde, Urban C. von. *The Johannine Commandments: 1 John and the Struggle for the Johannine Tradition.* New York: Paulist, 1990.

Wallace-Hadrill, Andrew. "Introduction." Pages 1–48 in *Patronage in Ancient Society.* Edited by Andrew Wallace-Hadrill. London: Routledge, 1990.

———. "Patronage in Roman Society: From Republic to Empire." Pages 63–87 in *Patronage in Ancient Society.* Edited by Andrew Wallace-Hadrill. London: Routledge, 1990.

Ward, Richard F. "Pauline Voice and Presence as Strategic Communication." *Semeia* 65 (1994): 95–108.

Whelan, Caroline F. "*Amica Pauli:* The Role of Phoebe in the Early Church," *Journal for the Study of the New Testament* 49 (1993): 67–85.

Williams, Ritva H. "Bishops as Brokers of Heavenly Goods: Ignatius to the *Ephesians.*" Pages 389–98 in *Life and Culture in the Ancient Near East.* Edited by Richard E. Averbeck, Mark Chavalas, and David Weisberg. Bethesda, Md.: CDL, 2000.

———. "The Mother of Jesus at Cana: A Social-Science Interpretation of John 2:1–12." *Catholic Biblical Quarterly* 59, no. 4 (1997): 679–92.

Wilson, Stephen G. *Related Strangers: Jews and Christians 70–170 C.E.* Minneapolis: Fortress, 1995.

Winkelman, Michael J. "Altered States of Consciousness and Religious Behavior." Pages 393–428 in *Anthropology of Religion: A Handbook.* Edited by S. D. Glazier. Westport & London: Praeger, 1997.

Wire, Antoinette Clark. "Performance, Politics and Power: A Response." *Semeia* 65 (1994): 129–38.

Wise, M. O. "Temple Origins and Structures." Pages 1167–69 in *Dictionary of New Testament Background: A Compendium of Contemporary Biblical Scholarship.* Edited by Craig A. Evans and Stanley E. Porter. Downers Grove, Ill.: InterVarsity, 2000.

Witherington, Ben III. *Conflict & Community in Corinth: A Socio-Rhetorical Commentary on 1 and 2 Corinthians.* Grand Rapids: Eerdmans, 1995.

Woll, Bruce D. *Johannine Christianity in Conflict: Authority, Rank and Succession in the First Farewell Discourse.* Society of Biblical Literature Dissertation Series. Chico, Calif.: Scholars Press, 1981.

INDEX OF MODERN AUTHORS

INDEX OF SUBJECTS

INDEX OF ANCIENT SOURCES